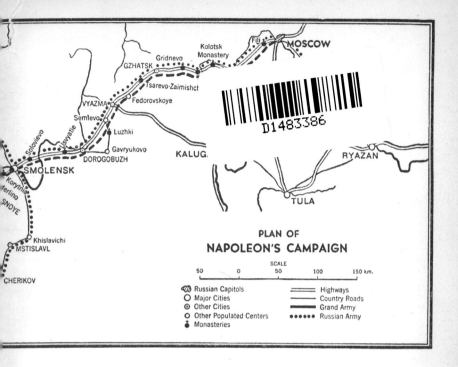

**PLAN OF
NAPOLEON'S CAMPAIGN**

SCALE

50   0   50   100   150 km.

🐎 Russian Capitols   ═══ Highways
○ Major Cities   ─── Country Roads
◎ Other Cities   ▬▬▬ Grand Army
○ Other Populated Centers ••••• Russian Army
🜊 Monasteries

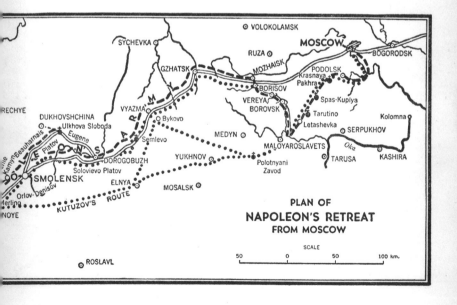

**PLAN OF
NAPOLEON'S RETREAT
FROM MOSCOW**

SCALE

50   0   50   100 km.

NAPOLEON'S INVASION OF RUSSIA, 1812

EUGENE TARLE

NAPOLEON'S
INVASION
OF RUSSIA
1812

OXFORD UNIVERSITY PRESS

NEW YORK   1942   TORONTO

TRANSLATED BY G. M.

CONTENTS

NAPOLEON'S INVASION OF RUSSIA, 1812

1

STORM CLOUDS

'THE storm of 1812 had not yet broken,' wrote Pushkin. 'Napoleon had yet to put the great people to the test. He was still threatening, still hesitating.' The poet was referring to the years immediately preceding one of the most momentous struggles in the history of western civilization.

The campaign of 1812 was more frankly imperialistic than any other of Napoleon's wars; it was more directly dictated by the interests of the French upper middle class. The war of 1796-7, the conquest of Egypt in 1798-9, the second Italian campaign, and the recent defeat of the Austrians could still be justified as necessary measures of defence against the interventionists. The Napoleonic press called the Austerlitz campaign 'self-defence' against Russia, Austria, and England. The average Frenchman considered even the subjugation of Prussia in 1806-7 no more than a just penalty inflicted on the Prussian court for the arrogant ultimatum sent by Frederick-William III to the 'peace-loving' Napoleon, constantly harried by troublesome neighbours. Napoleon never ceased to speak of the fourth conquest of Austria in 1809 as a 'defensive' war, provoked by

Austrian threats. Only the invasion of Spain and Portugal was passed over in discreet silence.

By 1812 no one in France took these fantasies and fabrications seriously, and they had almost disappeared from circulation.

The basic purposes of the new war were to subject Russia to the economic interests of the French upper middle class and to create an eternal threat against her in the shape of a vassal Poland, united with Lithuania and White Russia. If the plan worked out smoothly, there would be the additional prospect of gaining India, with the Russian army serving as an 'auxiliary force.'

Only by resisting this aggression could Russia preserve her economic and political independence. Only by fighting could she save herself from future dismemberment and the ruin incurred through the Continental blockade. Indeed, the Poles never even pretended that they would content themselves with Lithuania and White Russia; they hoped that in good time the French Caesar would help them to reach the Black Sea. In the circumstances, the War of 1812 was a struggle for survival in the full sense of the word—a defensive struggle against the onslaughts of the imperialist vulture.

This is what gave the war its peculiarly national character and impelled the Russian people to wage it with such heroic fortitude.

What, then, was the historical significance of the War of 1812? Lenin gives a clear answer to this question. In his view, the wars of the French Revolution, waged against interventionists in defence of revolutionary achievements, were, under the Directory and Napoleon, transformed into definitely aggressive wars of conquest; these aggressive, plundering, imperialist wars of Napoleon begot in their turn the movement of national liberation in the Europe he had subjugated; henceforth the wars of the European peoples against Napoleon became wars of national liberation.

The War of 1812 was the most typical of these imperialist wars; Lenin's term can be applied to it aptly and convincingly. The French upper middle class, especially the industrialists, demanded the complete elimination of England from European markets. Russia was not effectively maintaining the blockade—the only remedy was coercion. Napoleon made this the primary ground for war. The same French bourgeoisie, commercial as well as industrial, wanted to make Alexander I modify the customs tariff of December 1810, which was unfavourable to imports from France. Napoleon made this the second ground. He needed a base where men could receive political and military training for an attack on Russia. To this end, he made every possible effort to establish a powerful but submissive vassal on the Russian frontier, to create a Polish state in one form or another—this was his third ground for quarrel. No one knew exactly what Napoleon planned should the projected expedition against Moscow prove successful. He sometimes spoke of India, sometimes of 'returning by way of Constantinople,' i.e. conquering Turkey; he sent agents and spies to Egypt, Syria, and Persia well in advance (1810, 1811, 1812).

Another question: did this imperialist war of conquest promise the liberation of the Russian serfs, even as a by-product of Napoleon's greater designs?

By no means. There is no need for guesswork on this score. Soon after the invasion—indeed, before the bloody year had come to an end—Napoleon emphatically declared that he had never even considered liberating the Russian peasants. He knew that they were worse off than the serfs in other European countries. He even referred to the Russian peasants as 'the slaves.' He made no attempt to win the sympathy of the Russian peasantry by a decree abolishing serfdom; in fact, he feared that his invasion might cause a peasant revolution. He had no wish to create a gulf between himself and the landowning gentry, including the Tsar, because in Russia—so it seemed to him and so he said—he had not found any 'middle class,' i.e. that bourgeoisie without which he, the bourgeois Emperor, simply could not conceive the transition of a feudal or semi-feudal country to the new social and economic system. He had deliberately looked everywhere for this middle class on which to base the new political order. He had tried to find a Russian middle class, but, for lack of either time or ability, he had failed. After that, he refused to interfere in internal politics. Of the two remaining social groups, the landowners seemed closer to him in spite of everything, while the prospect of a peasant revolution filled him with terror. He found the Russian peasantry in chains and he departed without the slightest attempt to loosen them. On the contrary: in White Russia and Lithuania he forged new shackles.

None of this was accidental. Napoleon never concealed his ideas and sentiments on the subject, though it was not until after the invasion that he expressed them. At the session of 20 December 1812, in the throne room of the Tuileries, Napoleon said with reference to the recently concluded Russian campaign: 'The war I am waging against Russia is a political war: I have conducted it without animosity. I wished to preserve her from the misfortunes she had brought on herself. I could have armed the larger part of her population against her by proclaiming the freedom of the serfs. A great number of villages petitioned me to do so. But when I learned of the brutal nature of this large class of the Russian people, I refused to take a measure that would have subjected many families to death, ruin, and the most dreadful sufferings.' These words require no comment. In no contemporary document, not in a single letter, do we find even the slightest indication that this casual reference to a 'great number' of petitions by villages ever existed. This was obviously a politically convenient invention such as Napoleon frequently used without compunction. And Napoleon was well aware that if he had freed the serfs, he could have armed them against the feudal Russian government. He knew it, but feared to use this weapon. Napoleon, emperor by God's grace, was not the man to liberate the Russian peasants. Shortly before the invasion, Alexander had addressed him in a letter, 'Sire, my brother.' No, the 'brother' of Alexander I, the son-in-law of Francis of Austria, was not likely to free any peasants.

And what else could he have said at that time? That very day, in the throne room at a reception for the State Council, he praised the Senate for its monarchical attitude, spoke of 'the benefactions of the monarchy,' fulminated against 'popular sovereignty,' 'the principle of rebellion,' and with lofty distaste referred to the Jacobins as 'bloodthirsty men.'

In a letter to his brother, King Jerome of Westphalia, on 18 January 1813, he gives a new version of his story about the petitioning Russian peasants. 'A large number of the inhabitants of villages implored me to decree their liberation, and promised to take up arms in my behalf. But in a country with an insignificant middle class—without which it was impossible to direct and

hold within proper bounds a movement once it had
been communicated to large masses—and when the
members of this class, frightened by the destruction of
Moscow, fled—I felt that to arm a population of slaves
was to doom the country to terrible calamities. I could
not conceive of doing such a thing [*je n'en eus pas
même idée*].'

Napoleon invaded Russia not as a liberator but as a
conqueror. He did not intend to abolish serfdom, but
only, in the event of victory, to send the peasant masses
to the Himalayas and to India as an 'auxiliary army'
(his own term). But he made the same fatal mistake
about the Russians as he had about the Spaniards.

. . .

When did the spectre of a war between the two empires first assume a degree of reality? Diplomats began
to think and talk about it early in 1810, and the general public towards the end of the same year.

But long before this, subterranean currents had been
undermining the Franco-Russian alliance.

On 2 December 1805, at Austerlitz, Napoleon inflicted a crushing defeat on the Austrian and Russian
armies. Even then the French clearly saw the difference
between the Russian soldiers and the incomparably
weaker and less courageous Austrians. In 1807 the Russian armies dispatched by the Tsar to save Prussia from
final defeat fought Napoleon in the bloody but inde-
cisive battle of Eylau (8 February). A second battle followed at Friedland on 14 June, and Napoleon was
victor. It was then that Alexander I made peace and
concluded an alliance with Napoleon. This occurred
shortly after Friedland, at a personal meeting between

Napoleon and Alexander in the town of Tilsit. Alexander did not forget these painful lessons. And he was not unaware of the widespread displeasure prevailing in Russia, particularly in the army, over the 'ignominious peace of Tilsit.' Humiliation was not the sole factor. Napoleon had forced Alexander to join him in the 'Continental blockade': Russia had obligated herself not to buy anything from, or sell anything to, the English, or to allow Englishmen into Russia; she also obligated herself to declare war on England. The blockade caused great suffering to Russian landowners and merchants; Russian trade declined and the state finances dwindled. This Franco-Russian alliance, entered into at Tilsit in 1807, showed its first fissure in the following year, during the September meeting of the two emperors at Erfurt; and the fissure widened in 1809 during Napoleon's war against Austria. Let us dwell for a moment on these two years: 1807-9.

In the panic following his Friedland rout, Alexander decided not only on peace, but on a decisive, almost revolutionary turn in policy.

It is not our purpose to give a complete picture of Alexander as a man and a sovereign. In the course of his career, he passed through several transformations. As heir to the throne he had been one person; after the murder of his father Paul—another; before Austerlitz— a third; after Austerlitz—a fourth; now after Tilsit, he became a fifth. And how many more changes he was to go through in 1814! How many more in the years of Golitsin and Arakcheyev! It was not just his moods that changed, but his relations to people, his opinions of people, his attitude towards life; indeed his whole character. One of his contemporaries likened Alexander to Buddha, who, according to Hindu legends, undergoes various 'transformations,' 'becomings,' 'avatars' in the course of his life, each time showing a wholly new face. Here we are interested exclusively in his transformation before the War of 1812 and during the war itself. What kind of man was he then? What were his aspirations? Alexander knew how to keep himself in hand as did no other of Russia's tsars, and indeed, as few autocrats anywhere.

In 1805 he had suffered an ignominious rout at Austerlitz, and it was absolutely impossible to throw the blame on anyone else. Everyone knew that the Tsar himself, against the will of Kutuzov, led the army to disaster, and that when all was lost he publicly burst into tears and fled from the bloody field. But the enemy was so dangerous and the nobility which surrounded the Tsar so hated and feared this enemy that they largely forgave Alexander for Austerlitz, merely because, in spite of everything, he refused to make peace with Napoleon, and because a year after Austerlitz he again took the field against 'the enemy of mankind.' This time the war was longer and even bloodier. There seemed to be some hope of washing away the disgrace of Austerlitz, so hard to bear because, after the victories of Suvorov and Rumyantsev, it was humiliating for Alexander to begin his reign with this crushing defeat. With a little exaggeration, it was possible, especially for the provincial landowners, to regard Pultusk and Eylau as victories. Then came the spring of 1807: Heilsberg and Friedland—a fresh rout, and moreover at the very gates of Russia. Full panic reigned in Russian headquarters. Immediately after the terrible defeat at Friedland, Alexander humbled himself, and sent Lobanov-Rostovsky to implore Napoleon for an armistice.

Soon afterward, the two emperors met on a raft on

the Niemen. They embraced, kissed, and in no time concluded a peace and an alliance as well. Yet in the very midst of all these ceremonies and fraternal rejoicings, a certain irritation was discernible. The officers made no great effort to conceal the fact that they were ashamed for themselves and the Tsar, and that in their eyes Tilsit was even more humiliating than Austerlitz. There was also a feeling of shame because of the humiliation suffered by the King and Queen of Prussia. All Europe was saying that Alexander had betrayed and sold them out. Literally saying, not writing or printing, for in Napoleon's time little was written in Europe, and less was printed. At a farewell dinner, Queen Louise bitterly reproached Alexander for his treacherous behaviour, then suddenly burst into tears—at that time not much more was needed to impress public opinion. What mattered was not the eclipse of the 'chivalrous' Tsar; not the craven violation of the oath he had sworn scarcely two years before, an oath of eternal loyalty and friendship to Frederick-William III and Louise; not even the necessity of embracing and flattering the same Bonaparte who in 1804, when Alexander protested against the execution of the Duke of Enghien, had so rudely and publicly reminded him in a note of the murder of Paul. All these were mere sentimentalities. In politics, tsars must put up with worse ordeals. What really mattered was that the Russian nobility, which in the minds of European governments represented Russian public opinion, was frankly indignant at the peace of Tilsit. Alexander returned from Tilsit wounded in his pride, and with a feeling that an invisible menace hung over him.

The nobility wanted neither the Continental blockade, with the catastrophic losses it caused Russian agriculture and commerce, nor friendship with the hated Napoleon, in whom they continued to see the child of the French bourgeois revolution and a threat to their rule. The nobility was dissatisfied, and from the history of the eighteenth century, Alexander knew what happened to Russian autocrats when they aroused the wrath of the nobility. The Tsar controlled himself, and concealed his irritation and anxiety, indeed all those feelings which later he had an opportunity to reveal. He was by no means lacking in will power. He had character, and could be adamant on occasion. He could be both patient and stubborn. He never had a mature statesman-like mind; for example, it was he, not Arakchéyev, who conceived the monstrous, criminal absurdity of military settlements. And once he had conceived an idea, the Tsar let nothing stand in his way—shunned no baseness or cruelty in carrying it out. To get his way in the matter of these military settlements, he was ready to line the whole road from St. Petersburg to Chudov 'with gallows.'

He returned from Tilsit with a well-defined plan, which, in his opinion, would not only erase his defeats and the ignominy of two lost wars, but also cover him with greater glory than even the Empress Catherine had had. No one but him seems to have thought the plan feasible; he clung to it all the more stubbornly. He intended to seize large territories from the Turkish Empire: Moldavia, Walachia, perhaps even Constantinople. Napoleon had thrown out this bait in Tilsit where the two emperors spent entire nights in private conversation. Napoleon 'gave' Turkey to Alexander, while Alexander 'gave' Europe to Napoleon. Of course, Napoleon meant to trick Alexander and give him much less than he was promising. In any event, he never for a moment considered yielding Constantinople.

But Alexander was not so easy to deceive. 'Alexander is too weak to rule and too strong to be ruled,' said Speransky, who knew him well. It can also be said that he was not profound or flexible enough to deceive Napoleon, but too crafty and subtle to be taken in by him for long.

Actually, Alexander did annex Finland in 1808. He did so at the suggestion of Napoleon, who wanted to punish Anglophile Sweden. This was not enough for Alexander. And more than this Napoleon would not grant.

Long before this, indeed since Austerlitz, Alexander had ceased to trust anyone. He knew that he was not respected—'they consider me a little fool!' as he said later. As he awaited Napoleon's attack, he was sure of one thing: a second Tilsit would not be forgiven him. And remote Siberia, whither he was preparing to retreat, would really be more acceptable and safer for him than the Winter Palace, should he again show himself as pusillanimous as on the raft at Tilsit. And he concluded that for him the real risk would be to call off the war prematurely.

> In 1812 he trembled,
> At Austerlitz he ran,

wrote Pushkin of him later. For him personally, in any case, the conclusion of a peace with a victorious foe would have been far more terrible than the worst of wars.

The classic Marxists called Russian tsarism the gendarme of Europe. After 1812 Alexander made Russia the universally recognized leader of world reaction, and

Russian diplomacy actively tried to crush revolutions the world over, even as far as Peru, Bolivia, and Mexico. But even in the first period of Alexander's reign, which by comparison with what followed came to be called his 'splendid beginnings,' even in these years preceding Napoleon's invasion, Alexander eagerly came forward as a knight in shining armour, defending thrones and altars against the insolent revolutionists. As early as 1804, the Tsar's note of protest against the execution of the Duke of Enghien caused French emigrés to call him 'the champion of legitimism.' In the summer and early autumn of 1805, before the campaign, it was Alexander more than anyone who strove to represent the war as an all-European intervention in French affairs for the restoration of the Bourbons. At Tilsit, he was forced to renounce this role. In 1810, however, the hope of throwing off the yoke of Tilsit arose in his restless and sometimes penetrating mind. In any event, he could hope to make his peace with the nobility by reversing his Tilsit policy. He could not hesitate for long. His whole past, all his convictions and most secret inclinations, drove him to take this road.

.   .   .

Early in 1810 Napoleon was busy choosing a bride. There were two candidates, and it was being said in diplomatic circles that he would soon make war on the country that refused him its princess. He was refused Anna Pavlovna, but received the Austrian Marie-Louise the moment he asked for her.

The commercial bourgeoisie—for example, the Hamburg merchants—were more optimistic and less penetrating than the diplomats. Now, at last, they asserted,

Napoleon will cease his wars, and Europe will have peace. It seemed to them that after Austria's defeat in 1809, and after Napoleon's marriage to the daughter of the Austrian Emperor, the power of the French Emperor had grown so strong on the Continent that England would soon consent to any peace, to avoid being made bankrupt by the Continental blockade.

Napoleon himself thought otherwise.

For him the Austrian marriage was the best means of securing his rear, if he should again fight Russia. To his rapprochement with Austria, as to all political combinations in this period of his rule, he attached chiefly strategic significance. He clearly saw that the main task was to crush England—and this was unthinkable as long as the coasts of the Baltic, White, and Black Seas remained open to English goods. Even more clearly he realized that without a new and decisive defeat of the Russian armed forces, this aim could not be achieved. Moreover, without this defeat, he could not fully secure his power over the northern European coastline, he could not subjugate Spain, and he could not expect the Germans to give up all hope of national liberation.

For these reasons, he began in 1810 to pursue his famous policy of 'the moving frontier'; more exactly, he did not begin it, but intensified it: by a mere stroke of his pen, he annexed a number of new lands to his Empire, sent his troops to garrison German fortresses, and gradually moved the spearhead of his power eastward, closer and closer to Russia. At the same time, he took the most stringent measures against violators of the Continental blockade.

Silence reigned in a terror-stricken Europe.

Prince P. A. Vyazemsky, Pushkin's friend, wrote at a

later time: 'Napoleon was equally terrifying to kings and peoples. No one who has not lived in this epoch can know, or even imagine, how stifling existence was at that time. The fate of every state, of nearly every person, depended more or less, in one way or another, if not today then tomorrow, on the whims of the Tuileries cabinet or on the military dispositions of Napoleon's headquarters. Everyone lived as under the threat of an earthquake or a volcano. No one could act or even breathe freely.'

The annexation of Holland to the French Empire in June 1810, the transfer of three French divisions from southern to Baltic Germany in August of the same year, the transport from the French Empire of 50,000 rifles to the Duchy of Warsaw and of an artillery regiment to the French-occupied Magdeburg—all these menacing symptoms of an approaching new storm—Russian diplomacy directly connected with 'the Austrian marriage' and the Austrian alliance with Napoleon. Napoleon no longer needed Russia; his power over Europe had a new support in Vienna.

In the second half of 1810, the Trianon tariff, as Nesselrode said, 'began to be carried out by armed force.' All over Europe English goods were burned in bonfires. Russia was gently asked to adopt similar measures, but the Russian government refused, explaining that this would be contrary to her 'independence and interests.' In December 1810 Napoleon annexed the Hanseatic cities Hamburg, Bremen, Lübeck—and took advantage of the occasion to grab the entire territory between Holland and Hamburg, including the Duchy of Oldenburg. Alexander's sister, Ekaterina, was married to the son and heir of the Duke of Oldenburg. Alexander protested. But Napoleon 'added a fresh humiliation'—he ordered his minister, the Duke of Cadore, to reject the Russian note of protest without even reading it. Finally, in December 1810, a new Russian tariff was issued, increasing the duties on all luxury articles and wines, the very articles imported from France.

From then on, relations between the two emperors grew steadily worse.

The more troops Napoleon poured into Poland and Prussia, contrary to the conditions of the peace of Tilsit, which stipulated their withdrawal from Prussia, the more vigilantly and zealously he insisted on the fulfilment of the blockade—the more did Russia's secret hopes centre on England.

In a report presented to Napoleon on 7 April 1810 by his Foreign Minister, the Duke of Cadore, the Emperor read: 'The British Cabinet has not lost hope of a rapprochement with Russia and Turkey, thus securing on the Baltic Sea, in the Archipelago, and on the Black Sea more useful outlets for her manufactures than it might obtain by any peace, even if this peace should temporarily open up to her the ports of France, Germany, Holland, and Italy.'

The Duke of Cadore feared that the English might succeed in this. A struggle of 'interests' was being fought round Alexander, he said, and England could achieve much 'by promises, advantageous offers, and alluring guarantees.' 'The venality of the St. Petersburg Court has always been an established fact. This venality was quite open during the reigns of Elizabeth, Catherine, and Paul. If in the present reign it is less public, if we still have in Russia a few friends inaccessible to English proposals, such as Count Rumyantsev, the Princes Kurakin, and a very small number of others, it is nevertheless true that the majority of the Tsar's courtiers, partly from habit, partly from attachment to the Empress Dowager, partly from vexation at the drop in their incomes through lower exchange rates, partly as a result of bribery, are secret partisans of England.' In this secret report, the Duke of Cadore frankly acknowledged the difficulty of preventing a possible rapprochement between England and Russia: 'How will it be possible to rupture completely the secret relations between England and Russia, when their more or less weighty common interests impel both courts to renew these relations?' It is necessary to remark that this minister—Champagny, who had received the title of Duke of Cadore—was only an obedient tool of his sovereign. His mission, as he saw it, was to play up to the Emperor and to echo his passions and thoughts. For instance, he put it down to his own credit that his predecessors had sought to conclude a peace with England, while he, the Duke of Cadore, stood for the continuation of the war. It was only necessary to complete the conquest of Spain: then all the ports of Europe would be closed. 'Once in Cadiz, Sire, you will be in a position either to break or strengthen the bonds with Russia.' Europe must be closed to English ships and goods from Cadiz to St. Petersburg.

In December 1810, after publication of the new Russian tariff, all Europe began to discuss the coming war between the two empires.

In a letter to his beloved sister, Ekaterina Pavlovna, dated 26 December 1810, Alexander referred to it for the first time: 'It seems that blood must flow again. But at least I have done everything that is humanly possible to avoid it.' This letter discussing the seizure by Napoleon of Peter of Oldenburg's duchy (Peter's son and heir, George, was the husband of Ekaterina Pavlovna) contains no other important passages, except for a significant list of matters which Alexander wished to talk over with his sister at their next meeting. He was then preparing for a journey to Tver, where his sister lived, and he actually did appear there in March 1811. In this list a prominent place is given to military matters, such as the organization of the army, the increase of its effectives, reserves, et cetera. If, by the brutal and brutally executed seizure of Oldenburg, Napoleon intended not only to secure the German Baltic coast, but also to vex Alexander, he certainly achieved his aim. But, more important, Alexander realized that this provocation was only a beginning—it was clear that Napoleon was not insulting him for nothing.

In May 1811, Napoleon recalled Caulaincourt, his ambassador to St. Petersburg. His reason was that Caulaincourt stood for peace with Russia and believed that Napoleon was provoking the Tsar deliberately and without justification. Caulaincourt left St. Petersburg on 15 May. 'Should Emperor Napoleon start a war,' Alexander said to him in leave-taking, 'it is possible and even likely that he will beat us. But this will not give him peace. The Spaniards have often been beaten, but for all that they are neither conquered nor subjugated, and they are closer to Paris than we are, and they have neither our climate nor our resources. We shall enter into no compromises; we have vast spaces in our rear, and we shall preserve a well-organized army. With all that at our disposal, we shall never be forced to conclude peace, no matter what defeats we may suffer. We may even force the conqueror to make peace. Emperor Napoleon expressed this idea to Chernishev after Wagram. He himself acknowledged that he would never have been willing to negotiate with Austria, if Austria had not preserved her army; and, with a little more stubbornness, the Austrians might have obtained better terms. Napoleon needs results as rapid as his own thoughts; he will not achieve them with us. I shall profit by his lessons. They are the lessons of a master. We shall let our climate, our winter, wage the war for us. The French soldiers are brave, but less enduring than ours, they are more easily disheartened. Miracles occur only in the presence of the Emperor, but he cannot be everywhere. Moreover, he will inevitably be in a hurry to return to his country. I will not draw sword first, but I shall sheathe it last. Sooner would I retreat to Kamchatka than yield a province or put my signature to a peace made in my conquered capital, a peace which would turn out to be a mere truce.'

Caulaincourt, to be sure, often over-idealized Alexander. In this instance, however, his testimony is extremely plausible. In general, we must bear in mind that the memoirs of Caulaincourt were written later, and several incidents seen in retrospect may have taken on a different light.

Caulaincourt feared a war with Russia. Upon his return to Paris on 5 June 1811, he was promptly received by Napoleon, to whom he conveyed the Tsar's words. Caulaincourt insisted that the idea of restoring Poland would have to be sacrificed in order to preserve the peace and the alliance with Russia. At the same time, he maintained that in no circumstances would Russia start a war. Napoleon contradicted him. As always during this period, Napoleon, ignoring the Russian peasantry, their serfdom, et cetera, emphasized instead his own conceptions: the Russian nobility was dissolute, decrepit, self-seeking, undisciplined, incapable of self-sacrifice, and, after the first defeats, after the beginning of an invasion, they would take fright and force the Tsar to sign a peace.

Caulaincourt strongly objected: 'You are mistaken, Sire, about Alexander and the Russians. Do not judge Russia from what others tell you about her. And do not judge the Russian army from what you saw of it after Friedland, crushed as it was and disarmed. Threatened with an attack for over a year, the Russians have made preparations and strengthened their forces. They have considered all possibilities, even the possibility of great defeats. They have made preparations for defence and resistance to the utmost.' Napoleon listened, but soon changed the subject—he spoke of his Grand Army, the inexhaustible resources of his World Empire, of his unconquerable Guard. In all history, he pointed out, no military leader had commanded such enormous forces, such troops, magnificent in all respects. At the same audience, Caulaincourt protested that it was unjust to demand that Russia fulfil in every particular the ruinous conditions of the Continental blockade, while Napoleon himself violated them in the interests of the treasury and French industry, by granting licenses for trade with England to individual merchants and financiers. Napoleon shut his ears to all these arguments. 'One good battle,' he replied, 'will put an end to all your friend Alexander's excellent resolutions, and to all his fortifications built on sand.'

With a feeling of despair, Caulaincourt saw that he was accomplishing nothing. Napoleon's confidence in victory was increasing month by month as his grandiose preparations took shape, and he refused to take any warning seriously. Russo-French relations were in a muddled state. In 1811, Alexander I and most of the Russian nobility were less afraid of Napoleon than he would have liked them to be. But Napoleon, who had so often and so successfully cut Gordian knots with his sword, refused to understand why he should forego this method at a moment when his sword was stronger and sharper than ever before. All of his efforts were concentrated on two problems: first, to complete his preparations for war, leaving as little as possible to chance; and, second, to arrange matters so that Alexander, and not he, would be blamed for the war.

On 13 May 1811, General-Count Shuvalov, Alexander's aide-de-camp, was received by Napoleon at St. Cloud. 'I do not want war with Russia,' Napoleon began. 'War would be a crime, because there would be no purpose in it. And I, thank God, have not yet lost my mind, or my wits . . . Surely no one can think that I would sacrifice perhaps two hundred thousand Frenchmen, to restore Poland? In any case, I am not in a position to fight. I have three hundred thousand men in Spain. I am fighting there to obtain control of the coastline. I have taken Holland because her king could not prevent the import of English goods. I have annexed the Hanseatic towns for the same reason. But I have no intention of touching the Duchy of Darmstadt, or other states that have no coastline. I shall not make war on Russia, unless she violates the terms of the Tilsit agreement.'

Napoleon went on in the same vein, pretending that he did not trust in Alexander's desire for peace, and alternating complaints with threats: 'The Russian troops are brave, but I am quicker in collecting my forces. As you pass, you will see an army twice as numerous as yours. I know the military trade. I have been at it a long time. I know how battles are won, and lost. I cannot be intimidated, threats can have no effect on me.' And in the same breath he pointed out to Shuvalov the advantages of friendship with him, the advantages of the Tilsit policy: 'Compare the war that was fought in Emperor Paul's reign with those that followed. The Tsar whose armies had been victorious in Italy acquired only debts by war. While Alexander, having lost two wars against me, acquired Finland, Moldavia, Walachia, and several districts in Poland.'

Shuvalov left convinced that Alexander must promptly decide whether he wanted peace or war with Napoleon.

Despite everything, Alexander feared this war, although he tried to banish his fears and avidly sought grounds for reassurance. In the summer of 1811 he thought war probable, but his mood was by no means triumphant. Writing to Ekaterina Pavlovna about the same Oldenburg affair, in which his sister was directly interested, Alexander remarked that he regarded the matter as hopeless: 'Is it possible to expect anything reasonable from Napoleon? Is he a human being who may be expected to renounce any acquisition, unless compelled by the force of arms? And have we the force of arms to compel him with?' Alexander, however, had the hope, a sort of instinctive certainty, that Napoleon's world rule could not endure: 'It seems to me more reasonable to look to time for assistance, and even to the very vastness of this evil. I cannot banish my conviction that this state of affairs cannot endure, that the suffering among all classes in Germany as in France is so great that patience itself must inevitably become exhausted.' It is true that Alexander also put his trust in the help of God, help which might reveal itself in special instances in the form of regicide (not in St. Petersburg, of course, but in Paris!), and he devoted a few warm words to a young man who, according to rumour, had lately fired a shot at Napoleon and then shot himself. The Tsar expressed the hope that the young man 'would find imitators.' 'In one way or another, this state of affairs must come to an end,' he repeated.

Finally, Napoleon made an open demonstration of his hostility. In 1811, Napoleon's birthday, 15 August, was being celebrated with the usual pomp. One of the features of this celebration was the grand reception for all diplomatic representatives in the large throne room at the court of the Tuileries. The Emperor sat on the throne. The ambassadors and ministers, in gilded uniforms and bedizened with stars and orders, appeared before him with low bows. Prince Kurakin, the Russian ambassador, was in the first row.

Napoleon descended from the throne, and, walking up to Kurakin, began a conversation with him. Kurakin, an old man, an aristocrat of Catherine's days, past master of all the secrets of the courtier's art, did not enjoy the full confidence of Alexander but had been sent to Paris largely because of his portly bearing. The Tsar's real representatives in Paris were rather Nesselrode, Councillor of the Embassy, and Colonel Chernishev. But at this solemn reception, Kurakin, of course, was the chief figure. Amid the incredible opulence of Napoleon's Court and all the courtly and worldly luxury of Paris, the old Catherinian courtier did his utmost to maintain his dignity and to deck himself out with a magnificence second to none.

The conversation of the Emperor with the Ambassador soon became strained. Napoleon began to accuse the Tsar of making military preparations, and of harbouring warlike intentions. He declared that he set no stock in the Tsar's indignation over his annexation of Oldenburg. The real cause lay in Poland. 'I do not intend to restore Poland. The interests of my peoples do not require this. But if you force me to go to war, I shall certainly use Poland against you. I declare to you that I do not want war, and that I will not fight with you this year, if you do not attack me. I do not like the idea of a war in the north, but if the crisis does not end by November I shall call for a hundred and twenty thousand extra men; I shall continue to do this for two or three years, and if I find such a system more wearisome than war, then I shall declare war on you . . . and you will lose all your Polish provinces.' Apparently, he said, Russia wanted to suffer defeats similar to those suffered by Prussia and Austria. 'Whether because of my luck, or the courage of my armies—or perhaps I know a thing or two about the military trade—the fact remains that I have always been successful, and I hope that I will again be successful, if you force me into a war.' Realizing the hopes his enemies put on Spain, Napoleon hastened to assure Kurakin that in time he would have seven hundred thousand men, 'a number sufficient to continue the war in Spain and wage war against you.' And Russia would be without allies. At this point Napoleon frankly revealed why after Tilsit he had thrust Prussian Bialystok upon Alexander, and, after 1809, Austrian Tarnopol. 'You count on allies, but where are they? Surely not Austria, from whom you seized three hundred thousand souls in Galicia. Nor Prussia, which will surely remember Alexander's seizure of the Bialystok district. Nor Sweden, which will recall that you have reduced her to half her size, by seizing Finland. All these injuries will be remembered,

all these humiliations avenged—the entire continent
will be against you.'

For about forty minutes Kurakin was unable to get
in a word. He did finally manage to murmur that
Alexander remained a true friend and ally of Napoleon.
'Words!' protested Napoleon and renewed his complaints against the machinations of England, which was
trying to start a quarrel between Russia and France.

Napoleon finally suggested that a new agreement be
worked out. Kurakin replied that he did not have
powers for this. 'No powers? Then write to the Tsar to
give them to you at once.'

The ambassadors of vassal and semi-vassal Europe
listened tensely to these prolonged accusations flung
publicly in Kurakin's face. The reception came to an
end. To all corners of Europe flew the news that an
assault on Russia by Napoleon was inevitable.

By November 1811 Alexander no longer dared to
leave St. Petersburg even to visit his sister: 'We are on
constant guard: everything is so on edge, so tense, that
military operations may begin at any minute. I cannot
leave the centre of my administration and my activity.
I must wait for a more opportune moment, and the war
may hinder me altogether.'

Towards the end of November, Ambassador Prince
Kurakin had no doubt of the inevitability of Napoleon's attack on Russia, and informed Chancellor Rumyantsev that Napoleon had issued a whole series of
military and administrative orders, which directly indicated the close approach of military operations. All
hope of preserving peace must be put aside: 'The time
has passed when we could delude ourselves with vain
hopes. The time is indeed approaching when, with

courage and unyielding firmness, we must preserve our national inheritance and the integrity of our present frontiers.'

The French Court began to treat Kurakin perfunctorily and even rudely. The old man asked for instructions should the expected break take place; he feared that he might be detained in Paris in the event of war.

·   ·   ·

At the beginning of 1812, Napoleon accomplished a task which he had thought very important, but which really presented no difficulty: he concluded military alliances with Prussia and Austria against Russia.

King Frederick-William III had exceeded all bounds in his fear of Napoleon. He trembled like an aspen leaf before his terrible conqueror. Before appointing a minister, the King ordered the candidate to find out whether or not he would be agreeable to Napoleon. The French Emperor did not withdraw his troops from Prussia; on the contrary, he sent additional troops, maintained his garrisons in her fortresses, and treated the Prussian monarch like a sergeant guilty of some breach of discipline, humiliating him on the slightest pretext, and even without a pretext. And King Frederick-William III had a gift for fright. That was his one real gift. Not one of Napoleon's marshals, not one of his own brothers whom he had placed on the various European thrones, was so grovelling, so panic-stricken in the presence of the Emperor, as the Prussian King.

As early as autumn 1811, Napoleon gave Frederick-William to understand that he faced one of two choices: either to enter into a close military alliance with him for a common war against Russia, or to say farewell to his crown, because in the event of his refusal, Marshal Davout had his instructions to occupy Berlin and put an end to the Prussian kingdom. His situation was clearly hopeless, especially in view of Austria's attitude. Metternich, the director of Austrian policy, had definitely decided that Austria must take part in the approaching war on Napoleon's side. At that time, Metternich had no doubt of Napoleon's ultimate victory, and even anticipated opulent favours from the French Emperor. In the event of Napoleon's failure, both sides —Russia and France—would be so weakened by war that Austria would be in the advantageous position of being able to sell her support to whichever side she chose. As early as 17 December 1811, Napoleon and Schwarzenberg, the Austrian ambassador to Paris, concluded an agreement which, shortly afterward, led to a Franco-Austrian military alliance. Austria pledged herself to put an auxiliary corps of thirty thousand men into the field against Russia. This force would be under the supreme command of Napoleon. In compensation, Napoleon agreed to return Austria's Illyrian provinces, ceded to him by the treaty of Schönbrunn in 1809. Austria, however, was to receive these provinces only after the conclusion of Napoleon's war with Russia; furthermore, Austria agreed to cede Galicia to Poland, once Napoleon had restored it.

The Prussian King no longer hesitated. As a final touch, he was informed that Napoleon had promised Prussian Silesia to Austria, in case Prussia refused to join him in a military alliance against Russia. Faced with the alternative of prompt dismemberment and ultimate destruction of his kingdom or complete submission to Napoleon's will, the King was not long in deciding.

On 24 February 1812, Prussia signed a treaty of alliance with Napoleon. She undertook to provide an auxiliary corps of twenty thousand men, and to replenish it steadily to make up for possible losses. Prussia also undertook to supply the French military forces with oats, hay, liquor, et cetera, in fixed and enormous quantities. In return, the Prussian King wheedled out of Napoleon the promise of some conquered Russian territories. The text of this remarkable clause runs: 'In the event of a fortunate issue of the war against Russia— if, notwithstanding the desires and hopes of both high contracting parties, the war takes place—His Imperial Majesty [Napoleon] pledges himself to give the Prussian King a territorial reward, in compensation for the sacrifices and losses which the King would incur in the course of the war.'

The papers of Mikhailovsky-Danilevsky, attached to the copy of this pact, contain this interesting note: 'Upon conclusion of this alliance with France against Russia, the King demanded the provinces of Courland, Lithland, and Estland from the French Government, in the event of a successful issue to the campaign.' When Maret, the Duke of Bassano, reported the Prussian demands to the Emperor, Napoleon maliciously remarked: 'And what about the oath at Frederick's tomb?' He was referring to the sentimental comedy with vows of eternal love and friendship enacted by Alexander I, Frederick-William III, and the Prussian Queen Louise in October 1805 in the Potsdam Mausoleum.

Few persons believed that the Austrians would put up a serious fight against the Russians. Langeron, hurrying to Russia near the beginning of the war, wrote frankly to Vorontsov from Bucharest, on 22 May 1812: 'Schwarzenberg commands 30,000 Austrians. This choice does not frighten me, because he does not hate us, and I hardly think that these 30,000 will fight with any heart against us.'

Others were less optimistic.

From 'A Detailed Inventory of Autographed Letters' written by Alexander to Barclay de Tolly, we learn of the Tsar's plan 'to parry Austria's thrusts against Russia by encouraging the Slavic peoples and helping them to unite with the discontented Hungarians.' The Tsar had even chosen the man 'to carry out this plan'— Admiral Chichagov.

The very idea of this adventure was largely based on his complete ignorance of the actual relations between 'the Slavic peoples' under Austrian rule and the Hungarians, but it shows that in April 1812, just after he had learned of the agreement between Austria and Napoleon, Alexander was filled with the greatest apprehensions. He could not be sure that the Austrians in 1812 would do what the Russians had done in 1809.

In other words, Alexander had to reckon with the participation of Austria and Prussia in the approaching war. Should Napoleon desire to march on Kiev, his right flank would be strongly reinforced by Austria. Should he desire to advance on St. Petersburg through Riga and Pskov, his left flank would be protected by the participation of Prussia. Should he decide to march on Smolensk and Moscow, the Prussians and the Austrians would press the Russian troops on the left and right flanks, driving them off the line of the Grand Army's central advance.

The situation was becoming increasingly difficult; matters were looking more and more threatening. But in the months of April and May, no concessions on Alexander's part could have prevented the war or even the advance of the separate detachments of Napoleon's army, moving slowly but steadily from the Rhine, the Elbe, the Danube, the Alps, the North Sea, towards the Niemen.

There were a few circumstances, however, which heartened Alexander and his entourage. As early as April, and again in May, Metternich deviously and in strictest secrecy informed him that Austria did not take her share in the coming conflict seriously. She would not even furnish the entire 30,000 men, and would not, in any case, advance beyond certain districts very close to the Austro-Russian frontier. These secret conversations continued even during the war: in this manner Metternich re-insured Austria against any eventuality. Furthermore, during these spring months, the Tsar found out that the Swedes would favour not Napoleon but Russia. This meant that there would be no need to scatter his forces in defence of Finland and the northern land and sea approaches to St. Petersburg.

Towards the beginning of the summer, there were other favourable developments.

.   .   .

From the very start of 1812, neither side had any doubt that war was near. An unexpected case of espionage added to the tenseness of the situation.

The Russian Government had learned much if not all there was to know about the French Grand Army.

At that time Alexander Ivanovich Chernishev, later
Minister of War under Nicholas I, was just beginning
his career. Though only twenty-eight, he had the rank
of colonel and aide-de-camp. Attached to the Russian
Embassy in Paris, Chernishev several times served as
courier, bearing letters from Alexander to Napoleon
and from Napoleon to Alexander. Chernishev won
Napoleon by his subtle flattery and his apt and quick-
witted remarks on the military subjects in which the
French Emperor so delighted. The smooth-spoken
courtier, young, brilliant, and handsome, was an absolutely unprincipled careerist. Subsequently the ruthless
executioner of the Decembrists, he aroused moral
loathing even in those inured to court life. During his
long life he won the favour of three emperors. The
three were strikingly dissimilar, but he knew how to
handle each: Alexander, Napoleon, and Nicholas. And
that was all he needed for his purposes. The favour
of Napoleon opened the doors to all the *salons* in Paris
and provided him with connections in the upper circles
of French bureaucracy. Early in 1811, Chernishev made
the acquaintance of Michel, who was serving on the
General Staff of the French army and who had long
been connected with the Russian Embassy. On the first
and fifteenth of every month, the French Minister of
War handed the Emperor a so-called 'Survey of the
Situation' of the entire French army, with all the numerical changes in its separate divisions, all the changes
in billeting, a complete list of fortnightly appointments
to commanding posts, et cetera. These reports found
their way into Michel's hands for a few hours. Michel
made rapid copies of them, and delivered them to
Chernishev for a suitable reward. This arrangement
went on smoothly and successfully for over a year, from

January 1811 to February 1812. But despite Chernishev's cleverness and Michel's discretion, the Imperial secret police finally smelled a rat, and in February 1812 Chernishev's apartments were thoroughly searched in his absence—unofficially, of course. A courier was also searched at the frontier. As a result, no doubt was left in Napoleon's mind concerning the real activities of the Russian Colonel for whom he had developed so much affection. By this time, Napoleon had pretty well decided that war with Russia was inevitable, but he could not and did not want to precipitate a break with Alexander. He needed another three to four months for preparations, and refrained from divulging his discovery. Following the secret and delicate yet ill-boding search of his premises, Chernishev decided that a longer sojourn on the banks of the Seine was unhealthy. He paid a respectful farewell call at the Tuileries and left for Russia. Before his departure he burned all the incriminating documents that might reveal to the Imperial secret police the one thing they wanted to know —who had given Chernishev access to the documents? The riddle was solved by mere chance. In his haste to depart, Chernishev had forgotten to have the rugs taken from his floors. Under one of the rugs, near the fireplace, the police, which promptly called at his rooms, found a letter written by Michel; it must have dropped there by accident. Michel was immediately arrested, tried, and publicly guillotined—on 2 May 1812. His trial, and that of three others, was deliberately held in public; Napoleon wanted to create the impression that Russia was planning to attack France, and was sending spies as a preliminary.

Although the information in the hands of the Russian Government was somewhat out of date by the time war broke out, it was so extensive as to retain much of its value. Furthermore, lesser agents in Paris, in Germany, and especially in Poland had provided more recent information on French troop movements and changes in the army.

Napoleon was infuriated by the disclosures of espionage. On 3 March, his Foreign Minister, the Duke of Bassano, wrote a cutting letter to the Russian Ambassador: 'His Majesty was deeply distressed by the conduct of Count Chernishev. He was surprised to learn that a man whom he had always treated kindly, a man who was in Paris not as a political agent, but as the Russian Emperor's aide-de-camp, who was the bearer of a personal letter to the Emperor, and for that reason enjoyed more confidence than an ambassador, had taken advantage of this position to abuse the most sacred human ties. His Majesty the Emperor is grieved that spies were introduced to him under a title inviting trust, and this in peacetime—though such conduct is permissible only in wartime and in a hostile country; the Emperor is grieved that these spies have been chosen not from the lowest class of society but from men whose position has placed them so close to the Tsar. I am too well acquainted with your sense of honour not to believe that you yourself are distressed by this affair so contrary to the dignity of sovereigns. If Prince Kurakin, the Emperor told me, had engaged in similar manœuvres, I should have forgiven him; but a colonel, enjoying the confidence of his sovereign and occupying a place so close to his person, is a different matter. His Majesty had only recently shown his trust in Chernishev by holding a long private conversation with him. The

Emperor had no inkling that he was conversing with a spy and bribe-giver.'

Of course, Napoleon's moral indignation did not prevent him from maintaining a host of spies in Russia. Nor did it deter him from beginning, in April and May, to print counterfeit Russian bank notes to meet the demands of the coming invasion.

While preparing all his forces for the invasion, Napoleon could do nothing to hasten the approaching break.

Certain internal French developments had a delaying effect. Chief among these was a serious bread shortage in some of the departments. Hunger riots broke out in Normandy, and had to be quelled by force of arms. Profiteers tried to enrich themselves on the people's misery by extensive and bold speculations. The Napoleonic administration proved unable to put a prompt stop to the fantastic rise in the price of bread.

Towards the end of February, the tone of Kurakin's reports changed. He began to think that Napoleon had not yet decided to make war, that he was still wavering, and that it was up to the Russian Government to do everything possible to avoid the terrible clash. But two months later—on 23 April 1812—Kurakin was again pessimistic: 'Everything points to the conclusion that the war was decided upon long ago in the mind of the French Emperor.'

On 27 April 1812 Napoleon granted Kurakin an audience. Kurakin had requested the evacuation of French troops from Prussia. 'What have your St. Petersburg people done with their heads, to think they can intimidate me with threats?' Napoleon exclaimed, though actually Kurakin had uttered no threats. Kurakin had merely mentioned Napoleon's tremendous armaments and his 'alliance' with Prussia, clearly directed against Russia. Napoleon simply failed to listen and spoke what was on his mind. He repeated his categorical refusal.

At the same audience, Kurakin heard from Napoleon himself that Austria, too, had concluded an alliance with France.

On the following day, Kurakin called on the Minister of Foreign Affairs. The Russian Ambassador was willing to give in on almost every point: Russia would withdraw her protest against Napoleon's annexation of the Duchy of Oldenburg and would negotiate for compensation to the Duke (a course which she had hitherto rejected); Russia would introduce into the tariff of 1810 special clauses in favour of French imports. But Russia still insisted on the evacuation of Prussia, as stipulated in the Tilsit agreement, and she reasserted her right to trade with neutral countries.

But all these proposals were futile. Kurakin asked for his passports, and, after a long delay, obtained them. Even after Napoleon's departure from Paris, the Duke of Bassano kept trying to tell Kurakin that war was by no means certain. This he did by order of Napoleon, who wished at any cost to forestall a Russian invasion of Prussia or the Duchy of Warsaw.

Napoleon was extremely indignant at the Russian demand for his evacuation of Prussia. He called it an arrogant ultimatum, and, having irretrievably decided for war, he seized upon this 'ultimatum' as proof that the Tsar was the aggressor. But he wanted to delay the war until June. He tried to procrastinate by engaging in negotiations, and sending the Count of Narbonne, his aide-de-camp, to Vilna. By this move he also planned to obtain a first-hand report on developments in the Russian army.

The Count of Narbonne, a prominent aristocrat and former minister of Louis XVI, was subtle and crafty. He failed, however, to outwit Alexander.

. . .

On 21 April, Alexander left St. Petersburg to join his army. On the very day of his departure, Chancellor Rumyantsev invited the French ambassador, Count Lauriston, to call. 'He instructed me in the name of his sovereign,' wrote Lauriston to Marshal Davout, 'to inform Emperor Napoleon that in Vilna, even as in St. Petersburg, he [Alexander] would remain his friend and his loyal ally; that he does not want war and would do everything in his power to avoid it; that his journey to Vilna was prompted by the approach of French troops to Königsberg; its purpose is to prevent his generals from making any move which might provoke an explosion.'

The impressions Narbonne brought back from his trip to Vilna can be summed up as follows: In no circumstances would the Russian army begin military operations first. It would neither cross the Niemen, nor occupy Memel. Alexander had not concluded any agreement with England, but would do so once the first shot was fired. If negotiations were begun, Alexander would yield on all points 'save one, which the Emperor [Napoleon] considers essential.' All the Russian projects revealed 'une grande incertitude' because Napoleon's intentions were unknown. On three very important questions, Narbonne could give no accurate information. He surmised that the Russians would give battle as

soon as Napoleon crossed their frontier; that there was
no pact between Sweden and Russia, although Sweden
'seemed' to be against Napoleon; and that peace between Russia and Turkey was still remote.

Actually, Russia and Sweden had already agreed on
all basic questions, and Alexander had the firm assurance that Bernadotte, called the heir apparent but in
fact the reigning Swedish king, would in no circumstances fight against Russia. Peace with Turkey was concluded shortly after Narbonne's visit to Alexander. Towards the end of his life, on St. Helena, Napoleon acknowledged that the invasion of Russia, in the face of
Alexander's agreement with Sweden and the conclusion
of peace between Russia and Turkey, had been a mistake. Thus we see how essential it was for him, in those
decisive days, to know definitely whether the two events
had actually taken place.

Narbonne further failed to realize that Alexander,
though willing to make concessions before the invasion, could not be so tractable once it had begun. 'Emperor Alexander seems prepared to lose two or three
battles, but he feigns determination to go on fighting
in Tartary if need be.' This is the earliest mention of
the formula that, with certain purely stylistic varia-
tions, Alexander kept repeating throughout the War of
1812.

What Narbonne meant by 'the one [point] the Emperor considers essential' is clear from the instructions
he received from Paris before his journey: 'In the final
analysis, there is between us and Russia a single but
very important question. This is the question of neutral nations and of English trade . . . The American
ships which enter Russian ports are really English ships,
and they sail in the interest of England.' The instruc-

tions provide Narbonne with arguments to be used in his discussions with Alexander: if these ships were actually American, England would pursue them and seize them, not defend them as she was doing. This was the chief point of disagreement. As to the restoration of Poland, let Alexander have no worry on that score: 'His Majesty [Napoleon] is not concerned with Poland. He has only French interests at heart.' Narbonne was also advised 'not to conceal the tremendous strength' of Napoleon: 400,000 men on the Vistula, two army corps in Berlin, one in Cologne, one in Mainz. And 'at the first cannon shot,' 200,000 men of the class of 1813 would be called to the colours. These instructions were dated 3 May, and they urged Narbonne to keep his eyes open, while in Russia, for everything concerning the Russian army, the political temper in Lithuania, et cetera.

In sending Narbonne to Alexander, Napoleon also counted on him to prevent the Russian forces near the Niemen from beginning military operations. He counselled him to use the most peaceful language. If, despite his efforts, the Russians should cross the Niemen, Narbonne was to feign astonishment, continue negotiations with Alexander, and even try to secure a truce. In general, 'to arrest by soft words the movement [of the Russian army] and give his Majesty [Napoleon] time to reach the front.'

In dictating his instructions, Napoleon cautioned his envoy that Alexander was no simpleton: 'His Majesty has commissioned me to tell you,' writes the Minister of Foreign Affairs, 'to be restrained and on your guard, to bear constantly in mind that you are dealing with a subtle and suspicious man.' Napoleon's fear had no foundation in reality. Russia was determined not to begin military operations. Narbonne's report of his meeting with Alexander, dispatched to Napoleon through Marshal Davout, did not deter Napoleon from his projected invasion. On the contrary he was reassured: the war would begin as he wanted it to—by his crossing the Niemen. The Russians were waiting in confusion. And promptly after the invasion, there would be a new Austerlitz.

Alexander feared to say so much as a single word to Narbonne; that might suggest capitulation to Napoleon; he considered Narbonne's very presence in Vilna compromising. Narbonne had arrived in Vilna on 18 May, and gained an audience with the Tsar the same day. On the following day, he again conversed with the Tsar, and dined with him. On the morning of the twentieth, without any sort of warning, Count Kochubey, Nesselrode, and someone else of the Tsar's suite came to pay him 'a farewell visit.' He had not been planning to leave. Next he received from the Tsar's kitchens some tasty provisions and wines 'for the journey.' He had scarcely time for astonishment at this gratuitous kindness when a courier appeared and respectfully informed His Excellency that his horses were 'ready' and that he might leave Vilna at six o'clock that evening.

There was nothing for Narbonne to do but take the most direct route to Dresden, where he joined Napoleon. War was now an absolute certainty.

●   ●   ●

Most European diplomats expected a victory for Napoleon. There were, however, certain factors which, while they did not even chances, merited serious consideration by both sides.

In the first place, there was Spain. Those observers were right who insisted that, after 1808, Napoleon was reduced to fighting with one arm, since an appreciable portion of his strength remained in Spain. The army with which Napoleon approached Borodino was no more than half the size of the one which even then, in the autumn of 1812, was fighting and perishing in Spain.

Among the French documents taken in 1812 was a report sent to Napoleon in 1810 concerning the endless carnage in Spain. 'France has over 220,000 troops in Spain, but the French control only points occupied by their troops. No improvement in public opinion is discernible; no hope of assuaging tempers, of attracting the leaders, of subjugating the people. New forces are still headed for the Pyrenees . . . Another 300,000 men will be mobilized and, perhaps, perish in this ruinous war. And, in the opinion of the best-informed, the most devoted, the most determined of the Emperor's aides, he will not succeed in subjugating the peninsula, not with all the forces of his Empire.'

That was how matters stood in 1808 and in 1810. That was how they stood in 1812.

The second circumstance favourable to Russia was the unexpected reversal in Swedish policy. The Napoleonic Marshal Bernadotte (Prince Ponte-Corvo) had been elected heir apparent to the Swedish throne. Oddly enough, the Swedes had chosen him in 1810 in the hope of pleasing Napoleon, though in reality the two men had detested one another for some time and Napoleon was merely irritated by the choice. The shrewd, skilful, audacious, ambitious Bernadotte, like many other of Napoleon's marshals, started out in the lower ranks of the French revolutionary army. In 1844, after

his death as King Karl XIV of Sweden, the entire
Swedish Court was horrified by the discovery of a tat-
tooed inscription on his arm. 'Death to Kings!' it read.
He had apparently failed to foresee that he would some
day found a royal dynasty—a dynasty which survives to
this day.

Promptly after his appearance on the Swedish scene,
Bernadotte entered into friendly relations with Alexander. He was supported by a large section of the
Swedish aristocracy, indignant at Napoleon's autocratic
procedure in annexing by a mere decree Swedish Pomerania, which had belonged to Sweden since the seventeenth century. Alexander promised to help Sweden to
acquire Norway.

It was vitally important for Russia to secure the neu-
trality of Sweden, and, if possible, to make her a friend
and ally. The unexpected appearance of Sweden's fleet
in 1790, in the midst of Russia's war with Turkey, and
the thunder of naval artillery in St. Petersburg were still
vividly remembered.

Bernadotte, the Swedish heir apparent, had long forgotten that he had ever been one of Napoleon's marshals, let alone a soldier of the French Revolution. For
him Alexander was a friend, Napoleon an enemy, a
powerful enemy, to be sure, yet not so dangerous as
Alexander could be. From Napoleon, Sweden was protected by the sea, upon which the English reigned supreme. But against Alexander, especially after Russia's acquisition of Finland, there was no barrier. And
Bernadotte assumed a friendly attitude towards Russia as early as the spring of 1812, though he knew that
this was distasteful to Napoleon. He warned Sukhtelen,
the Russian Minister in Stockholm, that he himself,
like Alexander, was menaced by assassins sent from

Paris. Bernadotte promised to give military aid to Russia if necessary.

Armfeldt, one of Alexander's closest advisers, did much to bring the two countries together. Energetic, shrewd, loathing Napoleon, the Swede Armfeldt emigrated to the Russian court, where he rapidly became intimate with Alexander and played a significant part in the period preceding the war. Schenbusch, Swedish representative in 1811, and his successor Löwenhielm in 1812, acknowledged Armfeldt's great merit in preparing and completing the agreement between Russia and Sweden. While urging Alexander to break with Napoleon, Armfeldt realized the weaknesses of the entire Russian administrative organism. 'I am waging an open war with the ministers on all matters relating to administration, finances, and tariffs,' he wrote in confidential letters from St. Petersburg. 'One must be here on the spot and in constant relations with the officials to realize how far this country lags behind the rest of the world. Russian officials are nothing but a pack of bears or polished barbarians . . . Frederick II used to say that Sweden was a hundred years behind the times: in my opinion, Russia lags a thousand years.' 'In Russia there are no laws to which anyone would submit.'

Armfeldt actively intrigued against Speransky and was the chief cause of his sudden disgrace and banishment.

On 26 April 1812, in the city of Örebro, Sweden, the important diplomatic negotiations were completed: Sukhtelen, the Russian Minister, and Bernadotte ratified an agreement. Henceforth, Russia could face Napoleon without fear of a sudden attack from the north.

The third event favourable to Russia was the conclusion of peace with Turkey.

Negotiations had been in progress for some time in Bucharest. Russia was represented by Kutuzov, Turkey by the Grand Vizier. Kutuzov was in haste to sign the peace which would release the Russian army of the Danube in time for action between the Dnieper and the Niemen in the great conflict. After six years of war, the Turks were exhausted, but they could have held out for a time, particularly as they knew of Napoleon's imminent attack on Russia. The Grand Vizier's only fear was that there would be no war between Russia and Napoleon, that they would reach an understanding enabling Russia to concentrate all her strength on Turkey. Kutuzov cleverly exploited the news of Narbonne's journey to Vilna. The Turks were convinced that it indicated a Russian peace with Napoleon—why else would Napoleon enter into negotiations with the Tsar?

On 22 May, Russia and Turkey signed a treaty of peace, advantageous to Russia. The border was set at the River Prut, Russia retained Bessarabia, and the Caucasus frontier was readjusted in Russia's favour. Russia renounced Moldavia and Walachia; both provinces remained in Turkish hands. But the main, priceless advantage of this Bucharest peace was that it released tens of thousands of Russian soldiers who had been fighting the Turks. They could now be directed towards the Russo-Austrian frontier, against the auxiliary Austrian corps under Schwarzenberg, who was planning to invade Russia at the same time as Napoleon. The unexpected and speedy conclusion of the Russo-Turkish peace greatly diminished the value of Austria's help to Napoleon. Napoleon flew into a rage, and called the Turks imbeciles—and considerably worse.

Such were the comparatively favourable conditions which seemed to offer hope for a successful Russian defence. Nevertheless the Court and the higher nobility were in a state of confusion. We can give only a rough picture of this mood, because we know of it chiefly from foreigners. Russian contemporaries scarcely referred to it, and Russian historians have long considered it their duty to extol the patriotic spirit of the 'upper' classes in the year of the invasion. But Bernadotte in Sweden, the German monarchs, and the Danish Court received one report after another from their ambassadors and unofficial observers, all stating that the Tsar himself was extremely perturbed and that a large part of his entourage was apprehensive and nervous. Some—the minority—thought that the Tsar had destroyed Russia by quarrelling with Napoleon; the majority were irreconcilable enemies of Napoleon and favoured the approaching war. Yet nearly all believed that Alexander would be incapable of coping with the threatening storm; they thought it would be a good thing to eliminate the Tsar in some way and replace him by a stronger and generally more suitable man. Foreigners—the Swede Levenholm, for example—scarcely believed their ears at the gossip that was going round the salons of St. Petersburg.

Speransky was sacrificed by Alexander to those influential aristocrats who saw the weakness of the Tsar and suspected that he might waver at a decisive moment and again submit to Napoleon. The alleged 'treachery' of Speransky, whom the aristocracy loathed and regarded as favouring an alliance with Napoleon, was a mere device intended to eliminate him. But the exile of Speransky failed to disarm those who mistrusted the Tsar. Levenholm writes that the Tsar himself knew how much he was mistrusted.

Such was the mood when Alexander suddenly left

with his suite to join his army in Vilna. Was it to save himself from these irritating and depressing reproaches and rumours? Did he think that his departure would dissipate the fears of the nobility that he was ready to submit? Be that as it may, Count Narbonne turned up unexpectedly a few days after Alexander reached Vilna. Alexander was forced—once and for all—to clarify his attitude in the eyes of all Europe. We have seen how Narbonne's journey to Vilna ended.

The Russian nobility saw the storm approaching with mixed feelings. With joy because it meant the end of the 'Tilsit servitude,' the ruinous Continental blockade, Speransky's dubious innovations directed against the nobility. With fear before the terrible, invincible conqueror, although there were a few who had a sort of instinctive confidence in victory.

Three weeks before Napoleon crossed the Niemen, old Count Vorontsov, the Russian Ambassador in London, foretold the outcome of the war with startling perspicacity. If not for the faded paper, the rusty ink, and other unmistakable evidence, the authenticity of this document might be held in doubt.

'All Europe,' wrote Vorontsov, 'is tensely awaiting the events which must take place between the Dvina, the Dnieper, and the Vistula. I fear only the diplomatic and political events; I do not fear the military events at all. Even if the operations should prove unfavourable to us in the beginning, we can win by stubbornly waging a defensive war and continuing to fight as we retreat. If the enemy pursues us, he will perish, because the farther he proceeds from his stores of provisions, his arms and munitions depots, the farther he penetrates a land without passable roads or provisions which he could seize, the more pitiful will be his condition. He will be surrounded by an army of Cossacks and in the end will be destroyed by our winter, which has always been our loyal ally.'

After the retreat of the Russian army had actually begun, the old Count wrote another letter to his son, Mikhail Semenovich Vorontsov, Major-General in Bagration's forces, urging the Russian military leaders not to lose heart: 'Let them have patience,' 'Let them not lose heart because of a few defeats,' 'We must have the tenacity and firmness of Peter the Great.' The very fact that the old Count wrote these letters in his own hand, and did not dictate them—apparently wishing to conceal them from London—demonstrates the significance he attached to his counsels. Clearly afraid that Alexander would lose heart, he expected his son to convey his counsels to the Tsar.

But only a few persons of his rank were so confident after the invasion had begun. To be sure, it was easier to remain calm in London than in Vilna.

. . .

On the morning of 9 May 1812, Napoleon, accompanied by the Empress and a part of the Imperial Court, started for Dresden. Officially, the purpose of his journey was to review the Grand Army on the Vistula; but everyone knew he was going to make war on Russia. The interminable train of imperial carriages moved speedily across Germany through Mainz, Wurzburg, and Bamberg. The Emperor was received with tokens of servile respect. The vassal German kings bared their heads and bowed deeply. But the populace that crowded the roadsides was silent. Now and again one of the Emperor's retinue caught a sullen glance. Napoleon himself, in his more lucid moments, must have realized that his loyal General Rapp, commandant of Danzig, had been truthful in reporting the German hatred of the conqueror.

The Germany of 1812 was not the Germany which Napoleon had crushed in 1806-7. On the surface, there seemed to be no change. It is true that as early as 1809, while Napoleon was engaged in the war with Austria, there had been one or two desperate attempts at revolt in North Germany, but they had found no support and were promptly drowned in blood. From then on, French oppression had met with no organized resistance. In 1810, Napoleon annexed the Hanseatic commercial cities, and the entire coastline of the North Sea. With similar disregard of existing treaties, he proceeded to make other annexations and to pour his troops into Prussia. But all this time a great transformation was taking place in Germany. Former sympathies, aroused by the introduction of the *Code Napoleon,* dwindled and died, as the majority of the population came to understand the purely predatory, imperialistic nature of Napoleon's conquests. Germany was reduced to a colony for the marketing of French goods; German industry, as the foe of French industry, was suppressed. The German people was ruled by Napoleonic governors like King Jerome Bonaparte, who received all central and a part of northern Germany (the Kingdom of Westphalia), the kings of Bavaria and Saxony, the princes of the Confederation of the Rhine. Other German thrones were occupied by intimidated and servile descendants of previous dynasties, such as Frederick-William III in Prussia. Napoleon knew that Germany was beginning to awaken; he knew of the newly arisen *Tugendbund* (League of Virtue), an organization of patriotic students. He viewed all this with suspicion, but the new movement did not yet strike him as dangerous.

As he moved eastward across Germany in May 1812, Napoleon was conscious of being Europe's dictator in the fullest sense of the word. He might think with vexation of the Spanish ruffians who insolently refused to yield. But he would have thought it absurd to worry about Leipzig or Göttingen students singing patriotic songs in taverns, or about the suspicious lectures of an obscure Professor Fichte. Kings, dukes, and princes of Germany rivalled one another in flattery and sycophancy; their only dream was that their lord and master should let them accompany him to Dresden. In 1810, in the Cathedral of Notre Dame in Paris, when Napoleon celebrated for the second time his marriage to Marie-Louise—the first ceremony had taken place in Vienna, where, in the absence of Napoleon, Marshal Berthier had acted as his proxy—five queens had carried the train of Marie-Louise's gown. European wits had whispered that the kings were envious of the queens, lamenting that Napoleon himself had no train, which they might share in carrying. Now, in the spring of 1812, the cringing servility was even more shameless.

The King and the Queen of Saxony had come a long way from Dresden to meet Napoleon.

Cannon thundered salutes, troops and burghers jammed the streets and squares, when the Ruler of Europe entered the capital of vassal Saxony.

The Austrian Emperor, Francis I, and his wife also came to Dresden to greet their all-powerful son-in-law. The King of Prussia asked Napoleon's permission to come to Dresden; Napoleon graciously consented, and the King arrived forthwith.

Napoleon treated them kindly. True, all these monarchs in conversing with him respectfully bared their heads, while he kept his hat on his head; sometimes he forgot to ask them to sit down; he did not offer to shake hands with everyone, and, when he did, it was not always promptly. But no one paid attention to such trifles. On the whole, he was benign; he did not shout at any of them, did not deprive anyone of his throne; all of them returned unscathed to their respective capitals.

All these Dresden festivities, this immense assemblage of vassal monarchs, were meant as a grandiose anti-Russian demonstration. It was in Dresden that Napoleon received the report of Count Narbonne, who rushed there from Vilna.

Napoleon bade farewell to his crowned vassals, and, leaving Marie-Louise and all his Court in Dresden, he set out to join the Grand Army, which, in several columns, was advancing towards the Niemen. He went by way of Posen, Torn, Danzig, Königsberg, Insterburg, Gumbinen. At daybreak, on 21 June, he arrived at the small town of Vilkovishko, a few kilometres from the Niemen. On 22 June he ordered his troops to move from Vilkovishko towards the river. The third regiment of Mounted Chasseurs formed the vanguard of the Grand Army.

There are about ten different estimates of the size of the Grand Army that crossed the Niemen. Napoleon spoke of 400,000 men. His personal secretary, Baron Fain, mentioned 360,000; Ségur—375,000; Fezanzac—500,000. The figures given by St. Hilaire (614,000) and by Labomme (680,000) clearly include the reserves stationed in Germany and Poland. Most of the estimates lie between 400,000 and 470,000. The number 420,000

is the most frequently mentioned in documents referring to the army that actually crossed the Niemen. The
30,000 Austrians under Schwarzenberg participated in
the war, but did not cross the Niemen. Napoleon's
main army comprised about 380,000 men, and the two
flanks—Macdonald's in the north, towards Riga, and
Schwarzenberg's in the south—together comprised from
60 to 65 thousand men.

Another 55,500 men were sent into Russia during
the months of July and August, and, at the height of
the campaign, Napoleon's army was augmented by the
corps of Marshal Victor (about 30,000 men), and by
march battalions numbering about 70,000 for replen-
ishment.

The next chapter will deal with the composition and
peculiar character of this army. Here I wish only to
note that, according to most contemporaries and eyewitnesses, the bulk of the army crossed the Niemen in a
cheerful mood. Almost all were certain of victory, and
a few enthusiasts mentioned India, whither they would
march after beating the Russians, and spoke of the
cashmeres and golden ingots of Delhi and Benares.

Napoleon moved swiftly among the interminable columns of his troops, surrounded by his retinue, overtaken by couriers and estafettes, dictating and distributing orders, overtaking corps after corps. His army, half
a million strong, caught only passing glimpses of the
squat, fat man in the grey coat and three-cornered hat,
now in a carriage, now on his Arabian horse, advancing eastward at a speed impossible for masses of cavalry.
This passing apparition, eyewitnesses relate, aroused the
most passionate curiosity. Whither was he driving this
countless armed mass? What were his precise aims?

We have pointed out that Alexander was a changeable

character, that in 1812 he was not the same man as before or after that date. The same is true of Napoleon.

As a result of his first big war—the conquest of Italy
in 1796—Napoleon, according to his own words, 'had
unlearned submission'—that is, submission to human
beings. But as a result of Tilsit in 1807, he began to
lose his capacity for submitting to realities and for taking them into account. 'I can do everything now,' he
said, soon after Tilsit, to his brother Lucien. Politics,
in his opinion, was made by big battalions. And who
had bigger battalions than he? As for economics, that,
too, he would bring to reason with his big battalions.
Once he conquered Europe and subjugated Russia, the
English would not sell a single pound of goods anywhere; they would go bankrupt and perish. Human
beings were children and slaves, he could do with them
what he pleased; but their kings were worse than slaves;
they were lackeys always ready to lick the hand that
beat them, they would always prefer the role of stewards
and overseers of Napoleon's possessions to any other
role, as long, and only as long as their redoubtable master had his 'big battalions.'

True, there was one most incomprehensible exception, which had long been a source of perplexity to
Napoleon. This was Spain. The Spaniards spat upon
French officers who led them to be shot. Napoleon offered them the choice: submission or death. The Spaniards spat on death. But Napoleon had long ceased to
reckon with reality. He had failed to conquer Spain;
he knew at the start of the war with Russia that he
would be forced to leave some 200,000 or more choice
troops in Spain. Nevertheless he decided forcibly to
enlist a large number of Spaniards in the Grand Army

that was marching towards the Niemen. We shall see
with what results.

This was but one indication of the change in Napoleon's psychology. To the end of his days he could not
comprehend the historical impossibility of a goal he had
come to consider fully attainable. Even after his career
was ended, he continued, in his confidential conversations on the island of St. Helena, to speak of his ideal, or
what he then thought expedient to give out as his ideal,
as extremely modest and harmless. If the campaign of
1812 had only succeeded—he maintained—he would
have been satisfied, he would have ceased to wage war,
he would have visited his domains, helped the suffering, established order and justice, et cetera. In other
words, absolute power over Europe was his minimum
programme, so to speak. To the end of his days, he
thought it very moderate!

In reality, as he travelled from Dresden to Vilkovishko in June 1812, exultantly cheered all along his
route by the French units of his immense army, Napoleon's dreams were far more ambitious, but he did not
repeat to his soldiers what he had said in confidence to
Count Narbonne. And this secrecy left the strongest
and most disturbing impression in the souls of those
who recalled this period after many years. The officers'
corps knew that this time even members of the Imperial
staff, even marshals, received only the briefest, most
general instructions, and that each marshal had his own
idea of the basic purpose of the war. In none of his
previous wars had Napoleon kept his army so much in
the dark concerning his objectives. Six weeks later, in
Vitebsk, when Count Daru dared to tell Napoleon to
his face that no one in the French army knew why the

war was being fought, he was completely right; Napoleon had good reason not to answer him. But now, with the countless hosts advancing in orderly, brilliant columns towards the Niemen, even the unknown was attractive.

Today, 125 years later, we know many things that contemporaries did not know. Yet when we try to reconstitute and formulate Napoleon's purpose, we do not, despite all our efforts, obtain a definite, logical, and well-founded picture. All we have to go by is several equally authentic and often contradictory utterances by the only man who could have answered our question. We have, for instance, an account of Napoleon's conversation with Narbonne after his arrival at Dresden from Vilna. As Narbonne's mission in Vilna was precisely to avoid achieving any results, the Emperor scarcely listened to his report and passed at once to a subject in which he was far more interested. 'Now we shall march on Moscow,' Napoleon said, 'and from Moscow why not turn to India? Let no one tell Napoleon that it is far from Moscow to India! Alexander of Macedon had to travel a long way from Greece to India, but did that stop him? Alexander reached the Ganges, having started from a point as distant as Moscow . . . Just suppose, Narbonne, that Moscow is taken, that Russia lies prostrate, that the Tsar has either submitted to a peace or has perished in some sort of a palace conspiracy, then tell me—will it be so impossible for the French army to reach the Ganges with the help of auxiliary forces? And once the French sword touches the Ganges, the edifice of England's mercantile greatness will tumble in ruins.'

Are we justified in concluding that the basic objec-

tives of the war were Moscow and India? Not at all!
For at the same time and in the same place, Napoleon
asserted that the Tsar was forcing him into a war by
his 'ultimatum' demanding the evacuation of French
troops from Prussia, that the aim of the war was to
make Alexander listen to reason, to dissuade him from
a possible rapprochement with England; that this war
was a purely 'political' war, i.e. undertaken for a definite diplomatic purpose; and that once this purpose
was attained, Napoleon would be ready to make peace.
We are faced with similar contradictions when we try
to define Napoleon's immediate strategic aim: did he
intend to conquer Lithuania and White Russia, and
then wait in Vitebsk for the Tsar to make overtures for
peace? Or did he intend to go to Moscow, and await
these overtures there? Each hypothesis can be substan-
tiated by Napoleon's own words. Small wonder that the
Grand Army, from the marshals down to the cooks,
had no idea why it was being led into Russia.

In November 1812, in battles near Krasny, the Cossacks captured a portion of Marshal Davout's baggage
train, and among other papers and plans found maps
of Turkey, Central Asia, and India, 'as Napoleon
planned that an invasion of Hindustan should be one
of the conditions of a peace with Alexander.' This was
confirmed by Alexander himself in a conversation with
the English General Wilson. The Tsar stated that in
refusing to make peace with Napoleon he had saved
India for the English . . .

Napoleon's army passed through Germany and soon
entered Poland. The 'liberation' of Poland was one of
the slogans, but actually it was only an incidental detail of the approaching war. Poland was designed pri-

marily as a reserve of man power for the Grand Army. Whether or not Napoleon would actually give her Lithuania and White Russia in the future—that remained to be seen. Napoleon pledged nothing.

In Vilkovishko, Napoleon stopped in the house of a landowner. Here, on 22 June, he wrote a proclamation to the Grand Army: 'Soldiers, the second Polish war has begun. The first ended at Friedland and Tilsit. In Tilsit, Russia swore to an eternal alliance with France; she vowed to make war on England. She is now violating her oath. She refuses to explain her strange behaviour, until the French eagles return across the Rhine, abandoning our allies to her will. Destiny drives Russia onward, her fate is inevitable. Does she think we have degenerated? Are we no longer the soldiers of Austerlitz? She forces us to choose between dishonour and war. There can be no doubt of our choice. We shall go forward, we shall cross the Niemen, we shall carry war into her territory. The second Polish war will be as glorious for French arms as the first. But the peace which we shall conclude will be well secured; it will end the ruinous influence which Russia has exerted on the affairs of Europe for the past fifty years.'

This proclamation also served as a declaration of war on Russia; Napoleon delivered no other. On 23 June, he rode along the bank of the Niemen with his retinue. Two bridges were in process of construction. A third was completed at midnight of 23 June. A fourth bridge near Kovno could also be used for the crossing.

On the night of 24 June, Napoleon gave the order to cross. The die was cast.

'At one o'clock after midnight an unaccustomed commotion could be heard on the River Niemen. The entire city heard it, and beyond a doubt everyone guessed that such a din could be produced only by the march of a great army. The beating of drums and several rifle shots were heard above Kovno . . . At six in the morning, advance units of the French and Polish troops unexpectedly entered the town and drew up in military formation on the square.'

During the entire night of 24/25 June, and the days and nights of 25, 26, and 27 June, Napoleon's army, in four uninterrupted streams, crossed the Niemen on three new bridges and one old one.

'My dear': wrote Napoleon to his wife on 25 June 1812, 'I crossed the Niemen on the twenty-fourth, at two o'clock in the morning. In the evening I crossed the Vilia. I have seized the city of Kovno. No serious engagement took place. My health is good, but the heat is extreme.' This was his first report on the beginning of the war.

'During the day of 24 June,' wrote Barclay de Tolly, 'the savage storm broke: Napoleon, believing himself unconquerable and thinking that the time had come to throw off his hypocritical mask, broke off all the negotiations continued until then for the purpose of gaining time . . . He drove sixteen foreign nations, oppressed under the iron sceptre of his lust for power, to war on Russia.'

Regiment after regiment, battery after battery, the French army crossed the Niemen at Yurburg, Kovno, Olit, and Merech, and drew up on the Russian side. Napoleon stood at one of the bridges exchanging salutes with one regiment after another. Having crossed the river with his Old Guard, he galloped, without his retinue, into a neighbouring wood.

No one was anywhere to be seen. Deserted fields, sand, an endless forest, extending as far as the eye could reach. Dead silence, not a soul, or a sign of a human habitation. A sullen, dark, boundless forest filled the whole horizon.

2

FROM THE NIEMEN TO SMOLENSK

LATE in the evening of 24 June, at Vilna, at a ball given in his honour, Alexander learned that Napoleon had crossed the Russian frontier.

At ten o'clock the following evening, he summoned Balashov, his Minister of Police, who happened to be in his suite. 'You undoubtedly will be surprised,' he told him, 'when you hear why I sent for you. I intend to send you to Emperor Napoleon. I have just received a report from St. Petersburg that our Ministry of Foreign Affairs has received a note from the French Embassy explaining that our ambassador, Prince Kurakin, has asked for his passports twice in a single day and that France regards this action as a rupture; in consequence, Count Lauriston has been commanded to ask for his passport and leave Russia. Though this is a very flimsy reason, it is, as far as I know, Napoleon's first pretext for making war on us. What makes it all the more paltry is that Kurakin acted on his own account, and not on my orders.'

'Between you and me,' Alexander added, 'I do not expect your errand will stop the war. But at least Europe will know, and this will prove once more, that we did not begin it.' At two the next morning, Alexander handed Balashov a letter for Napoleon, and bade his messenger to tell Napoleon that 'if he wants to enter into negotiations, they can begin at once, on one unalterable condition: his armies must retire beyond the frontier. Otherwise, the Tsar gives his word of honour that so long as a single armed French soldier remains on Russian soil, he will neither utter nor listen to a single word about peace.'

That very night Balashov left, and at daybreak he reached the advance posts of the French army in the little town of Rossienti. French Hussars first conducted him to Murat, then to Davout, who, very rudely ignoring his protest, took Alexander's letter and sent it by an orderly to Napoleon. On the following day Balashov was told to accompany Davout's army-corps to Vilna. Thus it was not until 29 June that Balashov reached Vilna. On the following day, Napoleon's chamberlain, Count Turenne, led him to Napoleon's study. 'It was the same room from which, five days previous, Alexander I dispatched me on my errand.' *

Balashov's own account is our only source for his conversation with Napoleon. It is quite clear that Bala-

* The account of Balashov's conversation with Napoleon is preserved in the Archives of Military Studies. It has several times appeared in print, with certain deletions and changes (in Mikhailovsky-Danilevsky, in Thiers). In a fuller form it appears in the Dubrovin edition: 'The War for the Fatherland in the Letters of Contemporaries' (1882), No. 19. But here, too, there are excisions, restored, I must remark, by Nikolas Karlovich Schilder, from marginal notes in a copy of the Dubrovin edition in the Public Library in A. D. Balashov's own hand. Of course, Balashov's exposition is not entirely trustworthy, and it is impossible to verify it, as neither Napoleon nor anyone in his retinue left us his version; while the precise and truthful Ségur, who was always with the retinue, speaks of this meeting in two casual pages (Vol. I, pp. 171-2), relying, moreover, for the most part on Balashov's Russian version.

shov wrote his notes many years after the event; certainly after the death of Alexander I, perhaps only a short time before his own death. The cover of the manuscript carries the inscription: '29 December 1836,' and Balashov died in 1837. Moreover, the Minister of Police, a court intriguer and clever careerist, was accustomed to taking great liberties with the truth when it served some advantage; he obviously 'stylized' his conversation with Napoleon, and particularly his own replies (for instance, that Charles XII had taken the road to Moscow via Poltava; that in Russia, as in Spain, the people were religious, et cetera). All of this is obviously pure invention. Surely Napoleon could not have suddenly asked Balashov so absurd a question as 'What is the road to Moscow?' As if his staff under Berthier hadn't worked out the entire itinerary in detail! It is clear that Balashov invented this silly question only to insert his reply, also devised at leisure, about Charles XII and Poltava. And Napoleon could not have said, 'In our day no one is pious any more,' because he had often said that even in France there were many religious people, and he was particularly convinced that Russia was a country of great piety where religious superstitions carried much weight. Undoubtedly, this question was invented by Balashov to bring in his equally fabricated answer that the Russians were as religious as the Spaniards. With these reservations, it is nevertheless possible to accept as authentic almost everything that Balashov put in Napoleon's mouth, because it fully agrees with similar wholly corroborated statements by the Emperor in conversations with other persons.

Balashov had two audiences with Napoleon on 30 June: the first immediately after the Emperor's breakfast; the second, during and after dinner. 'I regret that Emperor Alexander has such bad advisers,' Napoleon began. 'What does he expect to gain by this war? I have already seized one of his fairest provinces without firing a shot, and here we are, neither he nor I knowing what we are fighting for.'

Balashov replied that Alexander desired peace, that Kurakin had not been empowered by him but had asked for his passports and left of his own accord, and that there was no agreement between Russia and England. Napoleon retorted angrily that Alexander had insulted him by demanding the withdrawal of his troops from Prussia, et cetera. 'At this moment, a window was blown open by the wind. Napoleon went to the window (both of us were pacing up and down the room) and quickly shut it. When it blew open again—by now he was quite agitated—he no longer took the trouble to shut it, but tore the window from its frame and flung it outside.' Napoleon went on to say that he had not intended to fight Russia, that he had even sent all his personal carriages to Spain, whither he wished to go. 'I know that a war between France and Russia is no trifling matter for either Russia or France. I have made extensive preparations, and my forces are three times as large as yours. I know as well as you do, perhaps better than you, the size of your army. You have 120,000 infantry, and 60 to 70 thousand cavalry. In a word, under 200,000 men, all told. I have three times as many.'

Further, Napoleon asked if Alexander was not ashamed of having such odious and criminal intimates as Armfeldt and Stein. Stein, he said, was 'a scoundrel, banished from his own country.' (Napoleon had forgotten to add that he himself had ordered the Prussian

King to banish Stein for sympathizing with the Spaniards and striving to liberate Prussia from the French yoke.)

Another of Alexander's intimates was 'Bennigsen, who is said to have some military gifts, though I personally don't think so, but who has stained his hands with the blood of his sovereign.' These final words, 'of his sovereign,' were written by Balashov, but were later scratched out, either by him or by someone else, but so badly that they are still legible. There can be no possible doubt that Napoleon had actually employed those words: it was not the first time that he publicly reproached Alexander for the assassination of his father.

Napoleon did not succeed in concealing his irritation at Barclay's retreat from Vilna. He would have preferred Barclay to make a stand at Vilna. He would have been able to destroy him at once, and this would have very much suited Napoleon. 'I do not know Barclay de Tolly, but, judging from his first moves in the campaign, he is rather lacking in military talent. Never have you begun a war in such confusion . . . You have burned many stores. Why? Either you shouldn't have assembled them, or you should have used them according to their purpose. Did you imagine that I would merely have a look at the Niemen and would refrain from crossing it? Aren't you ashamed? From the time of Peter I, from the time when Russia became a European power, no enemy has penetrated your borders, and now I am in Vilna. I have conquered an entire province without firing a shot. If only out of respect for your Emperor, who for two months had been in Vilna with his headquarters, you should have defended it! How do you expect to inspire your armies, or rather, what is their spirit now? I know what they thought as they were

going into the Austerlitz campaign. They believed they
were invincible. And now they are sure in advance that
they will be defeated by my troops.'

Balashov protested: 'Since your Majesty permits me
to speak of this subject, I venture to say with conviction
that you are undertaking a terrible war! This will be
a war in which the entire nation will take part—a redoubtable mass. The Russian soldier is brave, and the
people are attached to their native land . . .'

Again Napoleon interrupted him, and again he spoke
of his forces: 'I know that your soldiers are brave, but
I have an infinitely larger number than you have.' Napoleon threatened that he would go to the ends of
Russia; that, if necessary, he would undertake two or
three Russian campaigns. He praised the Poles, their
ardour and their patriotism. 'How are you going to
fight without allies, when even with allies you could
accomplish nothing? When Austria was with you,
France itself was threatened by attack at various points.
But now, with all Europe behind me, how can you resist me?'

'We shall do what we can, Sire.'

Changing the subject a little, Napoleon said that
Alexander, by rejecting the Tilsit policy and the friendship of Napoleon, 'had injured his own interests as a
sovereign.' The Tsar would have received not only Finland but also Moldavia and Walachia, and, in time, the
Duchy of Warsaw. 'No, not now! But in time.' These
words are extraordinarily characteristic of Napoleon, in
particular of his attitude towards Poland. He had just
spoken with enthusiasm about the loyalty of the Poles
and their readiness to shed their blood for him, and
now he was offering to betray them in exchange for
some advantage or other to be derived from a future

friendship with Alexander. For Napoleon, individuals and whole nations were only pawns in his game. This was always so natural with him that he would probably have been thoroughly surprised if Balashov had pointed out to him the cynicism and the utter unscrupulousness revealed by his words about the Duchy of Warsaw. But neither Balashov nor anyone else ever thought of telling His Majesty the real feelings which Napoleon's frankness often aroused. In any case, his unexpected words must have given Balashov a malicious pleasure, considering that the Poles were at that very moment filling the streets of Vilna with cries of 'Vivat Caesar!' and blessing the heavens for having sent them a great liberator.

And again Napoleon began angrily to revile Alexander for having dared to surround himself with his, Napoleon's, enemies, and not even with Russian ones, but with foreigners.

Towards the end of this first audience, the conversation passed to insignificant matters. Napoleon inquired about the health of Chancellor Rumyantsev, about Kochubey. For some reason, he pretended that he could not recall Speransky's name, though he had personally met him at Erfurt in September 1808. 'Tell me, please, why did they banish . . . the man who used to be in your Council of State . . . What is his name? . . . Spi . . . Sper . . . I can't recall it!' 'Speransky,' Balashov prompted him. 'Yes!' 'The Emperor wasn't satisfied with him.' 'He was not a traitor, was he?' 'I don't think so, Sire. Such crimes are inevitably made public.' 'Was it some sort of abuse, then—an abuse of funds, perhaps?' Why Napoleon wanted to play this comedy is not known. He certainly remembered Speransky's name, and he knew about the Speransky affair as well as Balashov himself. And, of course, he also knew that this same Balashov, as Minister of Police, had deported Speransky from St. Petersburg. Napoleon received from his spies the most detailed information about Alexander's dignitaries, and all the court intrigues of St. Petersburg and Pavlovsk.

At the dinner to which Balashov had been invited were present, in addition to the Emperor himself, his Marshals Berthier and Bessières, and Caulaincourt, the Duke of Vicenza. After dinner, the conversation grew serious. '*Mon Dieu,* what do people want?' exclaimed Napoleon, speaking of Alexander. 'After being beaten at Austerlitz, after being beaten at Friedland—in a word, after two unhappy wars—he received Finland, Moldavia, Walachia, Bialystok, and Tarnopol, and still he is not satisfied . . . I am not angry at him because of this war. One war more—one more triumph for me . . .' And again he indignantly attacked Stein, Armfeldt, Wintzengerode. 'Tell Emperor Alexander that if he surrounds himself by my personal enemies, I must conclude that he wishes to affront me personally, and, consequently, I shall do the same to him. I shall drive all his friends in Württemberg, Baden, Weimar, out of Germany. Let him prepare a refuge for them in Russia . . . England will not give Russia any money; she has none herself. Despite their pacts, Sweden and Turkey will attack Russia at a convenient moment. Except for Bagration, Russia has no good generals. Bennigsen is no good: look how he behaved at Eylau, at Friedland! And now he is five years older. He has always been weak, has always made mistake after mistake, and what will he do now?' Then, for the second time, he mentioned the murder of Paul, saying that Alexander 'knew of the crime' committed by Bennigsen. 'I hear that Emperor Alexander himself will take command of the army. What for? That means assuming responsibility for the defeat. War is my profession. I am used to it. It is not the same with him. He is an emperor by right of birth. He should rule, and appoint a general to command the army. If the general does his job well, the Tsar can reward him; if not— he can punish and discharge him. It is better to have a general responsible to the Tsar than for the Tsar to be responsible to the nation, since tsars, too, are answerable for their actions. This should not be forgotten.' 'Then,' writes Balashov, 'after pacing for a while, he walked up to Caulaincourt and, striking him lightly upon the cheek, said: "Well, why don't you say something, you old St. Petersburg courtier? . . . Are the horses ready for the General? Give him my horses, he has a long journey ahead of him!"'

Balashov's audience was at an end. He did not know what took place in the Emperor's study after his departure. The scene is related by Ségur, who also mentions Napoleon's final sally before Balashov's departure, though in a slightly different form—(he must have heard it from one of the attendant marshals). 'Well, Emperor Alexander has friends even at my Imperial headquarters,' said Napoleon to Balashov, and pointing at Caulaincourt he added: 'Here is a champion of your Emperor. He is a Russian—in the French camp.' Caulaincourt was deeply offended by this, says Ségur, and no sooner had Balashov left the room than Caulaincourt, in a trembling voice, asked Napoleon why he had humiliated him. Caulaincourt declared heatedly that he was a Frenchman, a good Frenchman; he had proved it and would prove it again.

There and then, Caulaincourt gave vent to his pent-up emotions. As Ambassador to St. Petersburg, he had made great efforts to strengthen the Franco-Russian alliance; later, after his recall, he had persistently tried to dissuade Napoleon from fighting Russia. In Balashov's presence, the Emperor had done his utmost to insult Alexander; with his departure, the last feeble hope of averting the dangerous adventure was gone. Caulaincourt now declared that he would prove himself a good Frenchman, precisely by repeating that this war was 'impolitic' and dangerous, that it would destroy the army, France, the Emperor himself. Moreover, as his Emperor had offended him, he wanted to leave, and he asked to be put in charge of a division in Spain, 'where no one wished to serve,' so that he might be as far as possible from his Emperor who had so sorely humiliated him. Napoleon tried to calm him, but in vain. Caulaincourt left the room unreconciled. On the following day, Napoleon put an end to the quarrel by formally commanding Caulaincourt to remain, and by showing him every possible kindness.

Caulaincourt was not a man to be easily upset, and Napoleon's witticism can hardly account for his extreme emotion on that day. Caulaincourt had endured worse from Napoleon. We know from Caulaincourt's own later writings and from his intimates that even long before the fatal campaign, he had the feeling that an abyss was opening beneath his feet. Most probably his constant worry about the Russian expedition had thrown him off his balance.

·   ·   ·

Balashov returned to Alexander and reported his conversation with Napoleon.

It was war, finally and irrevocably.

After some hesitation, Alexander decided not to publish any solemn manifesto. Instead, an order was issued to the troops on 13 June 1812, announcing Napoleon's invasion and the opening of hostilities.

In an unpublished draft of a manifesto, Alexander wrote of the 'distressing bonds' which he 'voluntarily' laid upon himself with a view to preserving peace. First he addressed the Poles, exhorting them not to trust Napoleon and to think of the servitude awaiting them if they yielded to him: 'Who does not know of the enslavement of all Western countries under the yoke of the French Emperor? Who had not found out that the newly established States are merely new vassals and victims on the altar of the French Emperor's glory?' The manifesto then referred to Napoleon's refusal to ratify the agreement on Poland, to the occupation of Germany by French troops and their gradual approach to the Russian frontiers, to Napoleon's seizure of all the possessions of the Duke of Oldenburg, which, the Tsar explained, was a personal affront to himself, because of his kinship with the Dukes of Oldenburg. Finally the manifesto went on to the most important point of all: 'Striving to reduce us to the ruin and impotence which is the lot of all the powers submitting to his rule, he has demanded that we should cease all trade, on the pretext that certain neutral ships entering our ports have been furthering the expansion of English industry and aiding her settlements in eastern and western India.' Alexander denied that he had permitted trade with England; on the contrary, he stressed the 'strong measures' he had taken against trade with the English.

But 'no agreement or any unfair interpretation of our obligations to France could constrain us to a ruin-

ous extermination of all our sea commerce.' This would
have been all the more 'unreasonable,' since the French
Emperor himself permits his country to trade with
neutral governments and even allows certain private
persons to trade with England. Equally unfounded were
Napoleon's grievances against the Russian tariff of 1810.
'This arrogant pretension to dictate the internal administration of a sovereign state is in itself so improper
that its confutation requires no extensive argument.'

Despite all this, the manifesto continues, Alexander
desired to make all possible concessions, including
changes in the tariff in favour of French industry and
trade (specifically in wines), and was even willing to
withdraw the Russian protest in connection with Oldenburg. Russia asked only that East Prussia and Pomerania
be cleared of French troops and insisted on the right
of 'neutral trade, indispensable to the very existence
of our Empire . . . It seemed incomprehensible to our
mind, which was far from harbouring any ill design,
that the French Emperor, responsible for the tears and
groans of so many nations, should once again cast aside
all respect for divine judgment, for the judgment of
Europe and the entire world, in a manner so harmful to
the best interests of his own Empire that, in return for
our extraordinary moderation, he should attack a country which has not harmed him in any way. We were
still hoping that he would stay his hand from executing such terrible designs, when he and his army violated the borders of our Empire.'

But there was no time to publish the manifesto.
Scouts reported that Napoleon was marching on Vilna,
with Murat and his cavalry heading the advance. It
was promptly decided to abandon Vilna for the 'forti-

fied camp' at Drissa, built according to the design of General Phull, a member of the Tsar's suite. This General Phull was doubtless one of the strangest figures in Alexander's entourage. He was a learned theoretician. At the beginning of every war, he marked out the most elaborate and detailed plans, which never came to anything. Phull began his career in the Prussian army. In 1806, when war broke out between Prussia and Napoleon, Phull (then on the General Staff of the Prussian army) devised an infallible plan for the crushing of Napoleon. The war began on 8 October. On 14 October, exactly six days later, Napoleon and Marshal Davout destroyed in one day the entire Prussian army in two simultaneous battles at Jena and Auerstadt. In this terrible hour of Prussian history, Phull startled everyone by bursting into laughter like a madman and jeering at the defeated Prussian army for not having followed his plan. The words 'like a madman' are used by Clausewitz, who had witnessed the incident. (*Er lachte wie ein halb Wahnsinniger über die Niederlage unserer Heere.*) After this catastrophe, Phull went to St. Petersburg, where he began to instruct Emperor Alexander in the art of war. Alexander had faith in the genius of this irritable, stubborn, supercilious failure, who after six years knew not a word of Russian, and despised the Russian generals for their ignorance of strategic principles.

Acting on Phull's advice, Alexander, without consulting either Barclay or Bagration, ordered the construction of a 'fortified camp' in the tiny town of Drissa on the Dvina. According to Phull's plan, this camp, in which 120,000 men were to be concentrated, could, because of its central position between two main roads, hinder Napoleon from advancing against St. Petersburg

or Moscow. When Napoleon had suddenly crossed the
Niemen, the Russian army was actually ordered to retire to Sventsiani, and thence to Drissa. A few generals
were bold enough to warn the Tsar that 'only a madman or a traitor could have conceived the camp at
Drissa,' whose sham fortifications would be unable to
hold out for even a few days. The Russian army, Alexander was told, was threatened with encirclement and
ignominious capitulation.

Clausewitz, who served Barclay's army in a minor
position and had studied this camp shortly before the
First Russian army entered it, arrived at this conclusion: 'If the Russians had not voluntarily abandoned
this position, they would have been attacked from the
rear, and, regardless whether they numbered 90,000 or
120,000, they would have been driven into the semi-
circle of trenches and forced to capitulate.'

Phull's clumsy plan, a poor imitation of Frederick II's
Buntzlow camp, was, of course, abandoned a few days
after Napoleon's invasion. Nevertheless, the fantastic
idea had caused much harm. The principle of such
'fortified camps' requires the defender to operate with
two separated armies: one army defends the camp and
holds back the besiegers, while the other, manœuvring
in the open field, harries the besieging forces. By the
very nature of the Lithuanian–White–Russian forest
region, the Russian army was anyhow divided into two
parts; this was all the more necessary because no one
knew which road Napoleon would choose for his advance. As long as they adhered to the plan based on the
defence of Drissa, these two Russian armies did not,
and could not, make any attempt to unite. For several
days, the First Russian Army remained in the camp

on the left bank of the Dvina, opposite the little town of Drissa, about a hundred kilometres from Dvinsk.

According to eyewitnesses, the Tsar arrived at Vilna firmly convinced that Phull's plan was good. Everyone else was against it. But no one had anything reasonable to suggest except Barclay de Tolly, and his opinion was not respected. His advice was to retreat and not risk a general battle at the frontier, which would lead to certain disaster. Alexander and his suite clearly underestimated the strength of the French army concentrated on the Vistula and the Niemen. They were familiar with Napoleon's method of overawing his foes by an appearance of invincibility, and this may explain why Alexander mistrusted the rumours concerning the immensity of the French army. Besides, Alexander's intimates must have considered the huge forces Napoleon had left in Spain. They also knew that Napoleon had been forced to distribute garrisons at many points of his immense empire extending from Antwerp and Amsterdam to the Balkan mountains; from Hamburg, Bremen, and Lübeck to Naples, Calabria, and Apulia; from Danzig to Madrid. After the first few days of war, however, these comforting illusions vanished, and extravagant hopes yielded to confusion.

The Russian army had no sooner entered the Drissa camp than it began preparations for getting out of the trap. The Tsar ceased to speak to or even look at Phull, formerly his inseparable companion.

When Napoleon invaded Russia, the Russian forces were scattered along a front of 800 versts. Some claim that Barclay de Tolly first intended to give battle, but was soon compelled to abandon the idea because the French army had turned out to be much larger than the Russian General Staff and the Court had supposed.

Towards the end of June, Bagration had six divisions, while Napoleon faced him with almost twice that many —eleven divisions. Barclay had twelve divisions, and Napoleon was moving about seventeen against him.* According to Count von Toll, the original plan provided for offensive operations, and only the 'immeasurable superiority of his [Napoleon's] forces, concentrated on the Vistula between Königsberg and Warsaw, and certain political considerations' caused a change in the plan. 'It was decided to wage a defensive war,' because, of the 360 to 400 thousand men available in Russia at the moment—this number included the troops of the Don and the Guard—only 220,000 men, even counting the army of Tormasov, could be sent against Napoleon. And even this figure was only on paper.

The Russians decided to retire. 'To be sure, this course involved the sacrifice of certain provinces, but, of the two inescapable evils, it was necessary to choose the lesser—and rather lose a part for a time, than the whole for ever.' These words of Count von Toll show the anxiety of the Court and the General Staff while they were awaiting Napoleon's ultimate decision in Vilna.

This first loss of Russian territory greatly dismayed Alexander's entourage.

'How terrible!' wrote Shishkov, the Tsar's secretary in the first days of the war. 'To lose Vilna only five days after the opening of hostilities! To run away, to abandon so many towns and territories to the enemy, and with all that, to boast of such a beginning! What more could the enemy wish for? Nothing, except perhaps to advance unhindered to the very gates of our two capitals! Oh, merciful Lord! My words are washed in bit-

* Thus wrote Alexander to Saltykov from Drissa.

ter tears!' Such were the feelings aroused in Alexander's intimates by the loss of Polish-Lithuanian Vilna. How then would the loss of purely Russian territories affect them?

Napoleon supposed that when he crossed the Niemen, the Russian army directly opposing him numbered approximately 200,000 men. He was mistaken. Actually, on the day of the invasion, and not counting the southern army of General Tormasov which faced the Austrian army corps of Schwarzenberg, the Russian High Command disposed of the following forces: the army of Barclay (First Army) consisting of 118,000 men; the army of Bagration (Second Army), of 35,000 men; 153,000 men, all told. During the retreat to Drissa, Bobruysk, Moghilev, Smolensk, these armies were reinforced by garrison troops and reserves, and their original number was increased to 181,000; but we must deduct from this total the army of General Wittgenstein, consisting of 25,000 men, assigned to guard the roads leading to St. Petersburg, and 7,000 men lost in battles; thus only 149,800 men remained; these should have been in Smolensk on 3 August, when, at last, the armies of Barclay and Bagration came together. Actually, however, only 113,000 men reached Smolensk, or 36,800 less than had been anticipated. Illness and death from disease accounted for the difference. The extent of the losses greatly disturbed Quartermaster General von Toll, and in his recollections he is even inclined to question the original figures: at the moment of Napoleon's invasion, in his opinion, the two armies—Bagration's and Barclay's —comprised not 153,000 men, but 15,000 less. The tremendous reduction of the Russian army through disease and defection is established beyond doubt. And according to both Russian and French reports, numerous Lithuanians deserted at this stage.

For one reason or another, only 113,000 men were in Smolensk. And these not for the defence of Smolensk, but of Russia.

As to artillery, the Russian army was relatively well equipped.

A reorganization had been begun by Arakcheyev in 1806. As early as 1808 there were 130 artillery companies with 1,550 guns. In the spring of 1812, there were 133 companies with 1,600 guns. Between 1805 and 1812, certain technical improvements were made in gun-carriages, and ammunition boxes were introduced. Note in passing that no further improvements were introduced until 1845, although artillery construction had made considerable progress in Europe during this period. During the entire first half of the nineteenth century the Russian artillery was never so close to the French in effectiveness as in 1812, 1813, and 1814. After that the relative position of Russia deteriorated steadily, culminating in the rout at Sevastopol.

Generally speaking, the Russian forces were relatively better equipped with artillery than the Grand Army. The Russians had approximately seven guns to every thousand men, while Napoleon had only four guns to the same number of men. Of course, the French actually had more guns than the Russians, because the French army was considerably larger. But at Borodino when the armies became numerically equal, the Russian artillery did achieve a certain preponderance. The organization of the Russian artillery, the creation of special artillery brigades in each division, and other details had been borrowed, in the years 1806 to 1812, from

Napoleon's army—Napoleon had taken his principal measures in artillery reorganization as early as 1805. Each Russian infantry division consisted of 18 battalions, and had roughly 10,500 men. Each infantry regiment consisted of two battalions of the line and one reserve battalion being trained in the rear. A cavalry regiment consisted of six squadrons and one of reserve. There were 48,000 men in the cavalry. The artillery was divided into companies, each company numbering 250 men. In all, there were 133 artillery companies in Russia during the spring of 1812. According to the calculations of Count von Toll, the Russian army at the beginning of the 1812 campaign, including the Caucasus front, Georgia, and Crimea with the province of Kherson, numbered: 283,000 infantry, 14,000 cavalry, 25,000 artillery, and, in addition, 30,000 Don Cossacks and the Guard, defending St. Petersburg. Napoleon, not counting the garrisons throughout his Empire and the few hundred thousand fighting in Spain, had 360,000 infantry, 70,000 cavalry, and 35,000 artillery. This number does not include the auxiliary units of Napoleon's 'allies,' Austria and Prussia.

The main weakness of the Russian army was the ignorance and military incompetence of many officers, even generals, although we should not overlook the group of progressive officers, from among whom some of the Decembrist leaders were to emerge. In 1810, Russia had abandoned the old Frederickian military system and introduced the French system, but after only two years the change could scarcely have had a decisive effect on the fighting ability of the army. Another weakness was the barbarous discipline. Much use was made of the bastinado. The principle was: beat two to death, train the third. The Arakcheyev principle, fully supported by the Tsar, the principle of parade grounds on which a regiment was transformed into a kind of corps de ballet, had by 1812 almost crowded out the tradition of Suvorov, which consisted of preparing a soldier for war and not for His Majesty's reviews. The third weakness of the Russian army was the outrageous rapacity of the authorities: the thievery of the 'commissioners' and other ranks in the Commissariat, and the embezzlement of public funds by many officers of various ranks, who enriched themselves by filching the soldiers' rations and stole their pay. The lot of the rank and file was wretched. Suicides were not infrequent, particularly after a war was over. To be wounded or killed in battle seemed better. than having your jaw dislocated or running the gauntlet in time of peace. In wartime, bestiality was less pronounced than in times of peace.

Of course the picture is not all black; not all the officers were beasts and thieves. Some of them were close to the rank and file. And there were generals idolized by the soldiers, such as Bagration, Kulnev, Konovnitsin, Rayevsky, and Neverovsky. Herzen later insisted that the average officer of Alexander's day was more humane than in the days of Nicholas, after the Decembrist revolt; moreover, during the terrible year which is the subject of this book, even the hangman Arakcheyev had temporarily quieted down.

Barclay left Vilna on 26 June and moved towards the fortified camp at Drissa. Even then he, as well as Alexander and his entourage, had become convinced that the camp at Drissa was an absurdity.

On 8 July, Alexander arrived at Drissa and made a detailed inspection of the camp. Alexander was organically lacking in any understanding of war and the business of war. Among the Romanovs, beginning with Paul, this deficiency was congenital. It seems likely that all of them—and, in particular, Alexander I, Nicholas I, Constantine, and Mikhail Pavlovich—were so passionately addicted to drilling and parades just because the strategy of real war was organically alien and incomprehensible to them.

In his present perilous circumstances the Tsar grew quite tame. He was no longer the self-confident and light-headed officer who, against Kutuzov's will, had led the Russian army to the massacre and shame of Austerlitz. On his tour of inspection around Drissa, the Tsar, according to witnesses, listened in silence to the words of Michaud, Barclay, Paulucci. And the words and the faces of these men said that the Drissa camp was the absurd invention of a stupid German, a trap from which they must flee without loss of time.

Alexander himself had lost all inclination to defend his professor. He had to think of his own salvation.

Barclay, with his army of 100,000 men, entered Drissa on 10 July. On 16 July, taking all his troops, baggage trains, and stores, and accompanied by the Tsar himself, he abandoned the camp and moved towards Vitebsk. The first important stop on this road was Polotsk. Since Vilna, and more particularly since Drissa, the General Staff had been faced with a perplexing problem: how to get rid of the Tsar? In Polotsk it was happily solved. To remove Alexander Pavlovich without appearing disloyal was a task requiring great tact. During these first days of the war the Tsar had already caused great confusion and damage.

Secretary of State Shishkov, who was with the Tsar, rendered this very important service to the Russian army. Shishkov saw clearly that Alexander's presence in

the army was ruinous for Russia. But how get rid of
the Tsar, who was both touchy and spiteful? 'Knowing
that he deemed his presence with the troops absolutely
necessary, and that he considered it ignominious not to
be with them, could I hope that my words and arguments might overcome in him his own prejudice and
pride?' Shishkov had talked this ticklish matter over
with several persons; all agreed with him, but no one
was bold enough to speak to the Tsar. 'A few even said
that if someone should suggest such a thing to the Tsar,
the Tsar would consider him a criminal and a traitor.'
When Alexander wanted to include the words, 'I shall
always be with you and shall never abandon you,' in
an order to the army, Shishkov in desperation decided
to act. He directly advised the Tsar to eliminate these
words, and shortly afterward persuaded Balashov and
Arakcheyev to help him in his design.

The three courtiers resolved to send the Tsar a col-
lective letter urging him to leave the army. They could
not, of course, use the real argument, i.e. that his presence was harmful because he meddled in military
affairs, confused and irritated the generals, and poked
about with his retinue of babblers, whisperers, and
parasites. The authors of the letter so feared the invasion that they resolved to abandon all etiquette and
implore the Tsar to get out of Barclay's and Bagration's
way in this terrible hour. But it was necessary to clothe
this incivility in an acceptable form. The three of them
worked hard over their letter, which occupies four
large pages written in a minute hand. One of their
arguments is curious: 'The example of sovereigns who
have led their armies cannot serve as a model for the
reigning Tsar and Emperor, because they had special
motives. Peter the Great, Frederick the Second, and our

present enemy Napoleon have had to do it: the first, because he had raised regular troops; the second, because his entire kingdom was, so to speak, transformed into a military force; the third, because he has come to the throne, not by birth, but by chance and good fortune. None of these reasons exists for Alexander the First.'

The Tsar might have regarded this juxtaposition of his person with Peter, Frederick, and Napoleon as a gibe, if he had not known that all three authors were far from intending irony. The Tsar, indisputably a subtle and intelligent man, concluded that if three such persons wanted him to help the army by his absence, it was absurd to be stubborn.

'If our Sovereign and Emperor should find it convenient, without waiting for a decisive battle, to entrust his military forces to the complete management of the Commander-in-Chief, and himself to take his leave of them . . .' the three dignitaries timidly insisted.

Alexander's shrewd sister, Ekaterina Pavlovna, equally understood that the army would not gain the slightest benefit from the Tsar's presence, but that the harm might be very great. Alexander even complained that his sister was driving him from the army: 'If, as you say, I wished to drive you from the army, the reason is this: of course, I consider you as capable as your generals, but you must act not only the part of an army leader, but also that of a sovereign. If one of them should do his work badly, censure and punishment await him. But if you should commit an error, everything would fall upon your head. This would destroy faith in the sole arbiter of the destinies of the Empire, who should be our support,' et cetera. In a word, it was

deemed best for the Tsar to exercise his talents anywhere else, but not in the army.

So Alexander abandoned the army.

In Polotsk, after the retirement from Drissa, Count
Tolstoy, the Lord Chamberlain, took Shishkov aside
and whispered in his ear: 'Do you know that a carriage
for Moscow has been ordered for tonight?' Shishkov,
according to his own statement, 'could scarcely believe
his words. My joy was indescribable, and the warmest
prayer poured from my lips to the Bestower of all blessings, the Heavenly Creator.'

Having warmly thanked the Maker of the heavens
and the earth, Shishkov sat down to write a manifesto
to the Russian people. The Tsar, who was leaving for
Moscow, had entrusted him with this matter. Shishkov
and the others could not have been happier at the news
of a victory. It was quite apparent that they considered
the absence of the Tsar as the first condition for a successful defence against the invading enemy, and in the
manifesto Shishkov prudently promised that 'we' shall
be in various parts of the Empire. To speak more precisely would have been dangerous, because Shishkov
was privately convinced that the Tsar was harmful no
matter where he was. The most loyal author of the
treatise 'On the Old and New Style' cleverly concealed
his real misgivings with stately, archaic expressions.

. . .

Barclay became the sole commander of the First
Army and gave the order to fall back on Vitebsk. His
Chief of Staff was A. P. Ermolov, his Quartermaster-
General Count von Toll.

There have been many debates about 'Barclay's

plan.' There is some little evidence that Barclay de Tolly, from the very beginning of the war, and even for a long time before, had believed that the most correct strategy in a struggle with Napoleon was to utilize the immense, sparsely inhabited, almost impassable expanses of Russia, to lure his army as far inland as possible and there calmly await its inevitable destruction.

But there is considerably more evidence, some of it originating with Barclay himself, that he retreated only because it was utterly impossible to halt the Grand Army, and that with the slightest chance of successful resistance he would have accepted a general engagement. But even all this allegedly indisputable evidence does not solve the question. Considering the terrible pressure experienced by Barclay from 24 June, the date of Napoleon's invasion of Russia, to 29 August, when he finally learned of his replacement by Kutuzov, he could not have expressed himself otherwise than he did. He should have stressed the fact that he fell back only for accidental causes, and that actually he was impatient to engage in battle and was only trying to find a better position. He should have spoken as he did, even if he had really avoided battle deliberately and retreated with the object of luring the enemy inland. Ermolov, his Chief of Staff, was a friend and secret correspondent of Bagration. And Barclay was well aware that Bagration roundly abused him 'and all renegade Germans.' He also knew that Rostopchin, the Governor-General of Moscow, suspected him of treachery; that a chorus of panic-stricken landowners was echoing this cry, trembling with fear lest Napoleon abolish serfdom in the territory he occupied.

In other words, Barclay's loud-voiced (and for practical purposes meaningless) protestations of his desire to give battle were only weak attempts at self-defence, and we have no right to base any conclusions upon them.

Military critics are prone not to count Barclay as a great military leader, and he is not looked upon as an equal of Kutuzov and Bagration.

We quote the opinion of Liprandi, an eyewitness who fought in the War of 1812 as Head-Quartermaster of the Sixth Corps, and subsequently wrote a remarkable critique of the military literature on 1812: 'I venture to conclude that neither before Smolensk nor until Moscow itself did we have any defined plan of action. Everything happened according to circumstance. When the foe was distant, our leaders showed determination to give general battle, and according to all calculations they thought they would win. Once the foe approached, everything changed. The retreat was resumed, and this, too, was justified by accurate calculations. The whole immense correspondence of Barclay and of Kutuzov himself clearly proves that they themselves did not know what they would or should do.'

This does not mean that Barclay's actions were irrational. Liprandi forgets that the retreat from Drissa was a manœuvre, that a new operational plan was in effect, having as its main objective the union of the two Russian armies. Barclay's great merit did not consist in having at an early date advocated the strategy of luring the enemy inland. Many others had advocated that plan long before the war began, including Prince Bernadotte, and even the untalented Phull. But it must be remembered that, as Napoleon said, battles are won not by those who make the plans, but by those who take the responsibility for carrying them out and do carry them out. Even granting that Barclay had hesitated before reaching Vitebsk, the fact remains that after Vitebsk he pursued the course he had resolved upon with great moral courage and with no regard for obstacles or adverse criticism. The most recent military theoreticians have expressed disapproval for certain of Barclay's acts in the course of his withdrawal. They have called him inconsistent, because of his intention—which remained on paper—of giving battle at Tsarevo-Zaimishche, et cetera; but they themselves recognize that the position at Tsarevo-Zaimishche, chosen by Barclay, would have been more advantageous than Borodino. In an interesting two-page essay on Barclay, written in 1858 for the *New American Cyclopedia*, Karl Marx expresses a similar view. And he quite correctly notes that from the opening of hostilities the withdrawal of the Russian army was 'not a matter of free choice, but of stern necessity.'

Barclay's conscience bade him save his troops, and he had enough firmness and strength of will to carry out the task systematically. He was acting under great moral stress—his own General Staff headed by Ermolov was secretly agitating against him, and Bagration, the commander-in-chief of the Second Army, known as the most competent of all Russian military leaders, quite openly charged him with treason. The agitation against Barclay came from above. The generals and colonels taught the rank and file to call Barclay de Tolly by the nickname *Boltai da i tolko*—'Bark and that's all' (literally: 'talk and there's nothing more to it'); the commanding officers told them that Ermolov had allegedly petitioned the Tsar 'to promote him, Ermolov, to the rank of a German,' since Germans received rewards. From above came the rumours that Vollzogen, a member of Barclay's staff, was one of Napoleon's spies. All this, even before Smolensk, made Barclay's position extremely difficult. Confidence in the Commander-in-Chief was undermined, and every new stage in the retreat intensified the malicious rumours about Barclay.

It was hard for him to parry Bagration's thrusts. Barclay had neither a heroic career nor a brilliant reputation in the army; he did not reflect the radiance of Suvorov's glory and he was not endowed with an iron character—in brief, he lacked everything that Bagration had in such abundance. A diligent military organizer, by origin a Scotsman (and not a German, as has often been erroneously said), he had gained Alexander's confidence by his executive ability. As Minister of War, the cautious strategist instinctively hit on the correct tactics; he had the civic courage to buck the current as long as humanly possible.

Count von Toll, the Quartermaster-General of the First Army (Barclay's), maintains in his remarkable memoirs that, at the beginning of the war, positively no one on the Russian staff at Vilna had the least idea of the part which the colossal expanses of Russia would play. This was realized only as the war progressed. The retreat had been dictated by Barclay's reluctance to risk the destruction of the army in the first days of the war. The opinion of Count von Toll would in itself carry much weight, even if it were not confirmed by a number of equally incontrovertible documents originating with Barclay himself. Barclay was not guided by any 'Scythian plan' of luring the enemy inland; he merely retreated under pressure of superior forces. The 'Scythian plan' was not discussed by the Russians until long after the war, and indeed the first to speak of the Scythians was Napoleon himself in 1812.

There are few documents relating to the state of mind among the peasants, nobility, and landowners at the beginning of the war. But certain facts may be regarded as firmly established. From the very first day of the invasion most of the nobility was in terror lest the conqueror, as he advanced inland, would liberate the serfs and incite them to fight against the landowners. This was an old fear dating from the war of 1806-7. At that time, Rostopchin reported to the Tsar on these fears of the nobility and assured him that the Russian masses were saying that Bonaparte would free the people from serfdom. It goes without saying that in 1812, with Napoleon campaigning on Russian soil, these fears were particularly acute.

It is true that the French authorities, at the request of Polish landowners, promptly sent punitive expeditions against the revolting peasants. But these facts were unknown in St. Petersburg or in Moscow, or anywhere else in native Russia. Occupied Lithuania and part of White Russia were cut off; what happened there did not become known until afterward.

In the meantime, Napoleon was advancing towards Moscow, sweeping aside all obstacles. The higher nobility in St. Petersburg and Moscow and the great majority of the middle class and landowners were terrified at the possibility of a Napoleonic decree liberating the serfs; every new announcement of the continued Russian retreat filled them with despair. There is no doubt that most of the nobility, then the most active and politically influential class, held Barclay responsible for these repeated withdrawals and regarded him as a traitor, or at best, an ignominious coward.

Thus, the persistent discord between Barclay de Tolly and Pyotr Ivanovich Bagration was no simple quarrel between two generals, no mere disagreement on strategy. All persons close to the general staffs watched the struggle with passionate interest, and when Rostopchin, the Governor-General of Moscow, learned of it, he passed on the information to the broad circles of nobility. Prince Bagration was then in the prime of his strength and on the crest of his military reputation. His fame was many years old, dating from Suvorov's wars. It was known that Bagration and Kutuzov had been Suvorov's favourites, his disciples and aides, and that, of the two, Bagration had learned the Suvorovian tactics more thoroughly. Countless tales and legends circulated about him. He retained an extraordinary presence of mind in the most desperate situations and was known to risk his life in circumstances where the odds seemed a hundred to one against him. The rank and file knew this well. They worshipped Bagration as no one else except Kutuzov. The authorities were also aware of his daring qualities and repeatedly utilized them. In November 1805, during the retreat to Olmütz, Kutuzov, to save the Russian army from capitulation, sent a small detachment under Bagration against all of Napoleon's hordes, sacrificing the detachment to gain time. Bagration brilliantly carried out this mission and saved his own life only by the merest chance. There had been many such episodes in Bagration's life. He demanded heroism from others as well. To serve on his staff was considered dangerous but a high honour.

Another feature of this man was his uncontrolled temper. Not that he was inflammable. On the contrary, he amazed everyone by his impressive calm, taciturnity, oriental restraint, and dignity of manner. When, however, he found an object which seemed to him worthy of his wrath and hatred, his anger knew no bounds, and he did not and would not restrain the force of his blows; and the blows of his anger were often out of all proportion to the actual demands of the situation.

No one would have been surprised if at the beginning of the War of 1812 Alexander had named Bagration Commander-in-Chief. The Tsar did not do this; nor did he want to hurt Bagration's feelings by naming Barclay de Tolly. With characteristic timidity and indecision, he named them both: Barclay became Commander of the First Army, Bagration of the Second. Each was independent of the other. This subtle decision caused much confusion, and gave Barclay an army much larger than Bagration's.

Bagration regarded Barclay's tactics as bad. He was impatient to fight, but his insignificant forces could not face Napoleon's enormous army without being destroyed, and all his appeals to Barclay remained unanswered. Bagration's rage grew steadily, because, for want of support from Barclay, he himself was forced to retire, and this he considered ruinous for Russia.

Less than five days after the invasion, the discord between the two commanders was complete.

'But, Sire,' wrote Barclay de Tolly to the Tsar on 17 June, when he realized that Bagration was determined not to obey his commands, 'it is most unpleasant to see that Prince Bagration, instead of promptly executing Your Majesty's commands, is wasting his time in useless discussions, and even communicates his opinions to General Platov, thus putting into a muddle this general who, even without this, is but little developed and completely uneducated.' Barclay was vexed, because Bagration refused to believe that the commands from the staff of the First Army came from the Tsar himself. Bagration understood that this was a threadbare subterfuge, and that the commands had not been written by the Tsar, but by Barclay himself.

Bagration was in a state of almost uninterrupted irritation. He loathed and distrusted Barclay. 'I am not to blame for anything,' he wrote to Arakcheyev on 8 July. 'First they stretch me out like a gut, while the enemy broke into our lines without a shot. We began to retire, no one knows why. You'll get no one in the army, or in Russia, to believe that we haven't been betrayed. I alone cannot defend all Russia. The First Army should at once, without fail, go to Vilna—what is there to be afraid of? I am completely encircled and I cannot say yet where I shall break through.' Bagration wanted Arakcheyev to influence Alexander, and he even tried to frighten the Tsar with the spectacle of internal revolts: 'I implore you to advance against the enemy . . . or else it shall be the worse for us when the enemy comes, and perhaps on the domestic front as well . . . It does not befit Russians to run. We are behaving worse than the Prussians . . . One feels ashamed . . . I have no peace and I do not live for myself, God is my witness; I am glad to do everything in my power, but we must have a conscience and be just. You will go on retiring, and I am asked to break through. If my person can't be borne here, better have me released from the yoke which is on my neck and send someone else to command. But why torment the soldiers without purpose and without satisfaction?'

What then saved Bagration from inevitable capitulation? No, it was not only the crude errors of Jerome Bonaparte, King of Westphalia, but also Bagration's own brilliance. While in Slutsk, he received word that immense enemy forces were advancing on Bobruysk. Without losing a minute, he made a forced march towards Bobruysk to escape the trap, though he knew that Alexander would be vexed by this retreat. On 14 July, Platov, following Bagration's instructions, had a successful engagement with the French mounted chasseurs at the tiny town of Mir, flinging them back and destroying a part of their regiment. This somewhat retarded pursuit on the part of the French and enabled Bagration's main forces to retire comparatively undisturbed. Thus the worst danger was avoided. Bagration saved his army and baggage train, a feat which at that time no one, with the possible exception of Napoleon, could have equalled. Bagration arrived in Bobruysk only to receive Alexander's 'rescript' reprimanding him for not going to Minsk—a procedure which to Bagration seemed senseless and impossible. The same rescript included equally foolish counsels for the future. Fortunately, Bagration ignored them. Between 25 and 27 July, Bagration moved to Stary Bykhov and thence to Novy Bykhov, where he crossed the Dnieper with his entire army intact.

From the first days of the war, Bagration had been unable to mention Barclay without flying into a rage. 'One feels ashamed to wear the uniform,' he wrote on 15 July to Ermolov, who was his intimate friend. 'Honest to God, I feel sick . . . What a fool . . . Minister Barclay himself is running away, yet he orders me to defend all of Russia. They chased us to the frontier, set us up like a lot of pawns, and there we stood, our mouths agape, befouling [in the original text of the letter the expression employed is much stronger] the entire frontier, then ran away . . . I must confess, I'm so disgusted with the whole business that I'm nearly out of my wits . . .'

During these days and weeks of retreat he had sev-

eral times threatened to resign, to don a peasant's coat
and shoulder a soldier's pack, to turn private or civilian,
to discard the Russian uniform 'besmirched' by Barclay, and so forth. Later military theoreticians do not
agree with Bagration. Though some think that Barclay
should have given battle at Smolensk, his retreat from
Vilna to Smolensk has been recognized as a correct and
logical move.

.   .   .

For ten stifling July days, Barclay marched from
Drissa, via Polotsk, to Vitebsk. From his scouts and
reconnaissance patrols he knew that Napoleon with his
main forces was also advancing on Vitebsk. Even with
the entire army he had commanded at Drissa, Barclay
would have faced Napoleon's 150 to 200 thousand men
with no more than 100,000 Russians. In reality, Barclay
had less than 75,000 men, for he was compelled to di-
vert 25,000 men to reinforce Wittgenstein, who was
covering the threatened road to St. Petersburg.

The alarm in St. Petersburg was immense; the court
aristocracy began to leave the capital. The Empress
Dowager, Maria Feodorovna, widow of Paul I, was in a
panic, packing her things and making inquiries about
the safest places to go. Only after Alexander had returned to St. Petersburg, where he prudently remained
for the rest of the war, did Maria Feodorovna quiet
down somewhat. Constantine Pavlovich, the heir apparent, was in the same state of panic. But he placed his
hopes less on flight than on a speedy peace with Napoleon. For the time being, Constantine was still 'with
the army'; that is, he loitered about headquarters,
offered his advice, and so irritated Barclay that the
habitually taciturn and self-controlled general began

unjustly to upbraid his aides, since he could not very well scold the importunate prince, whose supercilious, pug-nosed physiognomy and absurd ideas recalled his father, Paul. General Wittgenstein, entrusted with the task of defending St. Petersburg, was mediocre and irresolute. The heavy responsibility of defending the capital depressed him. In the early days of the war, he had an unsuccessful clash with the French and was forced to retreat to Druya.

Among Wittgenstein's forces were many detachments of militia. The militiamen were not a whit behind the regular troops in bravery, stubbornness, or hatred of the foe. Here is a characteristic episode. Wittgenstein had ordered the army to retreat. 'The regular troops promptly obeyed the command,' writes a witness, 'but the militiamen violently protested. "We were brought here to fight," they said, "not to retreat!" The same order was repeated a second, and a third time but the militia refused to listen. The brave militiamen, still unfamiliar with military discipline, were consumed with desire to strike at the godless foe.'

In the end, Wittgenstein himself came out to plead with the militiamen. ' "Well, children," he said, "you cannot fight alone against the foe. Yesterday we drove him off, but today it is our turn to run. Behind us we have set up big guns; if you don't get out of the way, we can't fire them." "Let them fire, little father," they replied, "but we won't run from the enemy!" '

In the end, Wittgenstein somehow made them listen to reason. The militiamen 'retired, in vexation, saying to the General: "You have given the order and you are responsible." ' The artillery went to work and then the militia was ordered to attack the French. 'Like enraged lions, the militiamen flung themselves upon the foe, and quickly inflicted considerable losses.'

The militiamen who later on poured into Kutuzov's army were of the same mettle. Most of them were peasants, often no longer young. They wore bast-shoes or torn boots, and drab coats instead of uniforms. They fought with pikes instead of sabres and rifles.

General Wittgenstein had at his disposal 25,000 men. Advancing against him was Marshal Oudinot (the Duke of Reggio), with about 28,000 men, though at the beginning of the invasion Napoleon had issued orders to give him 37,000. The Emperor expected Oudinot to unite with Macdonald, who was besieging Riga, and to threaten St. Petersburg. Oudinot occupied Polotsk and advanced northward, striving, in accord with Macdonald, to flank Wittgenstein from the north and, by pressing him southward, towards the left flank of the central Napoleonic army, to crush his entire corps and open the road to St. Petersburg. But nothing came of the plan. Macdonald failed to execute his part of the manœuvre, and scattered his forces by besieging Riga and marching on the city of Dünaburg. He took Dünaburg but got stuck there. In his long fighting career, the famous Napoleonic marshal had been defeated only once—in Italy, by no less a talent than Suvorov. The cause of his present failure was not fear of Wittgenstein, who was far inferior to him as a tactician, but lack of confidence in his own troops. Of the 32,500 men Napoleon had given him, two thirds were Prussians and the remaining third nearly all Westphalians and Bavarians, with a small number of Poles. Of all these troops, the Prussians alone showed the slightest fighting zeal.

In the first period of the war, the Prussian generals

under Marshal Macdonald fought with a certain honest
enthusiasm, because, like their good sovereign, Frederick-William III, they hoped that Napoleon would reward Prussia with Russia's Baltic territories. The Russians supposed at first that the Prussians were partici-
pating in the war only for the sake of form, to avoid
angering Napoleon, and that they had no intention of
fighting seriously. But the Russians soon saw their mistake. 'Acting on the plausible assumption that Prussian
subjects would be forcibly drawn into the fighting
against us, we ventured to hope that they would show
but weak resistance to our forces. I therefore tried to
give some appearance of friendliness towards Prussia
and thus preserve their good will towards us; but I have
now sufficient evidence that in the enemy attacks on
forces under my command the Prussians have fought
desperately.' As a result, an embargo was imposed on
Prussian vessels then anchored in the port of Riga. The
Prussians not only fought fiercely, but looted the entire
region they occupied in 1812. Yet no sooner had Napoleon left Russia, than the Prussians switched over to
the Russian side.

Distrustful of the Bavarians and Westphalians in his
army, Marshal Macdonald remained inactive. Oudinot
was left without support, and, in his efforts to outflank
Wittgenstein, was himself outflanked. Just before meeting Wittgenstein between Kliastitsi and Yakubov, he
had been forced to detach a full third of his forces for
the defence of the bridges across the Drissa, while he
had dispatched another third under command of General Verdier to Sebezh. On 30 July, Wittgenstein
clashed with Oudinot's weakened forces and scored a
success, throwing the Marshal back to Polotsk. General
Kulnev, commanding Wittgenstein's rear-guard, set out

in pursuit of Oudinot. This Kulnev, with N. N. Rayevsky, Bagration, Neverovsky, and Kutuzov, was among
the few generals who had attained full authority over
the rank and file without sticks and whips. Kulnev had
played a large part in the conquest of Finland and had
shown himself so magnanimous and chivalrous towards
the conquered that the national Finnish poem by Rune-
berg, *The Tales of Ensign Shtoll,* contains a few warm
stanzas in his memory.

Yakov Petrovich Kulnev, however, had one weakness:
in the thick of battle he was carried away by his ardour
and often risked his own and other people's lives. At
Kliastitsi on 30 July, it was not his chief Wittgenstein,
but Kulnev himself who defeated Oudinot, taking
nearly the entire baggage train of the enemy and 900
prisoners. The following day, Kulnev, with his 12,000
men detached by Wittgenstein for the purpose, flung
himself impetuously in pursuit of the retiring Marshal.
Imprudently pressing forward, Kulnev ran into Oudinot's forces, which had suddenly stopped and quickly
drawn up in battle order. Kulnev was caught between
two fires and thrown back with severe losses. His detachment lost about 2,000 men and eight guns. When
the defeated detachment retreated under the fire of
French batteries, Kulnev 'walked mournfully in the
last ranks of his rear-guard,' exposed to the greatest
dangers. A French cannon ball struck him and tore off
both his legs. Death followed instantly. Having routed
Kulnev, Marshal Oudinot's detachment returned to
Polotsk, arriving on 2 August. There it long remained
inactive. Wittgenstein's army displayed no greater activity, contenting itself with an observational role. Macdonald remained hopelessly immobilized between Riga
and Dünaburg.

Napoleon did not learn of all the happenings on the northern front until he arrived in Vitebsk. What he heard there made him angry. To be sure, the 'victory' of Wittgenstein over Marshal Oudinot, which St. Petersburg and London had made such a stir about, turned out not to be much of a victory. But this was a minor matter. The important thing was that two Marshals in the north, Oudinot and Macdonald, would be unable to give Napoleon any substantial aid, and that the Russians need fear no serious diversion against St. Petersburg.

The Court also realized that the decisive operations would take place not on the roads to St. Petersburg, but on the roads to Smolensk and, possibly, Moscow.

Pressed by the enemy, Barclay and Bagration were falling back towards Vitebsk and Moghilev. The heat was frightful. The soldiers were starved and had not had a drop of fresh water for days.

It was a hard retreat. The officers' corps was none too competent. Some of the officers showed great bravery, but many were imprudent, negligent, and incapable of quick decision in an emergency. Neither Barclay nor Bagration could ever be sure that his orders would be executed.

A colonel with eight battalions of recruits entered the town of Velizh. He drew up one battalion on the square, and kept it under arms all night. He placed sentries all about, with strict orders to stick to their posts. Suddenly, French squadrons swept into town, mowed down the sentries and the battalion in the square, and occupied the city. Those battalions the French had not wiped out fled as fast as they could. Later it was learned that the colonel, who wore down his men by depriving them of rest and sleep, had ordered all cartridges to be stored in the carts, for the sake of tidiness. When the French attacked, the soldiers were without cartridges. There were many instances of this kind.

The Commissariat was in a lamentable state. Thievery attained incredible proportions. One day, towards the end of July, Barclay's retreating army entered Porechye. It developed that there was no fodder for the horses. What had become of the several thousand measures of oats and the 64,000 poods of hay, which had supposedly been bought with treasury funds and stored in Porechye? It turned out that the Commissioner of Supply had ordered the stores to be burned: his own strategic calculations had told him that Napoleon would seize Porechye. Ermolov smelled a rat and inquired when the order to buy the oats and hay had been issued and when they had been stored in Porechye? He found out that all this had been done only two weeks previous. And as the transport facilities were very meagre (nearly all the carts had been requisitioned by the army), it would have been impossible to bring all this fodder to Porechye in so short a time. The Commissioner's impudent lie was fully exposed: he had no thought of buying fodder and transporting it to Porechye; he simply set the empty warehouses on fire and pocketed the money. 'For such impudent thievery,' said Ermolov to Barclay, 'the Commissioner should have been burned with the stores.' But this was not done. It was hardly possible to burn the whole Commissary Department with all its personnel. The hungry horses trudged on.

The troops were not always fed either, but they helped themselves as best they could. In the same

Porechye where the Commissioner had patriotically fired stores of oats and hay, he had burned all other supplies for the same reasons. 'The soldiers robbed and pillaged in the deserted houses,' writes Ermolov. 'I myself drove them out, and even out of the church, I am sorry to say. I did not meet any of their officers whose duty it was to notice their absence. The cause of the extraordinary decrease of men at the front lies in this indifference to duty.'

The Commissary Department in 1812 was no less rapacious than in the previous war with Napoleon. But the plundering in East Prussia, in 1807, bad as it was, paled by comparison to what happened now, in the villages between the Niemen and Moscow. In their effort to 'leave nothing to the enemy,' the vanguard of the retreating Russian forces often consumed or carried away everything, leaving the centre and the rear-guard to make their way through empty villages or burning ruins. Commissary officials delivered an insignificant portion of their 'purchases' and sometimes nothing at all. Their usual excuse was that the enemy had 'captured' the baggage trains.

For all these reasons, discipline in the Russian army was much worse during the first half of the war than later, during the advance from Tarutino to the frontier. Barclay himself, in a later report concerning the supply services during the second half of the war, observes casually: 'We were helped by the improved discipline, which was restored spontaneously, so to speak. I must say to my regret that the retreating soldier refused to give up his right to destroy everything, although the enemy did not suffer much as a result, because he could always find intact villages on his march.'

Throughout the entire campaign, the Russian cavalry suffered cruelly from lack of fodder. 'For God's sake, do everything you can to get me some oats or rye; my horses are starved. Yesterday we found only 13 measures of oats. Ask Saint-Priest, General, to prepare some fodder for us,' wrote Vasilchikov, commander of a cavalry regiment, to his friend and superior Mikhail Vorontsov, at the very beginning of the campaign.

Sometimes starved soldiers plundered the villages through which they passed with such thoroughness that the peasants fled *en masse*. And such incidents took place at the very beginning of the war, when there were undoubtedly large supplies of provisions on hand, for which in the months before the war large sums had been paid. 'Hussars, Cossacks, recruiting parties' attack and terrorize villages; 'the peasants take flight.' But what was to be done? Surely, the soldiers could not be left to die of starvation. And this situation prevailed throughout the war. The military authorities knew better than anyone that it was impossible to root out this evil, to punish starving soldiers, while the looters in the Commissariat systematically robbed the Russian army.

The medical services were equally bad. The physicians were few and incompetent. The organization of care for the wounded was positively worthless.

'A large number of wounded officers and soldiers remain without further assistance after the first bandaging,' reports Villiers, the chief medical inspector of the Russian army, in the earliest days of the war. And conditions went from bad to worse. Those who had been wounded near Vitebsk at the beginning of July reached Vyazma only on 7 August, without even the most primitive medical assistance: 'Many of them arrived from Vitebsk unbandaged, because there were only two doctors,' wrote Kozodavlev, the Minister of the Interior,

to Alexander, on 7 August. 'There is a complete shortage of medicines and bandages, and the worms are eating many of the wounded alive.' And this was before
the defence and evacuation of Smolensk, in which there
were many thousands more wounded.

.   .   .

An hour after the Russian troops left Vilna, Napoleon appeared there with his advance guard. The bridge
fired by the departing Russians was still burning. Napoleon sat on a folding chair near the burning bridge
and began to ask questions. He continued to ask questions in the palace which Alexander had left but a short
while before. His most frequent question was: Why
hadn't the Russians given him battle and where did
they intend to make a stand?

When one of those questioned—the editor of the
Lithuanian Courier—said that the Russians had an
army of 300,000 men, Napoleon gave him the lie, and
handed him the crumpled and torn report of Barclay
de Tolly's chief of staff addressed to Barclay himself and
intercepted by the French. This document revealed
that the supplies allotted to Barclay's entire army sufficed only for 92,000 men. Even supposing that Bagration had an army as large as Barclay's, Napoleon could
conclude that the Russians had at the most 185,000
effectives. As we have seen, the actual number was
smaller. And Napoleon could not help knowing that
Bagration had fewer troops than Barclay, because the
Tsar himself was with Barclay's army, and Barclay's
army had to defend the Drissa camp and the road to
St. Petersburg. But before Napoleon could move against

the Russians, a number of urgent matters demanded his attention in Vilna.

'I am in Vilna and very busy,' wrote Napoleon to the Empress Marie-Louise soon after entering the city. 'My affairs are going well, the enemy has been outwitted . . . Vilna is a fine city with 40,000 inhabitants. I have moved to a pleasant house which only a few days ago was occupied by Emperor Alexander, then far from the thought that I would soon come here.'

He remained in Vilna from 28 June to 16 July. The Polish nobility lavished extravagant honours upon him. They called him the liberator and Father of Poland. It was some time before Napoleon could devote himself completely to urgent military matters.

Jomini thinks that Napoleon committed the greatest blunder of his life in tarrying so long at Vilna. According to this military historian, who took part in the campaign as a Brigadier-General in Napoleon's army, if Napoleon had not waited at Vilna but had promptly advanced towards Minsk, he would have overtaken Bagration and destroyed him.

But too many preoccupations of all sorts beset Napoleon in Vilna. He had to set Lithuania in order, to organize its civil government; to pursue a subtle, complex policy, avoiding specific promises to the Poles concerning Lithuania's annexation to Poland, with a view to keeping open the possibility of peace with the Tsar; he had to keep a vigilant eye on the increasingly acute situation in Spain; finally, without giving anything to Lithuania, he had to organize the systematic drainage of bread, hay, oats, and recruits from that country.

'I love the Poles on the field of battle—they are a brave people. But their legislative meetings, their *liberum veto,* their *Sejms* [diets], which they attend on horseback, with swords in their hands—I don't want all *that*,' Napoleon declared to Count Narbonne even before crossing the Niemen.

He conducted himself accordingly. He gave the Poles no guarantees, spoke ambiguously about the future 'resurrection' of Poland and the annexation of Lithuania, and arrogantly demanded supplies and soldiers. All these worries were overshadowed by a new fear, which after Vilna remained with him through the entire war.

In the first days of July, Napoleon began to take account of the inconveniences of the Russian climate, intensified by the impassability of the roads. While he was in Vilna, his marshals wrote him about it. 'We have been having terrible heat here; now we have heavy rains, which create difficulties and cause us great damage,' wrote Napoleon to his wife on 2 July.

Disease was taking a threatening toll in the ranks of the army. When Napoleon left Vilna, 3,000 wounded and ailing soldiers among the élite regiments billeted in the city were left behind, and at the end of July Napoleon learned that they were in a desperate situation, that they even lacked straw to lie on, and that no provisions were left in the stores. He wrote a severe order to the Duke of Bassano in Vilna, of course without the slightest practical result.

Worst of all were the unexpected difficulties of supply. The army advanced so fast that the baggage train could not keep up. Hunger and marauding resulted.

Napoleon had prepared colossal stores and a richly supplied baggage train, but all these interminable files of wagons were unable to catch up with the fast-moving army, and even before they reached the boundaries of Russia, the soldiers, deprived of regular rations, began to loot the population. They were still on the soil of their Prussian 'ally,' and already the wagons lagged behind. In the words of an eyewitness and combatant (Ross), 'a strange order was issued: all regiments must provide themselves with food and fodder for three weeks . . . Detachments commanded by officers were sent to the villages and farms to requisition the necessary supplies and bring them to their regiments. These detachments everywhere encountered others sent for the same purpose. No one dared return with empty hands, and as a result there was fighting over the loot. The barns and granaries quickly emptied . . . Stables were forced open, pack-beasts were harnessed, fodder and food were piled into carts; cattle for slaughter were tied to the carts—and marched off to the regiments. This order, quickly executed, had thoroughly cleaned out the inhabitants of the region. They felt the full impact of war before it had even begun.'

The herds of cattle prepared in Prussia were far away, and the wagons lagged behind. But even in the opening stages of the campaign, when supplies were still plentiful, the regimental bakeries and kitchens were behindhand in the preparation of meals. Napoleon was angry: 'Inform General Jomini,' wrote the Emperor on 22 July, to his Chief of Staff, Berthier, 'that it is absurd to say there is no bread when he receives 500 quintals of flour every day; that, instead of complaining, he should rise at four o'clock every morning and go in person to the mill and the commissariat and see to it that 30,000 rations of bread are prepared; that by merely sleeping and moaning he will achieve nothing; tell him that the Emperor himself, who is very busy, visits the commissariat every day.' Soon, however, neither flour nor meat, oats nor hay, was available from any source. Again marauding became the order of the day.

Another disturbing factor manifested itself from the very beginning of the campaign. In no Napoleonic war, with the exception of the Italian campaign of 1796-7 and the conquest of Egypt in 1798-9, had the troops looted so unceremoniously and so thoroughly devastated the occupied territory.

On 2 July, within a week after crossing the Russian frontiers, Napoleon signed a strict order to arrest all soldiers caught in the act of looting or marauding, to try them by court-martial, and to shoot them in the event of conviction. But even the frequent executions, which Marshal Davout never hesitated to order, did not stop the constant plunder on the part of the First Corps of the French army, occupying the Government of Minsk. The others were worse. Official exactions and requisitions, ordered by the French authorities, devastated the provinces of Minsk, Vitebsk, Vilna, Grodno, and Smolensk even more than the looting. By an order of Napoleon, dated 1 July, a governing board was created in Vilna for the administration of Lithuania and White Russia. Actually this board was entrusted with organizing requisitions of supplies (above all bread, straw, hay, and oats) from the landowners and peasants. The Board acted ruthlessly and for half a year completely impoverished the entire region under its control.

The Russian army retreated from Vilna so speedily that it had no time to collect the supplies stored along the road. In Vileika, General Colbert seized some 2,000 quintals of flour, from 30 to 40 thousand rations of biscuit, and a great quantity of oats. Napoleon was enthusiastic about this find, which could not have come in handier; French cavalry horses were dying by the thousands for lack of oats and the men were suffering keenly from hunger.

In Stary Lepel, the French found 750 sacks of flour and 327 tons of biscuit. In Orsha, too, Napoleon seized large stores.

These supplies, however, did not always provide the expected blessings. The army was moving fast towards Vitebsk, and means of transportation were lacking. Napoleon had just rejoiced over the discovery of an enormous quantity of flour in Orsha, yet a few days later he wrote angrily to General Grouchy to ask why he had not sent the flour to Glubokoye, where the centre of the Grand Army was concentrating. 'We are in the greatest need.'

The discipline of the Grand Army was far below its usual high level, which had aroused the admiration of military experts of all nations.

One of the victims of pillage, a Vilna landowner named Eismont, stammered that 'according to the Bible' the countless hosts of Pharaoh had perished in the Red Sea. But this historical comparison was not appreciated. 'When I made this observation to a few followers of Napoleon, my frankness almost cost me my life, for one of the madcaps drew out a dagger three feet long and ran at me crying: "Die, thou unbeliever in the might of the earthly god and his inscrutable order . . ." After that, I learned to keep quiet.'

The robbers, by the unanimous testimony of the Lithuanians and later of the Russians, were Bavarians, Prussians, Rhenish Germans, and Croats (the Croats belonged to the Italian army corps of Viceroy Eugène). The Emperor's Guard did almost no pillaging. This is not surprising: it was much more abundantly supplied than the rest of the army.

The army itself was not the same army as before. It no longer consisted largely of volunteers. It was oversized and international. The more experienced French officers observed the lack of discipline from the first day of the campaign. They foresaw many misfortunes and did not cease to repeat with alarm that the army robbed and pillaged, that the number of laggards and deserters was immense, and that the whole undertaking might suffer as a result.

'But it was written [in the stars], that in *this* campaign nothing would be done as was done in former campaigns,'—this characteristic observation occurs in a manuscript found on a captured French general, Chief of Staff of the Third Division of Cuirassiers.

Never before had Napoleon been compelled in the first days of a war to hear reports about deserters, laggards, soldiers who abandoned their regiments at night to form marauding bands. The Emperor ordered his Chief of Staff, Berthier, to convey the following order to Marshal Ney: 'Dispatch detachments of cavalry under the command of staff officers to catch the laggards, many of whom commit crimes and end up by falling into the hands of the Cossacks.' It was found necessary to issue this order as early as 4 July, when the campaign was only ten days old. The pillaging, of course, did not cease, but was continued under the guise of 'board received from house owners.'

This time the French were a minority in Napoleon's army. The majority consisted of Germans, Italians, Dutchmen, Portuguese, Illyrian Slavs, Croats, and Swiss. Among them, many hated Napoleon with all their hearts as the subjugator of their native countries, and had joined the army solely from fear. For many, desertion was their most cherished dream from the first moment they entered Russia. Others, of course, had hopes of enrichment, promotion, and all those benefits which Napoleon's army always received in such abundance during and after every campaign.

Napoleon's idea, however, of including Spaniards in his army on the sole ground that they were considered subjects of Jerome Bonaparte was a complete fiasco.

Napoleon was well aware that it would have been risky to organize regiments entirely of Spaniards—even under French officers. 'We are trying to form such regiments . . . but we don't count on them,' he wrote to Count Daru before the invasion of Russia. He preferred to mix a small number of Spaniards with purely French battalions. But this didn't turn out well either: the Spaniards remained Spaniards, loathing Napoleon.

The Spaniards impressed into the army by force refused to sacrifice their lives for the conquest of Russia, and even watched for an opportunity to continue their endless, irreconcilable war against the French. The French Lieutenant Couanier tells this story, which occurred on the advance from Vilna to Vitebsk: 'A burned forest lay to the right of our road, and when we came alongside I saw that a part of my battalion was about to go into it. I galloped in that direction to turn them back. How great my astonishment when suddenly the soldiers turned about and began to shoot at me . . . The conspirators were from among the soldiers of Jerome, and all, without exception, Spaniards. There were 133 of them, not a single Frenchman was mixed up with the brigands.' On the following day, the Spaniards were captured by a French cavalry detachment. The Colonel decided not to shoot all of them, but only half. Lots were thrown, there were white tickets and black. Sixty-two of the men drew black tickets and were shot on the spot; the Colonel pardoned the rest.

Incidents such as these show clearly that Napoleon's effort to increase the quantity of the Grand Army did not help its quality.

. . .

In Vilna, Napoleon had to organize two simultaneous operations, one against Bagration, who was withdrawing his Second Army to Nesvizh, the other against Barclay, who had left Vilna on 26 June with the First Army, consisting of about 100,000 men, for the armed camp at Drissa.

Bagration was in a particularly difficult position, and Napoleon promptly ordered strong forces to move against him. Marshal Davout set out from Vilna with 50,000 men, and marched through Oshmyani towards Minsk, flanking Bagration and cutting off his retreat. Napoleon ordered his brother, Jerome Bonaparte, with about 16,000 men, to advance against Novogrudok, to forestall Barclay who, on 29 June, was still on the Niemen. Bagration was threatened with capitulation or complete destruction.

At two o'clock on the night of 1 July, Napoleon sent to Marshal Davout the following order: 'There is no longer any doubt that Bagration has gone from Bezhenetz to Grodno, from Grodno to a point about 18 miles from Vilna, then set out in the direction of Sventsiani. I have organized three strong columns to pursue him. All three will be under your command.' At this moment, Davout was in Oshmyani.

Bagration's position seemed desperate. He had about 40,000 men, because two entire divisions had been thrown back on Volyn at the beginning of the pursuit. He was being pursued by Marshal Davout with 70,000 men, Poniatowski with 35,000, Jerome Bonaparte with 16,000, Grouchy with 7,000, and Latour-Maubourg with 8,000. French records (Belfort and others) tell us that even deducting 46,000 as deserters, sick, and marauders, 90,000 men would still remain, fresh, magnificently armed, with abundant cavalry. And yet Bagration escaped. The French commanders blamed each other for it. Fleeing with his customary skill and stubbornness from the hotly pursuing Davout, Bagration rushed southward, and he might have perished, had Jerome Bonaparte arrived in time to cut his retreat. But Bagration managed to get away before the French pincers closed on him.

Marshal Davout, in pursuit of Bagration, occupied Moghilev and Orsha, and moved on. Coming into contact with the army corps of Rayevsky and observing the Cossack patrols of Platov, sent by Bagration to conceal his own retreat with the entire Second Army, Davout slowed down. Here he made his fatal blunder, sending the army corps of Jerome Bonaparte, the most ungifted of all Napoleon's ungifted brothers, in pursuit of Bagration. To elude and befuddle Jerome was for Bagration a question of life and death. He evaded a terrible danger. If Davout had speedily and briskly pressed on with his entire force, the Second Russian Army would almost certainly have come to grief; in any case, the successful junction of Bagration with Barclay at Smolensk would have been impossible.

By 5 July it became fully evident to Napoleon that his Brother Jerome had permitted Bagration to slip away and that the first phase of the operation had failed. He also knew that the slightest error on Bagration's part might still destroy him. That Jerome had spoiled and confused everything as much as he could, Napoleon realized clearly: 'Inform the King of Westphalia,' he dictated angrily to Berthier, 'that I am extremely displeased with him for not giving his light troops to Poniatowski to pursue Bagration, harass him, and block his movement . . . Tell him that it is impossible to manœuvre more clumsily than he did.' And he added: 'Tell him that all the fruits of my manœuvres and the most magnificent opportunity in the war have been lost through his strange ignorance of the first rules of strategy.'

On 6 July, Napoleon gave new directions: 'We must either compel Bagration to move towards Moghilev or throw him towards the Pinsk marshes. In either case, the French units can reach Vitebsk before Bagration, who will then be cut off.' On the same day Napoleon subordinated Jerome with all his forces to the authority of Marshal Davout.

On 7 July, new information arrived and Napoleon's hopes revived. 'Bagration is in Novogrudok, pursued from all directions,' wrote the Emperor from Vilna to Viceroy Eugène Beauharnais. But he was mistaken. Bagration had again escaped.

On 7 July, Bagration sent a secret order to Colonel Gresser, who was stationed in Borisov with a detachment: 'Having learned that the enemy is probably at Minsk, I command you, as soon as he approaches within 30 versts, without awaiting further orders, to spike all guns, throw them into the water, and then, with the men entrusted to you, to withdraw to Bobruysk.'

Napoleon finally understood that his armies had not succeeded in surrounding Bagration, and probably realized that Bagration was no General Mack or Prussian general; and that despite everything he would bring his army to Smolensk in full preparedness for battle.

Again and again, Napoleon turned angrily against his ungifted brother, the unlucky Jerome: 'That you had not been informed of the number of troops Bagration had left in Volyn, that you did not know how many divisions were at his disposal, that you made no effort to pursue him, and that he was enabled to withdraw as calmly as though he had had no one behind him— all this is contrary to every military rule.'

In Nesvizh, Bagration learned on the evening of 10 July that Marshal Davout with his detachments had entered Minsk, that Jerome Bonaparte, King of Westphalia, was advancing against him from Novogrudok, and that French patrols had appeared on his left flank. He was in danger of being outflanked. Bagration immediately broke up camp and marched to Slutsk, where he remained for only one day—13 July. Following him as his rear-guard, was a cavalry detachment under Platov. This detachment aside from miscellaneous Cossack and cavalry units comprised a division of Grenadiers under M. S. Vorontsov. On 13 July, at Slutsk, Bagration had alarming news: Davout had dispatched his cavalry by direct road to Bobruysk. On the following day, the fourteenth, Platov, in command of his rear-guard, reported that large French forces were pressing hard on his troops, and that since 28 June he had had daily engagements with the enemy.

The fact is that Davout had occupied Minsk on 8 July, and advanced thence towards the Berezina. Bagration with his 45,000 men, again found himself in a critical position. He was retreating, his army stretched out thinly along the narrow road through the marshes. When Napoleon was apprised of the position of Bagration's army, he exclaimed: 'They are in my hands!' He apparently forgot for the moment that he himself had called Bagration the best general in the Russian army. Davout spent four days in Minsk. By a skilful manœuvre, Bagration swerved far to the south and reached Bobruysk. Here he crossed the Berezina and advanced towards the Dnieper. He intended to cross the Dnieper at Moghilev, but, having learned on the way that Moghilev had been occupied by the forces of Davout which had advanced from Minsk, he retired fighting. Ségur recognizes that in the course of this retreat, Bagration destroyed an entire regiment of light French cavalry. Bagration ordered Rayevsky to do his utmost to hold Davout at the tiny town of Dashkovka, and he himself marched to Novy Bykhov, where he crossed the Dnieper on 25 July. Another part of his forces crossed the Dnieper at Stary Bykhov.

On 23 July, Rayevsky, with a single corps—the 7th—made a stand at Dashkovka for ten hours. Then, between Dashkovka and Novoselov he fought a stubborn engagement against five French divisions under Davout and Mortier. When in the course of this fierce battle, a volley of grapeshot caused momentary confusion among the musketeers, Rayevsky, as contemporaries said and wrote, seized the hands of his two sons, and all three flung themselves into the fray.* Like Bagration, his immediate superior, Nikolay Nikolayevich Rayevsky was a favourite with his men. His behaviour at Dashkovka was nothing unusual for him in desperate moments of battle. This did not subsequently prevent Nicholas I from completely ignoring the old general's

* According to the poet Batyushkov, Rayevsky later denied the accuracy of this tale.

petitions on behalf of his son-in-law, the Decembrist Volkonsky.

On the morning of 24 July, Bagration ordered Rayevsky to proceed to Novy and Stary Bykhov, then by bridge across the Dnieper. To Rayevsky's surprise and joy, Davout did not pursue him. As a result of Rayevsky's resistance, the French Marshal was convinced that Bagration was going to Moghilev and would there accept a general battle; hence, he began to concentrate his forces at Moghilev. Actually, Bagration's whole manœuvre was intended to make the French think that he was going to Moghilev and would accept a general battle. And the earliest military critics and historians of the campaign, who had not been with the staff of Bagration, as, for example, Clausewitz, who was with Barclay, wrote that Bagration went to Smolensk 'after a futile attempt to break through at Moghilev.' The 'futile attempt' had fooled Davout for several days.

Once on the left bank of the Dnieper, Bagration was beyond reach of the French pincers. Marshal Davout learned of Bagration's crossing only twenty-four hours later, and promptly reported it to the Emperor. Napoleon was extremely displeased at Bagration's unexpected escape from what seemed his inevitable rout, capture, or complete annihilation. It is true that despite all the mistakes of Jerome (who had been dismissed for incompetence and had returned to his kingdom of Westphalia), despite Davout's own slowness and the time lost in Minsk, Davout had in part executed Napoleon's order: Bagration's army was prevented from reaching Vitebsk, and was able to join Barclay only in Smolensk. But this success did not seem much of a consolation to Napoleon, when compared to his original hopes.

In any event, he was determined to exploit at once Bagration's retreat and his separation from Barclay's army comprising the main Russian forces.

On 18 July, Napoleon had another piece of news: that Barclay with his army had abruptly abandoned the armed camp at Drissa and had gone to Vitebsk.

.   .   .

Once it was decided to abandon Drissa, Barclay set out immediately. This was on 14 July. On the eighteenth he was in Polotsk. Here he resolved to go to Vitebsk to forestall its occupation by Napoleon. On the twenty-third, Barclay with his First Army arrived at Vitebsk, occupied the city, and set up camp.

Here he intended to await Bagration and, as he said, give battle to the Grand Army, which was advancing on Vitebsk. To delay the French, Barclay sent the Fourth Infantry Corps in command of Count Osterman-Tolstoy against their advance guard. Osterman took the road to Beshenkovichi, but less than 12 versts from Vitebsk he ran into an advance detachment of French cavalry. The Russian Hussars put the French to flight and, carried away by their own impetus, ran into an enemy cavalry brigade, which slaughtered many of them and threw back the rest. This engagement took place at the little town of Ostrovno, 26 versts from Vitebsk, on 25 July.

To the aid of the retiring Russian Hussars came the main forces of Osterman-Tolstoy. As he approached Ostrovno, Osterman-Tolstoy saw before him a dense mass of cavalry: this was Murat himself, advancing ahead of the Grand Army. A stubborn battle ensued, which, with shifting success, lasted the whole day of

25 July. Osterman was informed that General Delzon's division, sent by Viceroy Eugène, threatened his right flank; at the same time, two French regiments from two brigades under Roussel and Jeanninot impetuously assaulted three Russian battalions and threw them back. Osterman beat a fighting retreat. The resistance of Osterman's detachment would have been broken, had not Barclay learned of the engagement and rushed reinforcements in command of Konovnitsin. At daybreak on the twenty-sixth, Konovnitsin's infantry division came to the succour of Osterman's defeated regiments, and the battle was resumed with redoubled violence, this time about eight versts beyond Ostrovno, near the village of Kakzvachino.

It goes without saying that Konovnitsin, like Osterman, was expected only to hold the French, to give Bagration time to get to Vitebsk, where Barclay had decided to give battle. To fight delaying actions, to form living barriers doomed beforehand to destruction without the least chance of victory, is the most difficult of military tasks—Pyotr Petrovich Konovnitsin and his soldiers did this on the bloody day of 26 July as successfully as Osterman the day before, and Neverovsky and Rayevsky a few days later, on the road to Smolensk. Konovnitsin, like many other competent military men, had incurred the displeasure of Emperor Paul I, had been expelled from the army, and had passed eight inactive years in a remote village. In 1806 he had finally been reinstated in the service and had distinguished himself in the conquest of Finland in 1808-9. He was a kindly soul. During the army's retreat to Moscow, according to his colleagues, he never refused his soldiers permission to take along with them any inhabitants who wished to exacuate. And the inhabitants brought all their movable possessions. As a result, his regiments looked like caravans. Like General Kulnev, he treated his soldiers in a comradely manner. Such an attitude went definitely against contemporary army regulations, and only his shrewdness, competence, and extraordinary bravery saved him from a new enforced retirement.

On his arrival to relieve Osterman-Tolstoy on 26 July, Konovnitsin was attacked from two sides: by Eugène Beauharnais and Murat. From eight o'clock in the morning until three in the afternoon, Konovnitsin fought an unequal battle under strong artillery fire and persistent cavalry attacks. About three o'clock, Murat and Eugène Beauharnais forced Konovnitsin from his positions, and he began to retreat. At this moment, Napoleon himself arrived at the scene of action. He immediately countermanded Murat's and Beauharnais's decision to give their forces, battered and exhausted after seven hours of fighting, a rest. He ordered immediate pursuit of the retreating Konovnitsin. Slowly, fighting every inch of the way, Konovnitsin, hard pressed by Napoleon's superior forces, continued his withdrawal until nightfall. Thus he reached the village of Komarovo, where new reinforcements sent by Barclay had previously arrived; late on the night of 26 July remnants of Osterman's detachment also entered the village. The remnants of Konovnitsin's detachment augmented by these reinforcements (commanded by Tuchkov, of the Third Corps) proceeded to join Barclay's army and take up positions in the outskirts of Vitebsk on the right bank of the Luchosa. The detachments of Osterman and Konovnitsin had left the road between Ostrovno and the Luchosa strewn with corpses, but had accomplished their task—they had gained two whole additional days for Barclay and Bagration.

On 26 July, Barclay, accompanied by Ermolov, his Chief of Staff, and officers of his suite, spent the whole day inspecting his positions. All that day he awaited a report from Konovnitsin telling him how much longer he would be able to hold back the French, and a report from Bagration about his chances of breaking through Moghilev to Vitebsk. The night brought answers to both questions. Late in the night of 26 July, Osterman and Konovnitsin arrived with what was left of their detachments after the engagements at Ostrovno and Kakzvachino; and on the twenty-seventh, shortly before daybreak, Count Menshikov brought news that Bagration had not succeeded in breaking through Moghilev and that Marshal Davout was marching on Smolensk.

A few hours before the arrival of Menshikov, Barclay had been informed that Napoleon himself, with his Old Guard, had suddenly appeared near Vitebsk. That evening the Russians could see the campfires of the French Guard along the edge of the Vitebsk woods. Barclay was forced to take an immediate decision.

The entire day previous, Ermolov had been telling Barclay that to accept battle at their Vitebsk positions meant almost certain defeat and the destruction of the Russian army—this while Ermolov still counted on the arrival of Bagration. Now, on the morning of 27 July, the situation was even less favourable, as it was now impossible to expect any aid from Bagration. Barclay decided to abandon Vitebsk and to go to Smolensk, leaving 3,000 infantry, 4,000 cavalry, and 40 guns under the general command of Count Pahlen at a point 5 versts beyond Vitebsk, as a covering force to delay

Napoleon if only for a short time, should the Emperor decide to proceed promptly from Vitebsk to Smolensk. On the night of 27 July, the Russian army noiselessly broke camp and slipped away.

How did the French army react to the events preceding Barclay's arrival at Vitebsk? How do French reports complement the picture of the struggle up to that point? The French accounts give the most vivid picture of the heroic Russian rear-guard actions.

According to French sources, Napoleon, after leaving Vilna, proceeded by direct road through Glubokoye and Beshenkovichi towards Vitebsk, in pursuit of the retreating Barclay.

Having ordered his army to follow this course, Napoleon became firmly convinced that an engagement was at hand. He knew that Barclay with the main Russian forces was in Vitebsk, and that Bagration would, in all likelihood, join him. In Beshenkovichi, on 25 July, Napoleon learned of Bagration's attempt on 23 July to break through to Moghilev, and of the Russians' defeat by Davout.

These reports only strengthened the Emperor's assurance that battle would be joined at Vitebsk and that Barclay would retreat no further. 'We are on the eve of great events. It is preferable that they should not be prematurely announced, and that news of them should follow results,' wrote Napoleon on 25 July from Beshenkovichi to his Minister of Foreign Affairs, the Duke of Bassano, then at Vilna.

So eager was Napoleon for a general battle at Vitebsk that while still advancing on the road to Vitebsk he ordered Murat and Viceroy Eugène not to hinder separate detachments of the Russian army from uniting with the main Russian forces. 'If the enemy wants to give battle, that is a piece of good fortune for us . . . For that reason, he should be allowed to unite his forces, because otherwise he might use their separation as a pretext for not fighting.' The Emperor wrote these words at four o'clock in the morning of 26 July, as he was leaving Beshenkovichi on his way to Vitebsk.

'The day after tomorrow we shall give a battle, if the enemy remains at Vitebsk,' wrote Napoleon on the same day to the Duke of Bassano in Vilna.

On 25 July the French advanced on Vitebsk. Napoleon spent the night of 25-6 July in a tent between Beshenkovichi and Vitebsk. The terrible heat continued, the soldiers marched 'in a flaming dust,' the veterans of the Grand Army recalled Egypt and the Syrian deserts. The summer was unbelievably hot. 'We are being stifled,' wrote Napoleon to the Empress.

Barclay was retreating towards Vitebsk. General Dokhturov with his rear-guard was parrying Murat's attacks. The Russians were marching towards Ostrovno. On 25 July, within only a few kilometers of the tiny town, the Eighth Hussar Regiment of French cavalry sighted soldiers advancing in the same direction. As they were marching on the road to Beshenkovichi, where various detachments of the multi-raced Grand Army often unfamiliar to one another kept appearing from all possible directions, Murat's Hussars calmly proceeded at a distance of a hundred and fifty paces behind the unknown soldiers, taking them for their own. Suddenly the strangers opened fire, and big guns began to thunder. These soldiers were the Russian rear-guard, which had been ordered to delay the enemy as long as they could. The French and the Russians approached Ostrovno fighting. In the woods round

Ostrovno, Count Osterman, commanding the rear-
guard, stood his ground with remarkable stubbornness.
Only when Viceroy Eugène's troops came to Murat's
assistance did the Russians begin to retreat. Murat and
Eugène set out in pursuit. But on the following day,
26 July, towards evening, the Russians made a fresh
stand, after the divisions of Konovnitsin and Pahlen
had reinforced Osterman. The battle in the woods was
resumed. The Russians charged three times and each
time overthrew separate French detachments. One of
these attacks destroyed a Croat battalion belonging to
Eugène's forces; the cavalry of Murat also suffered heav-
ily. Panic seized the French. Without an order, the
artillerymen turned back their guns, and a part of the
infantry began to run, followed by some cavalry units.
Finally, Murat restored order, and the battle of the
woods continued. The French losses were relatively
large. The alarming part of it was that a section of the
French army had almost suffered a real defeat, in what
was obviously nothing but a rear-guard delaying action.

On the evening of the twenty-sixth Napoleon himself
came to the scene of this action, the woods extending
from Ostrovno to Vitebsk. He was followed by his main
forces. By now the Russians had reached Vitebsk and
were entering the city. Late that evening, the French
advance echelons reached the edge of the wood close to
the plain upon which Vitebsk is situated. A tent was
erected for Napoleon at a point close to the plain. During the night the Emperor looked at the many fires
round the city and in the city itself. All night long
everything was alight in the distance among the Russians. There was unceasing movement. It was hard to
tell what was going on. What was Barclay up to? Would

he fight at Vitebsk? Would there be a new Austerlitz tomorrow, the twenty-seventh, or the day after tomorrow?

In the morning the movement in and round the city had not ceased. The Russians did not attack Napoleon, and Napoleon decided that he would not attack on the twenty-seventh but on the twenty-eighth. He even thought it advantageous that Barclay had decided to postpone the battle. All day long French troops kept pouring from Beshenkovichi in an uninterrupted flow. There were constant minor clashes accompanied by intermittent bursts of gunfire. Murat at the head of a small detachment engaged the Russian cavalry, but was repulsed. Both sides left a few dead on the field. But as early as eleven o'clock in the morning, Napoleon ordered that all this foolishness be stopped. He had more serious business: to study the positions of tomorrow's battle and inspect the French units which kept arriving throughout the day. When the army retired for the night, the Emperor told Murat that at five o'clock in the morning he would start the battle. As on the previous night the Russian positions were illumined with fires. Napoleon went to his tent, while Murat rode away towards the advance posts of his cavalry, which of all French forces was closest to the city and to the Russian positions.

At daybreak an orderly came running to Napoleon with a message from Murat: during the night Barclay had slipped away . . .

Once again Napoleon's hopes for a speedy denouement collapsed. Victory had seemed in his grasp, and again had eluded him.

•   •   •

Napoleon was fully aware that from the purely military, tactical point of view, it was absolutely essential not to pause at Vitebsk, but to pursue Barclay and Bagration without delay, and prevent their junction in Smolensk. Only five or six days remained in which this could be accomplished. 'But the heat was so terrible and the army so large that the Emperor decided it must have a few days of rest.'

At least five times during the first days of his stay in Vitebsk, Napoleon peremptorily asked his subordinates to find out the exact number of divisions in Bagration's army. 'It is still a riddle to me—are there four or six divisions in Bagration's army?' he complains angrily on 2 August. This was the work of Platov's Cossacks operating as Bagration's rear-guard; the French cavalry reconnaissance never succeeded in penetrating that barrier.

This long, unusually sultry day of 28 July brought a number of disappointments to the Grand Army and many to Napoleon and his suite.

At first Napoleon refused to believe Murat. He would not believe that the Russian army could have broken camp so silently in the night and disappeared without a trace. Fearing an ambush and sudden attack, the Emperor ordered his men to approach the abandoned Russian camp with the greatest precautions. A deathly silence reigned there. The French drew nearer; finally they entered—the camp was empty. Not a soldier, not a single bit of equipment. They went into the city: not a soul in the streets. The few inhabitants who remained in their houses could give no information about the road taken by the Russian army. They didn't even know it had gone. For several hours cavalry detachments sent by Napoleon scoured all the roads round

Vitebsk. Exhausted by the frightful heat, tormented by thirst, one party after another returned in the afternoon without the desired information. The sand in which the horses' hooves sank, the clouds of burning and blinding dust, the complete absence of water made reconnaissance impossible. One of the detachments had seen a Russian unit in the distance and had even attempted to engage it. But the French were unable to find out whether it was Barclay's rear-guard or merely a detachment sent out to mislead the enemy.

Napoleon had to decide what to do next. The same evening (28 July) he summoned Murat, Eugène Beauharnais, and Marshal Berthier. This was not exactly a military council—Napoleon disliked military councils and made his own decisions, but during this campaign, in exceptionally difficult circumstances, he sometimes consulted a few members of his staff before deciding on a course of action. This time the consultation began with a slight unpleasantness for Murat, the King of Naples. During the reconnaissance that morning a French cavalry detachment had stumbled upon the supposed Russian rear-guard, engaged it, and had been beaten back with the loss of several horses and men. Murat who, even as King of Naples, feared Napoleon as much as when he had served him as a simple colonel, had concealed this little incident from the Emperor. But Napoleon heard of it from some other source. It was a trivial matter, but it did not improve the Emperor's temper.

The main problem remained: where and when would Barclay give battle? It was clear that he had gone to Smolensk. Despite the lack of precise information, Napoleon could even guess that he had gone by way of Rudnya. But this was relatively unimportant. If Barclay had gone to Smolensk to join Bagration, who had given Davout the slip, it seemed possible that he would finally make a stand there. This would have been logical, for in Vitebsk Barclay would have been compelled to fight without Bagration; in Smolensk he would have the advantage of fighting side by side with him. But Napoleon did not come to this conclusion at once. At first he thought that the Russian army would continue its endless withdrawal. As the French lines of communication were even then overextended, he thought it advisable to put an immediate stop to this strange campaign, conducted like no other war since the remote times when the endlessly retreating Scythians lured the invading enemy into the torrid desert steppes. The Scythians had ruled two thousand years before, over a mere part of this immense territory which now belonged to their heirs—the Russians. The Russians had perhaps inherited their strategy and tactics as well as their territory. If the Russian army was retreating from weakness, that was one thing; but what if this were a deliberate strategic plan—? 'Never do what your enemy wants you to do' . . . that was one of Napoleon's strictest rules. The Emperor concluded the conference with the solemn announcement that he meant to end the campaign in Vitebsk, organize conquered Lithuania and White Russia, strengthen his positions, replenish his army with fresh recruits, and await Alexander's peace proposals.

For Vitebsk, as for all of White Russia, came a time of great distress.

'Burning villages and suburbs everywhere!' wrote a witness to Napoleon's seizure of Vitebsk. 'Streets strewn with dead and wounded; fields soaked in human blood and studded with corpses; pillage, rape, and mur-

der of unarmed inhabitants—the picture defied all description. Even in the depths of the woods it was impossible to find a safe shelter; the monsters took special
delight in seeking out those in hiding, and treating
them in a most inhuman fashion. Yet no one dared
complain; it was forbidden. One Vitebsk landowner,
looted to the skin, his wife and daughter driven out of
their wits, ventured to make representations to the
French authorities in Vitebsk, bringing with him the
corpses of two of his serfs slain by the French. Instead
of the satisfaction he expected, he received warning
that if he should repeat the present performance, he
would himself be shot.'

Poniatowski with his corps was in Moghilev, Davout
in Orsha, Murat in Vitebsk, Ney between Orsha and
Vitebsk, the Old and the Young Guard and Eugène
with the Italian army in Vitebsk, Dombrowski in Bobruysk.

The right (southern) flank of these forces was protected by Schwarzenberg, the Austrian 'ally.' The left
flank, beginning at the approaches to Riga and continuing to the north along the line of Riga-Dvinsk, was
under the command of Marshal Macdonald, whose army
included all the Prussian troops. With the force of the
Grand Army thus disposed, there was every reason for
confidence. But Napoleon abided for only two days by
the decision he had taken on the evening of 28 July.
'Only Napoleon himself could destroy Napoleon'—this
aphorism oft repeated after Waterloo was never better
illustrated than in Vitebsk, in the last days of July 1812.

The Emperor stayed in Vitebsk one day, a second, a
third, a fourth. It was plain to his retinue, his Guard,
that he was irritated and dissatisfied. Then, suddenly,
without summoning a new council, he began to dis-

cuss his decision with his colleagues. At first they
thought that he wanted to be convinced again. But they
were mistaken. He had already made a new decision,
diametrically opposed to that which he had so solemnly
announced to his marshals on 28 July.

He had made up his mind to end the war that year.
And there was only one way of ending the war in 1812:
to destroy the Russian army.

In other words, Barclay had to be overtaken and destroyed before his junction with Bagration. If Barclay
had already joined Bagration, it would be necessary to
destroy them both.

Most unpleasant news reached Napoleon while he was
in Vitebsk. On 2 August a courier came from the right
flank, informing him that the forces of Tormasov had
defeated General Reynier. Three French battalions had
perished. The day following receipt of this news, Napoleon wrote to Prince Schwarzenberg that he had abandoned his original idea of incorporating the Austrian
corps into the centre of the Grand Army, since he
could no longer expect that General Reynier would
succeed in resisting the pressure of Tormasov without
Schwarzenberg's aid.

So it happened that a month and four days later, at
Borodino, Napoleon, by his own dispositions, was deprived of 30,000 men.

In Vitebsk, eyewitnesses tell us, Napoleon wrote and
dictated a hundred letters a day, directing all the affairs of his vast Empire, attending to diplomatic business, to the endless, savage war with the Spaniards, and
to the more immediate problems of the gigantic Russian
undertaking.

His mind retained its freshness. His boundless capacity for work, his lively interest in all the affairs of his far-flung Empire never left him.

At the beginning of August, Napoleon announced to his marshals that he would march on Smolensk.

The opinions of the marshals on this new decision were diverse. Murat was wholly in favour of continuing. Indeed, as soon as he discovered the retreat of the Russians, he had urged prompt pursuit. That day Napoleon had said to him: 'Murat, the first Russian campaign is finished . . . In 1813 we shall be in Moscow, in 1814 in St. Petersburg. The Russian war is a three-year war.' Murat did not believe this. Long wars were not in the spirit of Napoleonic strategy. Napoleon himself realized how difficult it would be to go on fighting for years so far from conquered Europe, which loathed him, with dubious 'allies' on his flanks. The delay would enable Russia to replenish her army and prepare further resistance.

Every courier arriving at Vitebsk brought news that matters in Spain were getting worse and worse, that the Spanish people continued to fight, to kill, and to die, but showed no inclination to capitulate. To begin a three-year war in Russia, with no end of the Spanish war in sight, seemed hazardous. The Emperor's intimates understood all this; yet, when Napoleon announced his new decision, Berthier, Duroc, Daru, and Caulaincourt—in direct opposition to Murat—came out against a new advance. Rarely had they ventured to disagree so definitely and stubbornly with their sovereign. The marshals, except for Davout, who was in Orsha, resolved upon an unusual course—frankness. General Duroc insisted respectfully but firmly that the Russians were clearly luring the Grand Army far inland, to its ruin. Berthier supported him. They spoke of the fearful loss of horses, the lack of fodder, the disorganization of supply, the poverty of the land deliberately devastated by the Russian troops, the endless expanses, the terrible heat, which was felling both men and horses. Duroc stubbornly stressed the ominous fact that Emperor Alexander was not suing for peace. Napoleon said he was aware of the dangers involved in a further advance, but that he would end the campaign in Smolensk. Duroc stood his ground. He insisted that even in Smolensk the Russians would not ask for peace.

Berthier and Duroc and Caulaincourt went on to stress the unreliability of the Austrian and German 'allies,' who had joined under the lash, fought under the lash, and would go over to the Russians as soon as they could escape the lash. Napoleon retorted that if the Prussians betrayed him, he would interrupt his war with Russia and turn westward against Prussia. He would make Prussia pay—for herself as well as Russia.

The first big conference passed in these fruitless conversations. In the end, the Emperor cried out angrily: 'I have made my generals too rich: they think only of pleasures, of hunting, of rolling about Paris in their magnificent carriages! They have grown sick of war!' The marshals kept silent, but were far from yielding. As soldiers, they did not dare to go on arguing with the Emperor after this scathing remark.

But there was one man at Vitebsk who was in a better position to speak. This was Count Daru, Secretary of State, Intendant General of the Grand Army, who knew the problem of supply better than anyone else. He knew that of the 22,000 horses that had accompanied the army to Russia (not counting the troops on the right and left flanks), no less than 8,000 had died during the advance from Vilna to Vitebsk. He

knew that both men and horses were very badly supplied, and that the further they went, considering the
rapidity of their advance, the worse conditions would
become, because the baggage trains simply could not
keep up with the troops and because the country was
a devastated, burnt-out, pillaged wilderness. All this
Count Daru knew well, and he did not conceal it from
Napoleon.

And that was not all he said. What was the reason
for this difficult war so far from France? 'Not only our
troops, Sire, but we ourselves fail to understand either
the aims or the necessity of this war.' The entry of
English goods into Russia and the Emperor's desire to
create a Polish kingdom were insufficient motives. Daru
thus gave tongue to everything that was in the minds
of Duroc, Caulaincourt, and Berthier.

Daru was a ponderous bureaucrat, cool, obstinate,
and hard-headed. He had touched several sensitive spots.
The timid, submissive Berthier was wholly on his side,
but since he did not open his mouth, Daru had to bear
the whole brunt of his disagreement with Napoleon.
The other marshals were absent from this conversation,
which went on for eight hours. Napoleon was all the
more irritated by Daru's words because he could not
fail to realize their gravity and truth.

Daru insisted that the war was incomprehensible, and
for that very reason not popular in France. It was 'not
national.' Daru's arguments pointed to a single conclusion: it was necessary to make peace. As the discussion
progressed, the Emperor's irritation mounted. He ex-
ploded when Daru repeated the advice of Duroc: to
await peace in Vitebsk, because neither in Smolensk
nor in Moscow would the chances for peace be any

better. 'I want peace, but it takes two to make peace. And Alexander is silent.'

Here Napoleon had expressed a thought that more than once had troubled his entourage. While Napoleon was still in Vilna and later during his advance through Lithuania and White Russia, they had expected that Balashov's first visit to the Imperial camp would be followed by a second, and possibly a third. Each time the 'negotiations' would become more advantageous to Napoleon, since the frightened Russians were bound to grow more accommodating as the Grand Army advanced. But Balashov's first journey turned out to be his last. The Russians kept retreating, burning everything behind them and devastating their country, yielding enormous territory to the enemy; but they maintained silence, and failed to show the slightest inclination to ask for peace. Had Balashov come to Vitebsk, he would have had a better reception than before. But Balashov did not come. 'What shall we do?' Napoleon asked Daru. 'Shall we remain in Lithuania? We would either have to ruin the country and turn all the inhabitants against us, or pay for everything to maintain the army. We would have to build fortresses for our protection. Or shall we go farther? Where to? To Moscow? The conclusion of peace awaits me at the gates of Moscow.' Napoleon could understand that Alexander would not ask for peace before a general engagement had taken place. 'If necessary, I shall go as far as Moscow, the holy city of Moscow, in quest of battle, and I shall win the battle.' After such a battle, Alexander could conclude a peace without dishonour. 'But should Alexander still remain stubborn, very well —I shall then begin negotiations with the Boyars or even with the population of this capital. It is large, united, and enlightened; these people will grasp their own interests, they will understand freedom.'

What did the Emperor mean by these words? Do they contain so much as a hint of the possible liberation of the serfs? Of course not. He could scarcely have regarded the Russian serfs as 'enlightened' and 'united.' He could have been referring only to the upper middle class, to whose interests he had subjected the whole of France, and upon whom, consciously and systematically, he based his rule in the vassal states.

Not once in the whole eight-hour conversation—or rather, monologue—did the Emperor utter a single word about freeing the Russian peasants from the yoke of serfdom; not once did he even suggest threatening Alexander or the Boyars with the abolition of serfdom. He wanted negotiations with Alexander; if Alexander failed him, with the Boyars; and if the Boyars failed him, with the 'enlightened' Moscow bourgeoisie. This was the Emperor's final word.

Napoleon had heard something of the traditional rivalry between Moscow and St. Petersburg. In his long conversation with Daru he greatly exaggerated the significance of this Muscovite fronde, the grumbling witticisms of the Moscow English Club against the St. Petersburg Court and St. Petersburg dignitaries: 'Moscow hates St. Petersburg. I shall take advantage of this rivalry. The consequences of such competition are incalculable.'

Obviously Napoleon's spies, who had long been informing him of what was being done and said in the high society of both Russian capitals, had greatly exaggerated the importance of the complaints they heard from wealthy Muscovites and the bureaucratic big-wigs in disgrace who lived in Moscow. Daru listened to Napoleon, who was clearly talking to convince himself, but was not reassured. Daru pointed out that hitherto 'His Majesty had always won in the gamble of war.' But now, desertions, disease, and hunger had diminished the Grand Army by a third. 'If we are short of provisions here in Vitebsk, what will happen later?' asked Daru. Foraging had produced no results: 'Officers sent out for provisions do not return, and when they do return it is with empty hands.' There was enough meat and flour for the Guard, but not for the rest of the army; and the troops were muttering. The Grand Army, he went on, had an immense baggage train, herds of cattle, and field hospitals, but all this was far in the rear, absolutely unable to catch up with the army. The sick and the wounded were left without medicines or care. We must stop now. Beyond Vitebsk came real Russia, and the population would meet the conqueror with even greater hostility: 'They are almost savage peoples, who have no property, no needs. What can we take from them? What will tempt them? Their sole possession is their life, and this they will carry away with them into the endless expanses.' Berthier supported this opinion, and assented to everything Daru said, but he did not venture to speak.

The Emperor was arguing with his own inner voice, which told him the same things that Daru spoke aloud. Suddenly and with great ardour, Napoleon recalled the Swedish campaign in the time of Peter the Great. 'I can see that you are thinking of Charles XII!' he exclaimed, though no one had thought of mentioning Charles XII. He himself, no doubt, had suddenly thought of the Swedish King, his direct predecessor as an invader of Russia. Again the Emperor was not answering Daru but himself. The example of Charles XII, argued Napoleon, proves nothing: the Swedish King was not the right man for such an undertaking. Besides, it was not admissible to generalize on the basis of one instance, the defeat of the Swedes; 'It is not the rule that creates success, but success that creates the rule, and if I should achieve success by further marches, my new success will create new principles.' Such was his line of reasoning. His habit of ignoring precedents, of dictating to history instead of learning from it; his assurance that no common standards and rules could apply to him are apparent in every word he said. Yes, the famous Swedish warlord met his doom, but that was his own fault; why, being 'only' Charles XII, should he have undertaken something that Napoleon alone, and no one else, was strong enough to achieve?

In the following days, the Emperor issued neither a final command to leave Vitebsk, nor any order to prepare for a prolonged stay.

He called no conferences, but spoke to Generals of the Guard and various marshals concerning plans for the near future. The majority were now for a continuation of the advance. Ségur ascribes this partly to their inner conviction, partly to a desire to please their sovereign by flattery—for they were all aware of the Emperor's desire—and partly to the soldier's habit of accepting superior decisions without argument. Moreover, Vitebsk seemed unfriendly and poor. The more soldiers collected in this tiny devastated town, far in advance of their baggage trains, the hungrier they became, the more horses perished. Many units lived almost entirely on a gruel made of oats. An epidemic of dysentery broke out.

Though his mind was made up, the Emperor delayed, awaiting a jolt of some kind.

The jolt came. On 10 August, the Emperor was informed that Marshal Sebastiani had been suddenly attacked near Inkov by the Russian cavalry, and had suffered losses. Hope revived that the Russians had halted somewhere near the left bank of the Dnieper.

Napoleon promptly gave orders to leave Vitebsk and advance against the Russians.

On 10 August, Napoleon informed Davout that he expected to cross the Dnieper at Rasasno, where he had ordered the construction of four bridges, and that he would cross to the left bank with 200,000 men. The Emperor made no secret of the heavy losses suffered by his army in encounters with Russian detachments, which were holding up the advance.

On 12 August, the first detachments of Napoleon's army left Vitebsk. On 13 August, in the wake of other detachments, the Old Guard, with the Emperor at the head, advanced eastward. On the night of 15 August Napoleon camped in Boyarintsevo. Reports arrived of Neverovsky's desperate resistance.

3

THE BATTLE OF SMOLENSK

AT one o'clock on the
morning of 13 August Napoleon left Vitebsk. He spent
the night of the thirteenth in his field tent near Rasasno. On the fourteenth and fifteenth, he crossed the
Dnieper with his entire army. Ney and Murat flung
themselves on Neverovsky's detachment, which had
taken up a position on the road from Lad to Smolensk.
Neverovsky resisted desperately, with great losses, and
slowly retreated towards Smolensk. He had orders from
Bagration to hold up the enemy as long as possible.

Concealing his route from the Russians by complex
manœuvres under cover of the woods, Napoleon
planned a rapid advance to Smolensk along the left
bank of the Dnieper. But Neverovsky, with his 27th
Division, stood in his way.

On 15 August Ney had fought his way into Krasnoye,
and from Krasnoye he advanced on Smolensk, delayed
by the stubborn resistance of Neverovsky's small detachment.

Dislodged from the small town of Lad and from
Krasnoye, Neverovsky, desperately battling an enemy
with five times superior forces, continued his retreat

towards Smolensk. Count Ségur describes this retreat as 'lion-like.' Neverovsky was a careful strategist. Before an engagement he would, when possible, inspect the battleground with his men, and explain the problem that faced them. During this murderous retreat, his soldiers fought with complete disregard of danger; the roads were strewn with Russian corpses. 'The Russian cavalrymen seemed to be rooted in the ground,' wrote Ségur. 'A number of our first attacks ended in failure about twenty paces from the Russian front. The retreating Russians would again and again suddenly turn to face us and throw us back with rifle fire.'

When Neverovsky entered Smolensk, his forces were reduced to a sixth of their original strength.

Near by, Bagration was manœuvring in the scorching heat. He was without food or fodder, he had no way of strengthening his positions, and meanwhile the enemy, division after division, was crossing the Rudnya in pursuit. 'I have no hay, no oats, no bread, no water, no positions,' wrote Bagration to Ermolov on 10 August. On 3 August, Bagration had succeeded in uniting with Barclay. 'The First Army, which has spent two days here, has taken everything, and eaten everything . . . The enemy might make a feint from Rudnya and actually advance to Smolensk; that would be bad and shameful.' Bagration demanded that Barclay 'should not exhaust the army for nothing.' He pleaded: 'Let someone else be entrusted with this work, and release me.'

Bagration was definitely reluctant to remain with Barclay, 'the Minister,' as he referred to him with deliberate formality. '. . . I am being treated without frankness and with unpleasantness beyond the power of words,' wrote Bagration on 10 August to Arakcheyev (for the Tsar's attention, of course). 'It is the will of my sovereign. I cannot get along with the Minister. For God's sake, send me anywhere, if only to command a regiment in Moldavia or in the Caucasus. But here I do not want to be. The whole headquarters is so full of Germans that a Russian cannot breathe, and the whole thing doesn't make any sense. Honest to God, the changes that take place every minute are driving me crazy . . . My 40,000 are called an army, and I am ordered to stretch them out like a thread, and pull them in all directions.' He firmly demands to be relieved of his duties. 'I thought I was truly serving my Tsar and my Fatherland, but I find that I am serving Barclay. I must admit that I don't want to.'

Moved by Bagration's recriminations, egged on by Ermolov, impressed by Platov's daring cavalry raid on Marshal Sebastiani at Inkov, where several Frenchmen and part of a baggage train were captured, Barclay decided to forestall the attack on Smolensk and moved his vanguard to Rudnya. But almost immediately he cancelled the order. For a time, he seemed 'to lose his head' (according to Clausewitz). On 13 and 14 August, his army moved aimlessly, now towards Rudnya, now away from Rudnya. On the evening of the fifteenth, Barclay was informed that Neverovsky's decimated unit had been flung back towards Smolensk. There was nothing to do but abandon everything and rush towards the city.

According to Barclay de Tolly, Napoleon was approaching Smolensk with 220,000 men. Barclay could directly oppose them with a mere 76,000, because Bagration and his army had to defend the road to Dorogobuzh.

In his 'Apologia,' published several years after

the event, Barclay finds all his actions without reproach. He says he intended to give battle at Tsarevo-Zaimishche, 'having placed his army in an advantageous position,' but at that very place learned that he had been relieved of his duties. 'Having revealed the truth in its entire nakedness, I offer to the severest judgment each and every one of my acts. Let anyone who desires indicate better measures that might have been sought and taken to save the Fatherland in the critical and terrible position in which it then found itself. After that, let hatred and slander continue to pour out their poison. I neither fear, nor respect them . . . If my explanations do not satisfy the incredulous, time shall justify me . . .'

Akhsharumov, author of the first official account of the War of 1812, published in August 1813, 'at His Majesty's command,' affirms that when the two armies finally united at Smolensk and Bagration became subject to Barclay de Tolly, the Russian army numbered exactly 110,000 men, while Napoleon, who had advanced from Vitebsk to Dubrovno, had with him an army of 205,000 men. These 110,000 were 'the bulwark of the nation, the sole barrier against Napoleon's ambition to dominate Russia and deprive all other nations of their last vestige of freedom. Opposed to Barclay was a great captain, who had been waging wars for 20 years, a favourite of Fortune, for 20 years a victor.' Akhsharumov is exaggerating: Napoleon had about 180,000 men during the bombardment of Smolensk.

Having learned that Napoleon had sent large forces towards Dorogobuzh to outflank Smolensk, Bagration promptly moved to occupy Dorogobuzh and prevent the enemy from cutting the main Moscow road. His army was small, but what most worried him was the conviction that Barclay would surrender Smolensk. On 17 August, he sent a note to Barclay from the inn of Volcheyki (near Smolensk): '. . . I humbly entreat Your Excellency not to retire from Smolensk, to try with all your strength to maintain your position . . . Your retirement from Smolensk would harm us greatly and could not be pleasing to the Tsar and the Fatherland.'

Bagration ordered Rayevsky's corps to proceed from Smolensk to meet the advancing French. The Second Division of Grenadiers was to precede Rayevsky, but, to his astonishment, this division did not budge for three hours. Rayevsky had to wait, losing precious time. The mystery was easily explained. In the words of Ermolov: 'The division was commanded by Lieutenant-General Prince Karl of Mecklenburg. Having spent the previous night with friends, he was drunk, and awoke very late the next day; only then was he able to order his troops to march.' The Prince of Mecklenburg knew that Bagration had no power to shoot him for this offence, because, after all, he was related to the Tsar. Why then should he deny himself a little recreation? About this time news arrived that on 15 August, in Krasnoye, the French army had attacked and defeated Neverovsky's forces, that Neverovsky was beating a fighting retreat, and that to save himself from annihilation he had asked Bagration for immediate assistance. The assistance came too late.

The remnants of Neverovsky's detachment were merged with Rayevsky's 15,000 men entrusted with the defence of Smolensk.

       .   .   .

On 16 August, Napoleon reached the outskirts of Smolensk and took up his quarters at a landowner's house in the village of Lubnya. This was his plan: the forces of Davout, Ney, and Poniatowski were to take Smolensk by assault; at the same time the forces of Junot were to by-pass Smolensk, advance along the main Moscow road and cut off the retreat of the Russian army, in case Barclay should again decide to evade battle and move back towards Moscow.

At six o'clock in the morning of 16 August, Napoleon began the bombardment of Smolensk, and soon launched the first assault. The first line of the city's defence was held by Rayevsky's division. All day the battle raged, with occasional lulls. During the night, Rayevsky's corps, whose losses had been tremendous, was replaced by the corps of Dokhturov. At four in the morning of 17 August the battle was resumed, and an almost unceasing exchange of artillery fire went on for thirteen hours—until five o'clock that afternoon. At that hour all the suburbs were enveloped in flames, and soon various sections of the city itself were burning. On the night of 17-18 August, the cannonade and fires grew in intensity. In the middle of the night, the Russian guns suddenly ceased firing; and shortly afterward the French heard explosions of tremendous force: Barclay had ordered his army to blow up the powder magazines and to evacuate the city. The Russian troops fought with great ardour, and did not feel defeated when Barclay issued his order to withdraw. Barclay saw that Napoleon was striving to force him into a general engagement, and to repeat Austerlitz on the banks of the Dnieper; he saw that Bagration would be unable to reach the field of battle in time.

Smolensk had to be abandoned at once; delay would

mean inevitable disaster. He knew the criticism he would come in for, but he saw no alternative; in any event, Barclay's fate had already been settled.

The destruction of Smolensk produced an indelible impression upon the French.

The whole long summer day, there had been no break in the bombardment. Again and again, attempts had been made to carry the city by storm. The remnants of Neverovsky's almost annihilated division had been incorporated into Rayevsky's corps. Under inconceivable difficulties, the Russian troops held their ground. Evening had come, the fires in the various parts of the city were clearly visible. There was something peculiarly sinister in the spectacle of the perishing city. 'The burning suburbs, the dense multi-coloured smoke, the red glow, the crash of exploding bombs, the thunder of cannon, the seething rifle fire, the beating of drums, the moans and groans of old men, women, and children, the whole people falling on their knees with arms outstretched to the skies—such was the picture that greeted our eyes and tore at our hearts,' says Ivan Maslov, who was there. 'Crowds of inhabitants ran from the flames, not knowing whither . . . The Russian regiments ran into the flames, some to save lives, others to sacrifice their own. A long line of carts rolled on slowly, bearing the wounded. In the deep twilight the ikon of the Smolensk Mother of God was carried out of the city; the dismal tolling of bells merged with the crash of falling houses and the din of battle.' Night came. The confusion and horror mounted.

At two o'clock on the morning of the eighteenth, following the explosion of the powder magazines, Cossacks galloped down the streets of Smolensk, announcing the retreat of the army and bidding all inhabitants wishing to leave the city to do so immediately, before the bridge across the Dnieper was burned. A part of the population fled in the wake of the retreating Russian troops; others remained. At four o'clock, Marshal Davout entered the city. The fires were still burning. Soldiers, mostly Poles and Germans, began to loot. The French, Dutch, and Italians, to judge by accounts, looted less than the others. About 2,000 persons fled from burning houses into the streets and later took refuge in the cathedral. Many of them remained there for over two weeks.

On the eighteenth, Napoleon awoke at dawn. Today, he thought, the general engagement would at last take place. But his aides pointed to a dense mass of troops moving eastward from Smolensk, beyond the Dnieper, and he realized that Barclay had again eluded him, and that the Russian command now regarded Smolensk only as a barrier, whose purpose was to delay pursuit.

The day before, as he had looked through his spyglass and seen the Russian forces entering Smolensk, Napoleon had joyfully exclaimed: 'At last, I hold them in my hands!'

But the Russian army had again slipped away.

The Russian troops fought so furiously at Smolensk that even the briefest, driest, most matter-of-fact French reports and memoirs mention a number of extraordinary exploits. The fiercely burning city had been abandoned by the Russians; several French columns entered the St. Petersburg suburb. The Russian rear-guard under General Konovnitsin and Colonel Toll fought desperately, and continued to hold back the enemy. Isolated Russian sharpshooters, scattered in gardens, fired at the approaching dense lines of French infantry and

at the French gun crews. The Russians refused to leave
their positions, though they knew that death was certain. 'Among these sharpshooters, one Russian chasseur
distinguished himself by his staunchness and bravery,'
writes Fabre de Faure, a French colonel of artillery.
'He placed himself right opposite us, on the very bank
of the river behind some willows, and we could silence
him neither by concentrating our fire on him nor by
the use of a big gun, which demolished all the trees
behind which he was operating; he continued to shoot
and did not stop until that night. On the following
day we visited this memorable position out of curiosity
and found the body of our foe, face downward, among
the broken and splintered trees. A non-commissioned
officer of the Russian chasseurs, he had been killed at
his post by one of our cannon-balls.'

According to amazed witnesses, the Russian soldiers
at Smolensk so thirsted for battle that their commanders
had to use swords to drive them from spots where they
were senselessly exposing themselves to slaughter by
grapeshot and bayonet. Here is a statement of the dry,
businesslike I. P. Liprandi: 'At daybreak the lines of
marksmen outside the city began to exchange shots.
This rifle fire became more intense as the advance
French file was reinforced. At ten o'clock Barclay de
Tolly arrived and stopped on the terrace of the
Malakhov gates . . . To the right of the gates, outside
the city, the Ufimsky Regiment had taken up its position. Constant "Hurrahs!" were coming from that direction, as the firing increased in intensity. I was sent
to remind the troops that they were not to advance beyond the assigned limit. I found the commander of
this regiment, Major-General Tsibulsky, in full uniform, mounted on horseback among his marksmen. He

replied that he was unable to restrain his men, who after exchanging a few shots with the French occupying the cemetery opposite them, repeatedly tried to dislodge them by bayonet assaults, without awaiting orders. Even as Major-General Tsibulsky spoke, there was a shout of "Hurrah!" from the line of men. He began to shout, *even to drive the marksmen back with his sword;* where he was, his command was obeyed, but only a few paces from him the cry of "Hurrah!" resounded again, and the men flung themselves on the enemy. The other regiments of this division acted likewise . . . during this encounter—their first—with the French . . .' 'The fierceness with which our troops— especially the infantry—fought at Smolensk is indescribable. Light wounds *were ignored* until the wounded fell from exhaustion and loss of blood . . .'

The Smolensk tragedy was all the more terrible because the Russian command had evacuated most of the seriously wounded from Moghilev, Vitebsk, Krasnoye, to Smolensk, not to mention the wounded from the detachments of Neverovsky and Rayevsky. These suffering thousands, without medical attention, had been gathered in the section of Smolensk known as the Old City. The Old City had caught fire during the first bombardment, and was reduced to ashes during the retreat of the Russian army, which was unable to save anyone from there. The French, on entering the city, came upon an unforgettable scene: 'The force of the attack and the impetuosity of the pursuit left the Russians time to destroy the bridge but not to evacuate the wounded,' write Colonel Combes. 'These unfortunates, abandoned to a cruel death, lay here in piles, charred, almost without human form, among the smoking ruins and flaming beams . . . The positions of many corpses indicated the horrible torments that must have preceded death. I trembled with horror at the spectacle, which will always haunt my memory. Choking with the smoke and heat, shaken by the terrible scene, we made haste to get out of the city. I felt that I had left hell behind me.'

'*Mon amie*, I have been in Smolensk since this morning. I have taken this city from the Russians, having slain 3,000 of their men and wounded thrice that number. My health is good, the heat is extreme. My affairs are going well,' wrote Napoleon on 18 August to the Empress.

Napoleon's lying bulletins and official reports of course gave no idea of the reality.

For the public, for Paris, for Europe, he could write anything he liked. To the Duke of Bassano he wrote, 'The heat is extreme, there is much dust, and all this is somewhat tiring. The entire enemy army was here; it was ordered to give us battle, but did not dare. We took Smolensk by frontal assault. It is a very large city, with solid walls and fortifications. We have slain three to four thousand enemy soldiers, their wounded were thrice that many; we found many guns here. Several divisional generals are said to have been killed. The Russian army is retiring, dissatisfied and disheartened, towards Moscow.' The Emperor himself, however, and his staff were not deceived by all this verbiage. 'After dictating this letter, His Majesty promptly threw himself on his bed,' runs a characteristic postscript, added by his secretary to explain the absence of Napoleon's personal signature. The truth is that Napoleon was exhausted, not only from the heat and the dust, but from all that was going on round him at Smolensk.

Cesare Loggie, an Italian officer who commanded a

unit belonging to the corps of Eugène Beauharnais, passed through Smolensk on the day after its capture by the French. In his *Recollections* he writes: 'The sole witnesses of our entry into devastated Smolensk were the smoking ruins of the houses and the corpses of our men and the enemy lying about pell-mell before burial in a common grave. The inner section of this unfortunate city presented a particularly gloomy and dreadful appearance. Not once since the opening of hostilities had we witnessed such scenes; we were greatly shaken by them. To the strains of military music, proudly and grimly we marched in among the ruins, where the unhappy Russian wounded wallowed in blood and mire . . . How many men were burned and smothered here! . . . I saw a cart filled to the brim with torn human limbs. They were being taken away for burial . . . On the thresholds of houses which had survived the flames stood groups of wounded imploring assistance . . . The only living people in the streets are French and allied soldiers . . . They roam the streets, in hope of finding something spared by the flames. The fire which is now put out has destroyed half of the buildings: the market, the warehouses, most of the dwellings . . . And here in the midst of these piles of ashes and corpses we are preparing to spend the night of 19-20.' In the Cathedral, dead, dying, wounded, old men, young men, women, and children were lying in a heap. 'Entire families, in rags, with horror in their faces, weeping, exhausted, famished, were huddled together on the slabs around the altars . . . They all trembled at our approach . . . To make matters worse, the majority of these unfortunates refuse the help that is offered them. To this day I see a dying old man stretched out to his full length in one corner, and, in another,

sickly babies clinging to the parched breasts of their
mothers.'

The countless Russian wounded abandoned in the
city received practically no medical aid. The surgeons
had no lint, and they made bandages out of oakum and
old papers found in the archives. Frequently the doctors did not show up for days. Even the soldiers, accustomed after sixteen years of the Napoleonic epic to
all kinds of horrors, were aghast at the scenes they witnessed in Smolensk.

Before Napoleon's invasion Smolensk had 15,000 inhabitants. A few days after the French occupation only
1,000 remained. The rest either perished, or, abandoning everything, fled. They ran straight ahead, anywhere, or voluntarily joined the Russian army as it left
the city.

Bagration was angry at Barclay's retreat from Smolensk. His letter to Rostopchin, written on 14 August
in the village of Dushka, was full of indignation: 'I
owe a great deal to General Rayevsky. He commanded
a corps, he fought with dash . . . Neverovsky's new
division fought with incredible bravery. But that
wretch, that scoundrel, that vermin Barclay gave up a
splendid position for nothing. I wrote him very seriously, I implored him in person not to withdraw, yet
no sooner had I set out for Dorogobuzh than he began
to follow me . . . I swear to you that Napoleon was in
the bag, but Barclay never listens to me and does everything that is useful to the enemy . . . I assure you that
Barclay will bring you the enemy within six days. I
must admit that I am thinking of leaving Barclay and
joining you, I'd much rather fight with the Moscow
militia."

Bagration was impatient to fight, although, in the

same letters, he admits that the Russians had only 80,000 men (by his reckoning), while Napoleon was stronger. 'I cannot take the command from Barclay, because the Tsar does not desire it, though he knows what is going on.' The more details reached Bagration of the magnificent behaviour of the Russian troops at Smolensk, the greater his rage: 'It is painful and sad, and the entire army is in despair, because they gave up the most dangerous place, and all for nothing.' He was convinced that Smolensk could have been held: 'Our troops fought and are fighting as never before. With 15,000 men, I held them back victoriously for over 35 hours, but he refused to make a stand for 14 hours. This is shameful, a stain on our army. As for him, it seems to me, he shouldn't go on living. If he reports that our losses are great, he is lying. We lost perhaps four thousand, no more than that, surely less. But suppose it were ten, what of that—it's war, after all.' Bagration says the Russian troops were magnificent at Smolensk. 'Our artillery, my cavalry, truly dumbfounded the enemy . . .' Before battle, Barclay had given Bagration his word of honour that he would not withdraw, and he had broken his pledge. 'It's impossible to fight in such a fashion, and we may bring the enemy to Moscow soon,' wrote Bagration to the Tsar on 19 August—that is to Arakcheyev, for the Tsar. Bagration demanded that 100,000 men should be massed near Moscow: 'either defeat the enemy or give our lives at the walls of the Fatherland, that's how I see it—there is no other way out.' Above all, he is perturbed by rumours of peace: 'To make peace—God save us from that! After all the sacrifices and after such extravagant retreats, to make peace! You will arouse all Russia against you, and

every one of us will be so ashamed that he will cast off
the uniform . . . The war is no ordinary war now, but
a national war, and it is necessary to uphold our honour . . . One should command, and not two . . . Your
Minister may be all right in ministerial matters, but
as a general, he is not merely poor but worthless; yet
they have put the fate of our country in his hands . . .
The Minister is most amiably bringing a guest to the
capital.'

Bagration was also angered and worried by the quantities of Germans at headquarters: 'The entire army is
suspicious of aide-de-camp Vollzogen. He is Napoleon's
man more than ours, yet he is the Minister's adviser.'
During the retreat from Smolensk, according to Bagration, the Russians lost more than 15,000 men, nearly
four times as many as were lost in the battle itself: 'I
am not to blame that the Minister is irresolute, cowardly, senseless, and slow, that he has every bad quality.
The entire army weeps, and curses him to death.'
Bagration demanded reinforcements, and advised mix-
ing the militia among regular troops, 'because if they
are allowed to fight by themselves, the results will be
terrible.' 'Oh, it's sad and painful,' concludes Bagration. 'Never before have we been so humiliated and
afflicted as now . . . I'd rather get a knapsack and fight
as a private than share the supreme command with Barclay.'

* * *

At daybreak on 19 August, Marshal Ney left Smolensk
by a circuitous road, avoiding the burning St. Petersburg suburb. His scouts informed him that the Russian army, which had left Smolensk on 18 August, had
taken the road not to St. Petersburg but to Moscow.

Ney sent scouts ahead on both roads, and then moved promptly after the Russians. Near Valutino Hill, Ney was stopped by the Russian rear-guard. An engagement followed, lasting the entire day of 19 August. The Russians stubbornly resisted. The French lost 7,000 men, the Russians about 6,000. When darkness fell, the artillery fire ceased on both sides. At night, Barclay abandoned his positions and went eastwards. The retreat of the Russians continued.

According to Count Ségur, the French held that the victory at Valutino had been too dearly bought. The fierce resistance of the Russian rear-guard, the high French losses, the death of Hudin at the end of the battle, one of Napoleon's best generals, and finally, the impossibility of pursuing the retreating Russian regiments—all this bore little resemblance to the victories that Ney and the other marshals had grown accustomed to winning. Indeed, it was only after Ney had ceased firing that the Russians followed suit and began their further withdrawal. The meaning of this was only too clear to Ney.

News of Valutino reached Napoleon in Smolensk, whither his dying favourite, Hudin, was brought to him. To be sure, Valutino had been a mere rear-guard action, the French had remained in possession of the field, and the Russians continued to retreat. But Napoleon, like Marshal Ney, clearly understood the meaning of the event.

'There was almost as much glory in the Russian defeat as in our victory,' said Count Ségur, who was then with the Emperor. This was a most ominous sign, and it was not the first time that such a sign had perturbed the Emperor in Russia. Had the Russians actually fled at all, since the beginning of the campaign?

Was it really possible, except in the bulletins for the benefit of the public, to call the battle at Krasnoye and Neverovsky's retreat—this even before Smolensk—a victory for the Grand Army? Except in Spain there had never been an instance of isolated soldiers hiding behind bushes and resisting an entire company. Never had a cannon been brought into action against a lone chasseur surrounded by his enemies. And how many such chasseurs had perished prior to Smolensk, and at Smolensk itself! To judge by accounts of witnesses, the capture and devastation of Smolensk and the battle at Valutino gave Napoleon plenty to think about.

Earlier, Napoleon had dispatched Marshal Junot's corps to outflank Smolensk to prevent Barclay and Bagration from uniting on the Moscow road, in case of a Russian retreat from Smolensk. This Napoleon had done, knowing that the two Russian armies would join forces either in Smolensk or on the Moscow road, a short distance east of Smolensk. Marshal Junot, however, having sent advance patrols to occupy the village of Preobrazhenskoye, about two kilometres from the spot where he had crossed the Dnieper, gave his troops a respite. His patrols were caught napping by the Russians, while his main forces, in accordance with Bagration's plan, were held back in a stubborn engagement near the village of Sinyavin. When at last Junot crossed the marshes to the Moscow road, he was too late—the united Russian army was proceeding towards Dorogobuzh. The Austerlitz which had eluded Napoleon in Vitebsk again slipped through his fingers between Smolensk and Dorogobuzh. Murat, the King of Naples, was furious. Transmitting to Junot a sharp censure from Napoleon, he added for himself: 'You are unworthy to be the last dragoon in Napoleon's army.' This broke

Junot's career and he did not long survive the disgrace. Unable to endure the Emperor's disfavour, he lost his mind a few months later and soon died.

At three o'clock in the morning of 19 August, Napoleon arrived at Sinyavin. He inquired in great detail about everything that had taken place during the battle, and commanded that General Tuchkov III, who had received a bayonet wound and been taken prisoner, be brought before him. The Emperor was extremely indignant at Junot's conduct on the field of battle, and gave orders to let him know it. Then Napoleon distributed rewards to soldiers who had distinguished themselves in the battle of Valutino. He gave the awards personally and with extraordinary lavishness; and he asked the soldiers to name comrades who had distinguished themselves. Privates and officers were showered with favours, ribbons, and promotions, and a thunderous 'Long live the Emperor!' resounded among the men. All this was intended to raise the morale.

Upon his return to Smolensk, however, Napoleon promptly sent an aide-de-camp for his prisoner, General Tuchkov III. This was the Emperor's first direct step to secure peace. Like all subsequent efforts, it brought absolutely no results. '*You*, gentlemen, wanted this war, not I,' he said to Tuchkov, as he entered his study. 'To what corps do you belong?' 'To the Second, Sire.' 'That is Baggovut's Corps. And what relation of yours is the General Tuchkov who commands the Third Corps?' 'He is my own brother.' Napoleon asked Tuchkov III if he would write to Alexander. Tuchkov refused. 'But could you write to your brother?'— 'To my brother, yes, Sire.' Then Napoleon uttered the following words: 'Inform him that you have seen me, and that I have asked you to write him. Tell him I shall greatly appreciate it if he brings to the attention of Emperor Alexander, direct or through a Grand Duke or through the Commander-in-Chief, that there is nothing I want so much as to conclude peace. We have burned enough powder and shed enough blood. We must end this some time.' Napoleon added threateningly that Moscow would surely be occupied and ravaged—a dishonour for the Russians, since 'for a capital to be occupied by an enemy is equivalent to a girl losing her honour.'

Napoleon also asked Tuchkov whether anyone, the Senate, for example, could prevent the Tsar from concluding peace, if the Tsar himself wanted peace. Tuchkov replied in the negative. The audience then came to an end. Napoleon ordered the captive General's sword returned, and sent him to Metz; Tuchkov gave Marshal Berthier his letter to his brother, containing an account of his conversation with Napoleon. Berthier dispatched it to Barclay's headquarters and Barclay sent the letter on to the Tsar at St. Petersburg.

It remained unanswered.

The battle of the Valutino cannot be regarded as a French victory; more accurately, it was a strategic defeat.

.   .   .

Again, Napoleon was faced with a difficult problem. What was the balance sheet of the Smolensk operation? What inference for the future could he draw from the deliberate burning of the city, the flight of its inhabitants, the transformation of the provincial capital into a smoking shambles? To this there could be but one answer: the possibility of the Russians asking for peace was definitely ruled out. People who destroyed not only their villages but even their large cities were not likely to seek the earliest possible peace. In Vitebsk there had still been a faint hope that Alexander would send an emissary with proposals for a truce, but amid the ruins of Smolensk, this hope vanished. Balashov would not come again . . .

From his twenty-seventh year, Napoleon had in all his wars occupied the post of Commander-in-Chief. From his staff and from his generals, he neither expected nor received any kind of advice on matters of general strategy. Their business was to execute commands, not to express opinions on war aims. In this war, however, everything was different. A vague uneasiness seemed to be taking hold of Napoleon's retinue and staff. After several hours of deferential arguing in Vitebsk, Count Daru had grown silent, but it was clear even then that Napoleon had not convinced him and that the *Intendant Général* had stopped talking only because etiquette required that His Majesty should have the last word in any conversation.

Now, in Smolensk, the symptoms of uneasiness had become far more apparent and alarming. Napoleon had a talk with Murat—his brother-in-law, King of Naples, and chief of the entire cavalry. Murat, the courageous Murat, the dashing cavalryman, suddenly began to implore the Emperor to remain in Smolensk, to abandon his plan for a march on Moscow.

The conversation began in the presence of witnesses. It was continued without witnesses, but later Murat made no secret of what had taken place between him and the Emperor. For a long time Murat had implored Napoleon to stop. The Emperor replied that 'honour, fame, and a rest' would be found in Moscow, and only in Moscow. Murat then threw himself on his knees before Napoleon, saying: 'Moscow will destroy us!'

Murat was greatly shaken. The same day, amidst the bombardment of Smolensk, when the Russian batteries answered the French fire and began to shower cannonballs on Murat's position, he rode forward, and dismounted. General Belliard begged him to take cover. Murat, scarcely concealing the fact that he was seeking death, sharply refused. Then Belliard told him that because of him his entire staff would perish. 'Well, then get out of here, all of you, and leave me alone!' Murat shouted angrily. Unanimously the staff refused to go, and only then did he leave the perilous spot.

Whether Napoleon reconsidered his decision because of this scene with Murat, or because of the terrifying appearance of burning Smolensk, with its destroyed stores and houses reduced to rubble, is unknown. In any case, after riding through several streets strewn with dead and wounded, he uttered the words: 'The first Russian campaign is over.' (In another version: 'The War of 1812 is over.') But this hesitation proved only momentary.

Of course Napoleon knew that Murat was far from being alone in his conviction. He knew that his staff and suite, many officers of the line, and even the rank and file were critical of his plans. Disillusionment was great when, instead of peaceful quarters and abundant food, instead of a real rest in the great Russian city, the Grand Army found a city razed to the ground, entire sections reduced to ashes, an enormous, pervasive, and unceasing stench from thousands upon thousands of corpses rotting in the torrid sun, and innumerable wounded scattered about among the corpses. Foraging parties returned from the country without bread or oats. Horses were dying in increasing numbers. At night, the

French soldiers in the outskirts of the ruined city could see the distant glow of burning villages.

On the night of 24-25 August, Napoleon set out from Smolensk. The entire day he followed the Russian army on the devastated road. On both sides of the road, one could see the glow of distant villages and haystacks, deliberately set aflame. On 26 August, the Emperor was in Dorogobuzh; on the evening of the twenty-seventh in Slavkov; he spent the night of the twenty-eighth in a landowner's house in Rubki, near Vyazma.

'Everywhere we mowed unripe corn for fodder and almost everywhere we found complete devastation and smoking ruins,' wrote Pion, an artillery officer in the Grand Army, in August 1812. 'Thus far, we haven't found a single Russian in any of the houses and, when we approached the outskirts of Vyazma, I realized that the enemy was deliberately luring us far inland to surprise us later or wear us down with hunger and cold. Fires were burning not only in the path of the main army, but in other directions far and near. At night the entire horizon was aglow.'

On the morning of 29 August, Napoleon entered Vyazma. The Russian army continued to retreat eastward. 'I am in a rather handsome city,' wrote Napoleon to Marie-Louise from Vyazma. 'There are 30 churches, 15,000 inhabitants, and many shops with vodka and other useful objects for the soldiers.' On the night of 1 September, the Emperor left Vyazma, and at 2 o'clock in the morning reached Velishchevo. Rains had lessened the heat. 'It is already autumn here, and no longer summer,' the Emperor wrote to his wife. Moisture had settled the dust so the army could march more easily.

Villages, hamlets, stacks of hay and straw, stores had

been burned by the retiring Russian army. On the sides, somewhat away from the main road of retreat, the French, to their great joy, found cattle, houses, and inhabitants. In Pologo, near Smolensk, on 24 August, the corps of Eugène Beauharnais came upon 'what is for us an unaccustomed sight: near Prudisch were grazing cattle. We saw villagers, we saw houses, off the route of the marching troops and consequently left intact.' Officers and soldiers were sent to local inhabitants with orders to be conciliating and 'ask for one day's food and a few head of horned cattle.' Everything went off well, and the soldiers 'had a good rest.' But this was rather exceptional. If the Russians had no time to burn villages and stores situated too far from their road of retreat, the French who were pursuing them had no time for distant foraging.

Napoleon was taciturn on the road from Smolensk. His retinue and marshals were taciturn, too. With whom could he talk? With Caulaincourt? With Viceroy Eugène? With Murat? With Berthier? With his beloved friend Duroc? He was leading them to Moscow, and they did not conceal that in their eyes 'Moscow is our ruin.' They had all said as much—except the devoted Berthier, who said nothing. But Berthier had the same thoughts, and Napoleon knew it.

'Vive l'Empereur!' shouted the Old Guard each time he approached them. The Old Guard never asked him anything, nor could they give him any advice. They only gave their lives, whenever he demanded.

4

FROM SMOLENSK TO BORODINO

ON 18 July, Alexander I at last left his army at Polotsk. He was accompanied by his numerous suite, including A. S. Shishkov.

Shishkov convinced the Tsar that his appearance in Moscow was indispensable to raise the spirit of the people. We know, however, from Shishkov's reminiscences (not intended for publication) that he was far less concerned with where the Tsar should go, than with his departure from the army, since Alexander's presence could nowhere be more harmful than in the active army. 'Several days before this, the idea took possession of my mind that our position might improve if the Tsar could be induced to abandon his troops and return to St. Petersburg by way of Moscow.' But, of course, it was impossible to say this frankly to the Tsar; so Shishkov stressed the need of going to Moscow, the ancient, sacred capital, and so forth.

Everything turned out better than anyone had expected. Alexander with his suite arrived in Moscow on the evening of 23 July, five days after leaving the army. Arakcheyev, of course, was with him. In Polotsk, when Shishkov and Balashov explained that the Tsar's de-

parture would contribute to the salvation of the
Fatherland, the courtier said literally: 'What do I care
for the Fatherland? But tell me this: will the Tsar be in
danger if he remains in the army?' For Arakcheyev
the Tsar's departure from the army was above all a
means of saving his own skin from the danger of war.
Arakcheyev's cowardice, like his cruelty towards the
rank and file, was pathological. Now he had temporarily quieted down. His practice of dislocating soldiers'
jaws, of tearing out their mustaches, as well as of making them run the gauntlet 'of a thousand men a dozen
times' had to be abandoned till the times were more
suitable.

News that the enemy was breaking all resistance and
marching straight on the city had kept Moscow tense
for some time. Alexander's arrival did much to cheer
the capital. On 27 July, separate assemblies of the
nobles and merchants were held in the Kremlin. Recognized (though not elected) representatives of both
classes were invited to the Palace. The Moscow merchants expressed their readiness to help the Fatherland
by voluntary contributions amounting to 10,000,000
roubles. The nobility of the Government of Moscow
resolved to send 'up to 80,000' peasant serfs to the
militia and to contribute 3,000,000 roubles to the treasury. Citizens of 'various ranks' offered militiamen. In
addition, individual wealthy men and magnates from
among the nobility (such as Count Mamonov) pledged
themselves to raise and equip entire regiments. A national militia began to form. The morale of the people
gained enormously. Not fear but anger was the domi-
nant sentiment. Witnesses testify that in this terrible
moment all classes merged in one common emotion.
Better death than submission to the invading 'ravisher'!

Peasants, lower bourgeoisie, merchants, nobility—all vied with one another in their eagerness to fight Napoleon to the death.

Characteristically, official representatives of the Government shared least in this national fervour. According to his own memoirs, Rostopchin, Commander-in-Chief of Moscow, was occupied with quite other problems. He had learned that some nobles intended to question the Tsar at the Kremlin audience about the size of our forces, our means of defence, and other military matters. This 'parliamentarianism' seemed to Rostopchin out of place, and he promptly warned the would-be questioners. 'The intention was impertinent, improper, and dangerous at such a time; as to its being carried out, I was not worried at all, for I knew that the said gentry were as brave at home as they were cowardly away from home. I deliberately repeated in their presence that I hoped to offer the Tsar the spectacle of a loyal nobility and that I should be in despair . if any ill-intentioned person should violate the peace and should forget himself in the presence of his Tsar, because that person, before finishing what he had set out to say would start on an extremely long journey. To lend my speeches more weight, I had two carriages with post horses stationed near the palace, with two police officers attired like couriers, sauntering in front of them. When curious persons inquired about the purpose of these carriages, they were told: "For those who will be ordered to go." This explanation reached the ears of the assembly, and the braggarts did not utter a word throughout the whole conference, and generally conducted themselves like well-mannered children.'

The authorities made no preparations whatsoever for the immediate organization or arming of the militia, which was to have gradually replenished the losses in the army.

While in Moscow, Alexander became convinced that it was impossible to arm the Moscow militia. Not alone the Tsar, but even Barclay had been unaware of this. 'The dispositions in Moscow are excellent, the Government of Moscow has offered me 80,000 men,' wrote Alexander to Barclay on 26 July. 'The difficulty lies in arming them, because, to my great astonishment, we have no rifles left, whereas in Vilna you seemed to think that we had an abundant supply of them. For the time being, I shall form large detachments of cavalry, armed with pikes. I shall see to it that the infantry also are supplied with them [pikes], until we can obtain rifles.'

So great was the lack of rifles that, by an Imperial Command, issued in the same month, the Vologda nobility were requested not to raise a militia unit as they had intended, 6 souls out of every 100, but to send 500 huntsmen with their hunting rifles.

Most of the militia was armed in haphazard fashion. The 'Duke de Richelieu,' Governor-General of Novorossiysk, informed the Minister of Police on 26 July: 'We are arming the militia as best we can.'

To arm human beings with pikes and send them to fight Napoleon's army was as good as not arming them at all. At first orders were issued to raise a militia in six governments: Tver and Yaroslavl (12,000 men each), Vladimir, Ryazan, Kaluga, and Tula (15,000 men each). Together, this made 84,000 men, while the Moscow Government gave 32,000. Thus, a militia was raised comprising 116,000 men. But they received no rifles. 'I designated assembly points,' writes Rostopchin, 'and in 24 days the militia was ready, divided into com-

panies and provided with attire; but as there were not
enough rifles, we armed them with pikes, which were
useless and harmless.'

.   .   .

During the night of 31 July, the Tsar left Moscow
for St. Petersburg, where he arrived on 3 August.
The reports he received from the army in the days
that followed were far from cheerful. For the benefit of
the public one could be enthusiastic about Wittgenstein's victory over Oudinot and fail to mention that
on the following day this victory had turned into a defeat costing Kulnev's life. For the benefit of the public
one could also stress General Tormasov's success over
General Reynier on the Southern front, but Alexander
knew that this success was followed by a complete lull,
because Tormasov had neither the strength nor the
ability to exploit his advantage. There was some comfort in the obviously ambiguous behaviour of Napoleon's Austrian 'ally,' and in Schwarzenberg's apparent
unwillingness to endanger Tormasov's positions. But
all that was overshadowed by Napoleon's advance from
Vitebsk on Smolensk.

The panic among the aristocracy, in the Tsar's entourage, and in his family, grew by the hour. The first
as yet vague and obscure reports of the destruction of
Smolensk only served to intensify it. Ermolov, Bagration, and Bennigsen were declaring loudly that unless
a change occurred Moscow was lost. But who could replace Barclay? Fear rose to such a point that people began to tell the Tsar the whole truth, oblivious of etiquette. And it was little comfort to Alexander that his
own sister spoke more than anyone else, and spoke in

French. 'For God's sake,' Ekaterina Pavlovna adjured her brother, 'don't take the command upon yourself; we mustn't lose a minute in finding a leader whom the troops will trust, and in these circumstances you can't inspire any confidence. Moreover, should you suffer a defeat, it would prove to be an irreparable misfortune because of the feeling that would be aroused.'

Meanwhile the news from the army was such that no more time could be wasted in finding a Commander-in-Chief.

After the loss of Smolensk, Barclay's position in the army became untenable. In Dorogobuzh, all the corps commanders declared to Constantine, the heir apparent, that the condition of the army was poor and the struggle uneven, 'in particular if the army should continue to be commanded by Barclay de Tolly.' After this, Constantine, who was never distinguished by an excess of courage, asked Barclay for a passport with which to leave the army. Barclay tried to dissuade him, but Constantine left, declaring that he was perfectly acquainted with the situation and that he was going to St. Petersburg to prevail upon his brother to make peace.

Of course, Constantine's departure was promptly used against Barclay. It was said that Barclay 'had sent away' the heir apparent, and Constantine appeared 'in the very best light, notwithstanding his reprehensible conduct; the General is said to have removed him for loudly proclaiming the truth.'

Worst of all for Barclay was Bagration's furious campaign against him.

After the withdrawal from Smolensk, the relations between Bagration and Barclay grew increasingly tense. Bagration began to treat Barclay like a traitor. Finally, on 28 August, Bagration received the Tsar's rescript announcing Barclay's replacement by Kutuzov. On entering Maksimovka the same day, he wrote the following letter to Barclay, who was right there with the army, but to whom he chose to write rather than speak: 'Dear Sir, In my opinion, the position here is not good, and worse, there is no water. It is a pity for the men and horses. We should try to move on to Gzhatsk. But the best thing would be to join Miloradovich and have a good fight. It is too bad that we have been lured to this place, and that the enemy has been coming closer. It would have been better to realize this yesterday and gone on direct to Gzhatsk, than to be in a bad position, without water. Our poor soldiers complain that they have nothing to drink and no water to cook their gruel in. It seems to me that we should not stop here but move immediately; that we should reinforce the rear-guard with infantry and cavalry, and make a stand at Gzhatsk, where the new Commander-in-Chief can join us. That is my opinion. I am returning the plan, which was taken down incorrectly; it was done in too great a hurry. Very truly yours, Your humble servant, Count Bagration.'

We see that Bagration was unable to control his hatred and malicious joy. He wrote to Barclay of his replacement as if it were the most natural thing in the world and very fortunate.

Ten days earlier, on 17 August, Prince Volkonsky had brought Alexander a letter from Count Shuvalov, written from the army on 12 August—before the fall of Smolensk. This letter was most alarming and gloomy: 'If Your Majesty does not give both armies a single commander, then I must attest on my honour and conscience, that everything may be irrevocably lost . . . The army is so dissatisfied, that even the rank-and-file complain. The army has not the least confidence in the commander now in charge . . . The commissariat is very badly organized, the soldiers are often without bread, the horses have been without oats for days. The Commander-in-Chief is entirely responsible for this state of affairs; he plans the marches so badly that the Chief of the Commissariat can't do a thing. General Barclay and Count Bagration do not get along; the latter is justly dissatisfied. Pillaging goes on shamelessly . . . The enemy is free to do his harvesting, and his provisioning is secure.' Ermolov is efficient, but, with such a commander, he can do nothing: 'Another commander is necessary, one over both armies, and Your Majesty should appoint him without losing a minute; otherwise, Russia is lost.'

Alexander made up his mind. On the same day (17 August) he called a committee composed of Saltykov, the chairman of the Government Council, and Generals Vyazmitinov, Lopukhin, Kochubey, Balashov, and Arakcheyev. After examining Barclay's report and those of Bagration and other persons, the committee proceeded to discuss the question of a new Commander-in-Chief. It was a ticklish question. The nobility of both capitals and the mass of the army had long been talking of Kutuzov. All the members of the committee, however, were well aware that the Tsar could not endure Kutuzov, and that Kutuzov fully reciprocated his feeling. From seven until half-past ten in the evening these courtiers hesitated to make the Tsar swallow the pill. Finally, they took courage. So great was their emotion that the record of the proceedings is not wholly literate. It must be said, however, that the members of the committee, excepting Balashov and Count Kochubey, were not too careful about Russian grammar even when calm. This is the text of their resolution: 'Whereas the appointment of a Commander-in-Chief for the entire army must be based first on certain experience in the military art, distinguished talents, general confidence, and seniority, we unanimously propose for this choice the General of Infantry, Count Kutuzov.'

Alexander knew beforehand what would happen, and was reconciled to the verdict. Reports had been reaching him of the battles around Smolensk and of Barclay's withdrawal. He countersigned the committee's decision without delay.

In July, the nobility, amidst great ovations, had elected Kutuzov commander of the St. Petersburg militia. 'All the while they shouted in a single voice, that his place was not here, that he should command not the muzhiks of the St. Petersburg Government, but the army, which Barclay was sparing at the cost of surrendering Russia . . . His [Barclay's] name had become an object of hatred, no real Russian could pronounce it calmly; some called him a traitor, others a madman or a fool, but all agreed that he was leading us to ruin and betraying Russia.'

Such was the temper of the nobility in August 1812.

Alexander himself says he recognized the general exasperation with Barclay and acknowledged that the feeling was justified since, in his opinion, the 'Minister' had revealed indecision and 'disorderliness in the conduct of his business'; moreover, the differences between Barclay and Bagration had been constantly growing. Hence—so the Tsar informs his sister—he suggested to the 'small committee' that they choose a new Commander-in-Chief. The committee had chosen Kutuzov.

He could not help ratifying this choice, because 'Kutuzov is in great favour among the public both here [in St. Petersburg] and in Moscow.'

. . .

At the time of his appointment, Mikhail Illariono-vich Golenischev-Kutuzov was 67 years old, and he had exactly nine months left to live. In these months his name was to be associated for all time with one of the greatest events in Russian and world history. He will be remembered as the genuine representative of the Russian people in the most terrible moment of Russia's existence.

In the Court, among the aristocracy, Kutuzov, though a scion of the old nobility, had always been a stranger, and even if the Tsar's dislike of him had not been so widely known, the Vorontsovs, the Sheremetevs, the Volkonskys, and the Stroganovs would never have recognized him as one of 'their own.' In the time of Rumyantsev and Suvorov he had become a high-ranking general. Twice gravely wounded, he had escaped death by a hair's breadth. A Turkish bullet had put out one of his eyes in the battle of Alushta, when he was but 29 years old. Impressed by his conduct during the storming of Izmael, Suvorov called him his right hand and appointed him commandant of that city. In 1805, Kutuzov was considered the Commander-in-Chief of the Austrian and Russian forces, and by all powers and means resisted Alexander's desire to fight a general engagement with Napoleon. The battle—at Austerlitz— was fought, and lost. From that time on Alexander felt a strong dislike for Kutuzov. Later, someone tried to justify Kutuzov to him, saying that Kutuzov had tried

'to restrain' the Tsar from engaging in battle at Austerlitz; the Tsar had replied cuttingly: 'He didn't restrain
me enough.' Kutuzov was very shrewd, crafty, and
subtle. He had said once, he had said twice that Napoleon would whip the Russians and the Austrians, if
battle were joined. The Tsar refused to listen.—Well,
if the Tsar was so anxious to get a good drubbing, let
him have it! At the same time, Kutuzov could be an
adroit courtier; he had a good understanding of military intrigue and all other kinds of intrigue; he highly
valued power, honours, lustre, success. He disliked
Alexander, and had little respect for him. His patriotism was exceptionally deep. His strategic abilities were
indisputable and universally recognized. He was also a
remarkable diplomat, and had often rendered valuable
services in this field.

Suvorov placed him far above his other companions
in arms. 'He's crafty, crafty! And shrewd, shrewd! No
one will fool him!' he said of Kutuzov, whom he
esteemed also for his bravery. On the basis of a report
by Suvorov, Catherine II had written to Kutuzov on
25 March 1791, felicitating him on his 'distinguished
courage in the capture of the city and fortress of Izmael,
in the course of which you rose to new heights of skill
and fearlessness. Under strong enemy fire you sur-
mounted all difficulties, scaled the walls, and took possession of the bastion, and when the superior forces of
the enemy forced you to stop, you, serving as a model
of courage, stood your ground, overcame the powerful
enemy, consolidated your position in the fortress, and
continued to deal blows at the foe.'

His great strategic abilities, his calm, firm courage,
his long military experience, his exceptionally wide

popularity among the civilian population and the army —all this placed the old general in an exceptional position.

Kutuzov was occasionally sly; he knew how to use people for his purpose, as his intimates were well aware. 'Kutuzov, it might be said, did not so much speak as play with his tongue,' wrote his orderly, General Mayevsky. 'He was a Mozart or Rossini, who enchanted the ear with his conversational bow. No one was more apt at playing upon the emotions, and no one was subtler in the art of cajoling or seducing, if that was what he had resolved to do.' This 'subtlest of politicians' did not like to share his glory . . . 'He imperceptibly undermined anyone whom he suspected of sharing in his glory, just as a worm gnaws at a lovely and hated sapling . . ."—thus is he described by one who saw him daily. 'You had to watch for a chance to make him listen to you or sign a paper. He was reluctant to listen to reports or to sign his name on ordinary occasions.'

But on extraordinary occasions Kutuzov was always in the right place. Suvorov found him in his place on the night when Izmael was stormed; the Russian people found him in his place in 1812.

Only his sybaritism, laziness, and cunning caught the eye of the average observer. What, for example, did the gay, light-headed Frenchman, Langeron, see in Kutuzov? 'Kutuzov has left,' wrote Langeron to Vorontsov from Bucharest on the eve of Napoleon's invasion. 'He touched us deeply on his departure. He was very amiable and moving. Let the Lord give him a Field Marshal's baton, tranquillity, thirty women—but not an army.' Langeron did not understand the tremendous service which Kutuzov had just performed in concluding peace with the Turks, whom Napoleon was inciting with all his might to continue the war. Far less could the French emigré and careerist foresee Kutuzov's role in the coming storm. And Langeron was by no means alone in his judgment of Kutuzov. Yet, in 1812, there were many, among them those who scolded Kutuzov for being a sly courtier and an old lecher, who looked up to him in their confusion and expected salvation from him, and only from him.

Faith in Kutuzov was not limited to the nobility and the merchants. He enjoyed tremendous popularity in the army. To be sure, soldiers did not regard him with the same superstitious awe as Suvorov. Kutuzov's manner of dealing with them was quite different. Suvorov was the legendary hero, the sorcerer. Every instant he exposed his head to bullets; he flirted with grapeshot and it refused 'to take him.' Suvorov, the all-conquering, was worshipped by his soldiers. A Field Marshal who runs about camp in his shirt sleeves, who challenges his soldiers to fist fights, who at 70 refuses to put on a warm overcoat until winter clothing is sent to his soldiers, was bound to fill a special place in the heart of a soldier. Kutuzov had no such pretensions. But a reflection of Suvorov's glory lay upon him, as upon Bagration. The empty eye socket was a reminder of Suvorov's love for him. In talking with a soldier, he could be simple and good-natured. Suvorov's pranks and familiarities, which endeared him to the rank and file, would not have been becoming in the mellow, ponderous, corpulent old Field Marshal. When he spoke to a soldier, he tried to be like him, an unsubtle, simple Russian, a hearty and well-disposed grandfather.

He was loved and trusted in the army as no one else since Suvorov. Bagration, too, was loved, but this was something different. Bagration was taciturn, almost Oriental in his restraint. A hero in battle, yielding nothing in courage to Suvorov, he never enjoyed Kutuzov's wide popularity in the army, he was not quite 'their own,' though the men and officers directly under him deeply loved and respected him.

Immediately upon his arrival in Tsarevo-Zaimishche, Kutuzov appointed Barclay and Bagration commanders of the armies which had been under them before Smolensk.

Kutuzov was well aware of the giant he had to deal with.

'On one occasion Danilevsky permitted himself to use certain bold expressions about Napoleon. The Field Marshal [Kutuzov] interrupted the reading and sternly remarked: "Young man, who gave you the right to jeer at one of the greatest of men? Stop all this unseemly abuse!"'

But he did not lose hope of worsting Napoleon. If he could not 'defeat' him, then at least he would out-wit him. He would get the better of him by using all the means at his disposal—especially time and space. Of course, he did not reject active military struggle. But he did want to conduct the struggle with the smallest possible losses for the Russian people.

Even less than Barclay before him did he seek a general engagement with Napoleon. He did not seek it at Moscow, he did not want a single one of the battles fought after the destruction of Moscow. Tarutino, Maloyaroslavets, Krasnoye, and Berezina were none of his choosing. Barclay was at times confused, irresolute.

He spoke of taking the counter-offensive. Kutuzov, whose reputation and authority were incomparably more solid, conducted himself more calmly than his predecessors, and systematically carried out his idea of 'a golden bridge' for Napoleon that would take him out of Russia without superfluous bloodshed. In the final analysis, this strategy led to the destruction of the invading army. He methodically executed his plan, beginning with the advance on Tarutino—and continuing with the flanking 'parallel' pursuit until the foe was expelled from Russia. Both before and after Borodino his position was difficult. Again and again he resorted to cunning.

The difference between Kutuzov and Barclay was that Kutuzov knew the vast expanses alone would not suffice to defeat Napoleon; equally essential was the scorched-earth policy of the Russian people. Barclay had based all his calculations on the supposition that Napoleon would weaken himself by excessively lengthening his line of communications. Kutuzov counted on the fact that the Russian peasant would sooner burn his grain and his hay and his house than sell provisions to the foe, that in this scorched wilderness the enemy was sure to perish.

He knew that no one, including himself, would be allowed to yield Moscow without battle. It was with this responsibility that he received the superior command of the army. 'Kutuzov, it is certain, would not have given battle at Borodino, where he obviously did not expect to win. But the voice of *the Court, of the Army, of all Russia* forced his hand. We must assume that he looked upon this engagement as an inevitable evil. He knew the Russians and he knew how to deal with them.' Such is the opinion of Clausewitz, who had no love for Kutuzov but who guessed many of his secrets, though he never understood him completely.

On 29 August, the retiring Russian army arrived in Tsarevo-Zaimishche; here it was learned that Alexander had replaced Barclay by Prince Kutuzov. Barclay felt shaken and humiliated. 'Had I been guided by blind, senseless ambition,' wrote Barclay to the Tsar, 'Your Imperial Majesty would have received reports of battles and, even so, the enemy would be at the gates of Moscow, because we did not have sufficient forces to resist him.'

Barclay had endured humiliation after humiliation before Tsarevo-Zaimishche, and then came this new sudden affront, this unexpected blow. Nine days after his dismissal, the day after Borodino, Barclay said to Ermolov: 'Yesterday I sought death, and did not find it.' Ermolov, who took down these words, adds: 'Having had ample opportunity to know his firm character and extraordinary patience, it was with astonishment that I saw tears in his eyes, though he tried to conceal them. His affliction must have been great.'

Kutuzov found himself in the most difficult position. Soon after entering Gzhatsk with his army and ordering a further retreat, he wrote to Rostopchin, who in his alarm had asked him about the fate of Moscow: 'No decision has yet been made with regard to the question: to lose the army or to lose Moscow. In my opinion, to lose Moscow means to lose Russia.' This was before Borodino. After Borodino, Kutuzov interrupted the military council in Fili with the words: 'My order is to retreat,' meaning to yield Moscow; but on the same day, before the council, when Ermolov remarked on the impossibility of holding these positions (referring to the necessity of giving up Moscow), Kutuzov 'took me by the hand, felt my pulse, and said: "Are you well?" ' Up to the very last minute, no one, despite every effort, could figure out what Kutuzov really intended.

Yet all his actions show that if he refused to give up Moscow without battle he was determined not to fight another battle; and he didn't. He changed his mind and contradicted himself, but only because he wanted to show his soldiers that he was bitterly opposed to surrendering Moscow, and that if at the last moment he did surrender it, it was because of wholly exceptional, wholly unexpected and insurmountable difficulties. And he succeeded in giving this impression. To judge by the unanimous statements of witnesses, the army's confidence in Kutuzov was not shaken one whit after the surrender of Moscow.

Entering Mamonovo on 12 September, he gave the order: 'The Russian forces must engage in a decisive battle before the walls of Moscow.' Here, of course, he was deliberately misleading the army regarding his real intentions. Even while he was feeling Ermolov's pulse at Fili on 13 September, he definitely knew that on the next day he would pass through Moscow, and that immediately afterward the French cavalry would ride through the gates.

All his talk, ruses, and commands were but propaganda, whose value was brilliantly demonstrated. In the eyes of the common soldier he was no German, no traitor Barclay. He was a good Russian; he hadn't the least desire to retreat, but what can you do against God's will? Even at Fili, where the fate of Moscow was decided, Kutuzov let Barclay speak first. When Barclay said: 'The capture of Moscow will prepare Napoleon's doom,' Kutuzov merely subscribed to his words.

. . .

The temper of the people, above all the peasants and the army, both officers and rank-and-file, was such that although Kutuzov could successfully evade a second general battle, the first one was absolutely inescapable. 'Anyone who proposed giving up Moscow without a shot would have been a traitor in the eyes of the entire nation.'

Between Gzhatsk and Mozhaisk, the retreating Russian army was joined by 15,000 men under Miloradovich and 10,000 Moscow militiamen under Count Markov. After receiving these reinforcements, Kutuzov finally decided to pause and accept battle.

The die was cast. The Russian army stopped, and turned its front to the advancing Napoleon.

Kutuzov was beset by difficulties from all sides. The vultures of the Commissary Department were starving the army, stealing up to 100 per cent of the allotted funds, and blaming the lack of biscuit on 'capture by the enemy.'

In the days before Borodino and immediately after, the supply service was wretchedly organized. How the rank-and-file subsisted, no one knew; the generals and officers with money had plenty to eat, but those without funds went hungry too. 'Our General Miloradovich hasn't a penny; often after heavy exertions he asks for food. But most of the time we have nothing; he lies down and goes to sleep hungry, without reproaches or grumbling.'

And Miloradovich was equal in rank to Barclay de Tolly.

Kutuzov and his army were approaching the monastery of Kolotsk. The soldiers were hungry, the army had nothing to eat. Kutuzov was forced to ask Moscow for provisions; he exhorted Rostopchin to send the soldiers some food, lest the 'shortages' compromise every hope of success.

Every day, hundreds upon hundreds of horses died in the French army, and the situation among the Russians before and after Borodino was equally desperate: 'We continue to retreat, we don't know why. We lose men in rear-guard actions, and we lose our cavalry, which is barely moving. Thanks to that beast Sivers my regiment has been reduced to 400 men; other regiments fare no better. In brief, despite my best wishes and my disinclination to see the dark side of things, I believe that within two weeks we shall have no cavalry at all.' Thus wrote Prince Vasilchikov to the wounded Mikhail Semenovich Vorontsov on the fourth day after Borodino.

We have many more authentic documents, sharply contradicting Clausewitz's unfounded and over-optimistic view of the Russian supply service during the retreat. It is true that conditions among the French were even worse, but this did not make the Russian army any less hungry. Nevertheless, the Russian troops preserved order, discipline, and fighting spirit.

Hunger and privations struck the Russian soldier harder than Napoleon's bullets and grapeshot. 'The cause of the increase in the number of sick in the army must be sought in the deficiency of good food and warm clothing,' wrote Villiers, commander of the medical section in the army, to Arakcheyev on 24 September.

Villiers was strongly inclined to official optimism. 'Until now, the larger part of the soldiers have been wearing summer trousers, and many of their great-coats have become so worn that they can scarcely serve as a protection against the wet cold.'

. . .

On 28 August, Napoleon with his Guard entered the village of Semlevo. On the following day, Davout and the cavalry of Murat advanced upon Vyazma. The heat was unbearable; the French soldiers literally fought for a drop of muddy water from the swamps. The Russian rear-guard under the command of Konovnitsin set fire to all supply stores in Vyazma. When the French advance forces approached Vyazma, the whole city was in flames. The Russian rear-guard was still fighting, as it retired. The French found next to nothing in the scorched city, but discovered a few wealthy estates in the environs. The Cossacks, however, who were tirelessly scouring the country round the Russian army and were scarcely ahead of the French advance guard, had taken everything in sight. After their departure from Lithuania and their invasion of the purely Russian Governments, foraging became increasingly difficult for the French. The peasants consistently refused to sell them anything. They fled to the woods, hiding or burning their produce. Beyond Smolensk, this sabotage assumed menacing proportions for the Grand Army.

In Gzhatsk, four days before Borodino, Napoleon gave the following order to Berthier, his Chief of Staff: 'Write to the generals commanding army corps that we are daily losing many soldiers as a result of the inadequate methods of procuring provisions. Let them, in agreement with the commanders of various units, take the necessary measures to end a state of affairs which threatens the army with destruction; every day several hundred prisoners fall into the hands of the enemy; it is necessary, under threat of severe punishment, to forbid our soldiers to stray too far.' The Emperor commanded that a sufficient guard be provided to protect foragers against Cossacks and peasants.

On entering Gzhatsk, Napoleon ordered that at three o'clock in the afternoon of 2 September a general roll-call should be taken of all the fighting forces in Gzhatsk and the immediate vicinity. The result revealed 103,000 infantry, 30,000 cavalry, and 587 guns. But lagging detachments were still coming up.

In Gzhatsk, Napoleon wrote to Marie-Louise, apparently in reply to her letter about the drawings of Denon (illustrating the history of Napoleon's wars): 'I am pleased that you find some recreation in Denon's drawings of my campaigns. You must know that I have been exposed to endless dangers. It is nineteen years since I have been conducting wars, and I have fought many battles and laid many sieges in Europe, Asia, Africa. I shall try to end this war, in order to see you soon . . .'

After two days in Gzhatsk, the Emperor accompanied by his Guard continued his advance at one o'clock in the morning of 4 September.

Napoleon advanced by forced marches, pressing hard on Kutuzov's rear-guard, clearly determined either to force the new Commander-in-Chief into a general battle, or to enter Moscow on the heels of the retiring army. Napoleon followed Kutuzov, constantly encountering vigorous resistance from the Russian rear-guard.

On the second day after his arrival at Tsarevo-Zaimishche to join his army, Kutuzov, to the general astonishment, ordered a retreat. The rear-guard, commanded by General Konovnitsin, was under constant pressure by large French cavalry forces. But on 2 September, the Dragoons and the Cossacks succeeded in hurling back the Bavarian cavalry harassing Konovnitsin; this improved the situation for at least twenty-four hours.

Covered by the successful and stubborn resistance of Konovnitsin, Kutuzov, with Barclay and Bagration, reached the Kolotsk monastery on 3 September, and began to dig in. Kutuzov bade Colonel Toll inspect the position. Only a few of the early military critics of this campaign understood that the battlefield chosen by Kutuzov was the only one possible, for the simple reason that Napoleon with his main forces was now keeping Kutuzov's rear-guard within his range of vision, and Konovnitsin was forced to retire fighting every inch of the way. Kutuzov could, to be sure, speed up his retreat and leave Konovnitsin to his fate, but even then Napoleon, after smashing Konovnitsin would still have been able to overtake Kutuzov somewhere near Mozhaisk and make him accept battle. Kutuzov chose rather to stop near the Kolotsk monastery, fortify whatever position he found there, incorporate Konovnitsin's hard-pressed rear-guard into his main forces, and await Napoleon. The position for battle was none too good, and some military historians claim that it was quite bad, but it had to be accepted.

Napoleon followed Konovnitsin, giving him no respite. Suddenly, the Emperor was informed that a redoubt lay ahead. He surmised that it was an advance

fortification erected for tactical reasons. Later military
writers insist that this redoubt near the village of
Shevardino was one of the fortified points of the position chosen by Toll for the imminent battle, but that
it had been abandoned at the final inspection, where
it was decided to move the left (Bagration's) flank a
short distance eastward, to cover it with a Semenovsky
trench and earthworks, which were quickly erected.
These were the Semenovsky or 'Bagration' *flèches*,
which were destined to play an immense part in the
great battle. But Napoleon appeared before the Shevardino redoubt on the night of 5 September. Bagration's army had not entirely evacuated the Shevardino
position; some small Russian units remained in the
redoubt and round it. Napoleon directed enormous
forces against the redoubt. Several French cavalry attacks were beaten off by its defenders. Two French infantry divisions, which had managed to come up, and
three regiments of a third division pushed back
Neverovsky's division occupying the approaches to the
redoubt, and stormed the position. The Russian defenders cheered as they met the French troops. They
counter-attacked with bayonets and were all slain. The
artillerymen went on firing to the last moment, and
when the French broke into the entrenchments, they
made no attempt to flee, though the road to escape lay
open. Instead, they fought hand to hand and were all
killed at their guns. Late that night the battle came
to an end, a battle so unequal that the French could
not understand why it had taken so long. Silence
reigned in Shevardino; stumbling over corpses that
covered all the approaches to the redoubt, the French
returned to Baluyevo and Gridnevo in the dense darkness.

While this battle was in progress, Napoleon was receiving reports from his scouts, and his eyes scarcely left the spy-glass directed at the Russian positions. That very morning he had come to the conclusion that the most suitable point for breaking through the Russian lines was the left flank of the Russian army, and a village which was far in advance of the Russian centre. He had learned the name of this village: Borodino.

According to some military critics and observers, the battle before Shevardino was 'an unnecessary and unsuccessful battle,' because the enemy captured the redoubt and its defending batteries. This was also the opinion of Robert Wilson, the English commissioner attached to Kutuzov's headquarters, whose functions were formally vague, but in fact extraordinarily concrete. He spied on the Commander-in-Chief for two separate clients. His reports on the words and actions of the Field Marshal went to two separate addresses: to the English ambassador, Lord Cathcart, and to Tsar Alexander. When he wasn't too busy with his main occupation, he spied upon Emperor Alexander for the English Government. Alexander did not trust Kutuzov; the British Cabinet did not trust Kutuzov and trusted Alexander even less. The lesson of Tilsit was still too fresh in their memory, and one never knew what to expect from the Tsar. Sir Robert Wilson, a shrewd and vigilant observer, acquitted himself excellently of his complex tasks. His letters, reports, and memoirs furnish valuable information on the year 1812.

Wilson was extremely displeased with Shevardino. The Russian generals, too, were displeased. It had now become clear that Napoleon would fall upon the left flank, because the Shevardino redoubt had protected the left flank. The left wing was numerically the weakest. But it was commanded by Bagration: Kutuzov knew that this doubled its strength.

Towards the evening of 5 September, the Russian rear-guard commanded by General Konovnitsin was again attacked by the French at the monastery on the Kolotsk and thrown back to the village of Borodino. Napoleon advanced against the Russian army in three dense columns. Poniatowski's corps marched at the head of the left column; the right column was commanded by Viceroy Eugène; in the centre was the main force, with Napoleon, Murat, Ney, Junot, and the entire Guard at the head.

The Imperial Staff halted near the village of Valuyevo.

Late in the night of 5 September, Napoleon was sitting in his tent when Caulaincourt appeared. He had just come from the Shevardino redoubt. 'We didn't take a single prisoner,' he said. The astonished Napoleon began to ask whether the Russians had really decided to conquer or die. Caulaincourt replied that the Russians had been whipped to a frenzy by their commanders. Accustomed, moreover, to fighting the Turks, who took no prisoners, they had resolved to die rather than yield. This explanation was of course intended to minimize the significance of the Russian heroism. The reference to the Turks was absurd: Russian soldiers were little interested in their fate in captivity. The simple truth is that they defended their positions with courage—the French had occasion to learn this as the war progressed.

Napoleon slept very little that night. It seemed to him that the Russian fires were growing dimmer; then he heard a din and rumble from the Russian camp. The Emperor was seized by the fear that followed him throughout the war: did the Russians intend to withdraw under cover of night? After the Shevardino engagement, Napoleon decided that the imminent battle must primarily be fought with artillery. The rifle and bayonet were to play a subordinate part.

At the first gleam of dawn, the Emperor, accompanied by his suite and marshals, began an inspection tour of the positions. All day he remained on horseback, every now and then casting a glance at the Russian camp. Some sort of commotion was apparent, and all the while the sounds of a distant din reached him. At midday, the French learned that Kutuzov was inspecting his troops, and that the ikon of the Smolensk Mother of God was being borne round the Russian camp. Towards evening everything quieted down.

That day, Napoleon rode to the Shevardino redoubt and, apparently wishing to verify the report he had received in the night, asked a general of his suite who had been in the battle: 'How many Russian prisoners did you take yesterday?' 'They won't be taken prisoner, Sire.' 'They won't? Very well, then we shall kill them!' said Napoleon and went on. This brief dialogue is related by many witnesses, among them officers of a Cossack regiment.

The whole day of 6 September was passed in preparations. In the evening the following proclamation of Napoleon was read to the regiments: 'Soldiers, here is the battle you have so much desired! Victory depends upon you! We need this victory. It will give us a life of abundance, good winter quarters, and a speedy return to our native land. Conduct yourselves as you did at Austerlitz, at Friedland, at Vitebsk, at Smolensk, and may the most remote posterity speak of your conduct upon this day. Let them say of you: he was in the great battle under the walls of Moscow!'

The same order was read in a different version at daybreak on 7 September: 'Soldiers! The day which you have so much desired has come. The enemy army, which has been fleeing before you, now stands facing you. Remember that you are French soldiers! The winning of this battle opens up to you the gates of the ancient Russian capital; it will give you good winter quarters. The enemy will be compelled to seek his salvation in a speedy peace, which shall be a glorious one for us and for our loyal allies! Given at Main Headquarters before Mozhaisk, 2 September 1812. NAPOLEON.'

Towards the evening of 6 September, Colonel Fabvier, aide-de-camp of Marshal Marmont, arrived from distant Spain. The news he brought was not cheerful. In the battle near Aropile, the French, whose army in Spain was twice the size of the army now at Borodino, had suffered a fresh defeat . . . It grew dark. The Emperor commanded his army to go to sleep—the next day's action was to begin before daybreak. He himself went to his tent, but could not sleep. And he did not let Caulaincourt or Rapp get a wink of sleep. Every hour or so he went out of his tent to see if fires were still visible at Semenovsky and Borodino, and on Bagration's flank, between Utitsa and the Semenovsky ravine. The fires were burning, Kutuzov had not left the spot. The Emperor was suffering from a cold and not feeling any too well. He would start saying something to his aides-de-camp and break off in the middle of a sentence. Or he would spring a question and promptly forget it, not waiting for the answer. Suddenly he asked General Rapp, whom he had summoned to the tent: 'Do you believe in tomorrow's victory?' 'Without a doubt, Your Majesty, but it will be a bloody victory.' At this point, Napoleon unwittingly betrayed his intention of withholding the Guard or a certain part of his cavalry (50,000 out of his 130,000 men) from the impending battle: 'I have 80,000 [sic], I will lose 20,000, and with 60,000 I shall enter Moscow. There we shall be joined by the units remaining behind and later by the march battalions. We shall be stronger than before the battle.'

He spoke of many things, trying to forget his cold and his anxiety. He did not go to bed.

At dawn a messenger from Marshal Ney entered the tent. Five o'clock had struck and the Marshal wanted to know if he had the Emperor's command to begin the battle. The Russians had not moved from their positions. Napoleon suddenly cried out: 'At last, we hold them! Forward! We shall open the gates of Moscow!' Within half an hour he was at the Shevardino redoubt. The sun began to rise behind the distant Russian camp.

'The sun of Austerlitz!' exclaimed the Emperor.

5

BORODINO

HISTORY records few battles comparable to Borodino in bloodshed and fierceness. Its consequences were tremendous.

Napoleon destroyed almost half the Russian army and a few days later was in Moscow. Yet he failed to break the spirit of the Russian forces remaining after the battle and failed to intimidate the Russian people, which, after Borodino and the loss of Moscow, resisted more fiercely than ever.

The right wing and the centre of the Russian army were both commanded by Barclay de Tolly. Miloradovich was in immediate command of the right wing, consisting of two infantry corps, the Second and the Fourth (19,800 men), and two cavalry corps, the First and the Second (6,000 men)—25,800 men all told. Dokhturov was in direct command of the centre, comprising one infantry and one cavalry corps, altogether 13,600 men. The reserve of the centre and right wing was directly under Kutuzov himself (36,300 men). All in all, the right wing and the centre, including reserves, comprised 75,700 men. This entire mass of troops (the right wing and the centre) bore the name First Army, since its nucleus was Barclay's former First Army. The left wing was under Bagration, and as the nucleus of this left wing was the Second Army commanded by Bagration prior to Smolensk, the whole left wing retained the name Second Army, and Bagration himself was called the 'second Commander-in-Chief.'

The left wing comprised two infantry corps (22,000 men) and one cavalry (3,800 men), so that Bagration had, all told, a little over 25,000 men; his reserves numbered 8,300 men. Consequently, Bagration had at the beginning of the battle 34,100 men, or two-fifths as many as the First Army. In addition to these regular troops with reserves, constituting 110,800 men in all, the Russian army at Borodino was augmented by 7,000 Cossacks and 10,000 militiamen from the governments of Smolensk and Moscow. All in all, Kutuzov had 120,800 men under arms, not counting the Cossacks. His artillery consisted of 640 guns. These figures occur in many sources. Toll's figures are somewhat smaller: 'On this day the Russian army had under arms the troops of the line with artillery to the number of 95,000 men, 7,000 Cossacks, 7,000 militiamen from Moscow, and 3,000 from Smolensk. Altogether, this army had 112,000 men under arms, and 640 guns in its artillery.'

In his brief article on Borodino in the *New American Cyclopaedia,* based largely, as he himself indicates, on the *Memoirs* of Toll, Engels says that the Russian artillery at Borodino was stronger than the French and that it used heavier projectiles—six to twelve pounds as against three to four pounds. The efficient production of the Tula and Sestroretsk factories and the arrival of new armaments from England helped the Russian army in the struggle against the technically superior enemy. In any case, 1812 saw none of the shameful technical backwardness displayed by the Russian army in the Crimean campaign of 1854-5.

According to exaggerated Russian computations, Napoleon brought five infantry corps to Borodino: the First, Third, Fourth, Fifth, and Eighth; four cavalry corps, the Old Guard and the Young Guard. The infantry corps consisted of 122,000 men, the four cavalry corps of 22,500, the Old Guard of 13,000, and the Young Guard of 27,000. According to the computations of the Russian staff, he had 185,000 men and over 1,000 guns. The First Corps, largest of the five, comprised 48,000 men, and was commanded by Marshal Davout; the Third, commanded by Marshal Ney, had 20,000; the Fourth, commanded by Eugène Beauharnais, Viceroy of Italy, had 24,000 men; the Fifth, commanded by Prince Poniatowski, had 17,000; the Eighth, commanded by Marshal Junot, Duke of Abrantès, had 13,000. The entire cavalry of 22,500 men was under Joachim Murat. The entire Guard, the Old and the Young, was regarded as directly subordinate to Napoleon himself, the Commander-in-Chief of the Grand Army. But the immediate commander of the Old Guard was Marshal Mortier, and the commander of the Young Guard was Lefebvre, Duke of Danzig.

Actually, according to computations made by Clausewitz, who participated in the events and later wrote their history, Napoleon had 182,000 men when he came to Smolensk, but at Borodino he had only 130,000 men and 587 guns. Of the remaining 52,000, Napoleon lost 36,000 in the battles at Smolensk, at Valutino Hill, in the smaller battles and skirmishes between Smolensk and Shevardino, and by illness and desertion; 10,000 had been sent to reinforce the garrison at Vitebsk, and 6,000 were left at Smolensk.

These figures are given by the French military historians of the campaign, from whom, after critical verification, Clausewitz took them. They are today generally accepted.

.   .   .

The battle began with an attack by Delzon's division on the village of Borodino. The village was within the disposition of the right wing of the Russian army, commanded by Barclay. The French ejected the chasseurs stationed there, and a sharp skirmish took place on the bank of the river Koloch. Barclay gave orders to burn the bridge across the river. The villages remained in French hands. The Russian chasseurs suffered severe losses, but so did Delzon's infantry.

At five o'clock in the morning, a fierce battle developed on the left wing of the Russian army, at Semenovsky Gully, where Bagration was stationed.

Thither Napoleon directed Davout, Murat, and Ney (to whose command Junot's corps was assigned). The first attacks were repulsed by Russian artillery and dense rifle fire. His horse killed under him, Marshal Davout suffered a contusion of the head. In these first attacks on Bagration's positions, the French lost many commanders, including several generals and colonels. The fortifications round Semenovsky, 'Bagration's *flèches*' as they were called, had been hurriedly built, and were technically unsatisfactory; but the defence was so furious that, from five o'clock in the morning until half past eleven, the desperate attacks of the French were shattered with tremendous losses. At seven o'clock that morning, Napoleon ordered 150 cannon to

direct their fire against Bagration's *flèches*. After long
artillery preparation, Ney, Davout, and Murat assaulted
Semenovsky Gully and the *flèches* with tremendous
forces—Murat alone flung three cavalry corps against
the *flèches*. The attacking forces rushed fiercely upon
Vorontsov's Division and overwhelmed it, then upon
Neverovsky's Division, with the same result. Vorontsov's Division was almost entirely destroyed, and
Vorontsov himself was wounded. Neverovsky resisted
desperately, and more than once his battalions, bayonet
in hand, charged the onrushing masses of the French.
Murat, Ney, and Davout sent to Napoleon for reinforcements. But he refused them, expressing dissatisfaction that the *flèches* had not yet been captured.

A most sanguinary battle developed. In repeated attacks and counter-attacks, the *flèches,* now covered with
dead men and horses, several times changed hands.
Those who knew Prince Bagration could not doubt
that the *flèches* would remain in his hands as long as
he had breath to defend them.

For his part, Napoleon could not and would not renounce his plan, for he had firmly resolved first to
destroy the Russian left flank and then to make an all-
out effort against the centre. At first he had directed
only 150 guns upon Bagration's *flèches;* the number
had now been increased to 400—over two thirds of his
entire artillery.

He ordered a new concerted effort to storm the
flèches. Bagration decided to forestall the enemy by a
counter-attack.

'At this point an important event took place,' says
Fyodor Glinka, a participant in the battle. 'Grasping
the Marshal's intention and observing the menacing
movement of the French forces, Prince Bagration con-

ceived a great design. He gave orders, and the entire left wing in all its length moved quickly forward with fixed bayonets.' The Russian attack was hurled back, and Davout replied with a counter-attack. The French grenadiers of the Fifty-seventh Regiment, with rifles leveled but withholding fire, flung themselves at the *flèches*. They withheld fire to win time, and the Russian bullets mowed them down. 'Bravo, bravo!' cried Prince Bagration, impressed by the courage of the Fifty-seventh Regiment.

A volley of grapeshot came from the French battery aimed at the defenders of the *flèches*.

At this moment a shell splinter struck Bagration and smashed his shin-bone. For a few minutes he made a valiant effort to conceal his wound from his men, in order not to dismay them. But the wound bled profusely, and he began silently to slip from his horse. His men caught him in time, laid him on the ground, and then carried him away. The thing he had most feared, which had caused him to conceal his pain, now came to pass: 'In an instant the rumour spread that he was dead,' writes Ermolov, who took part in the battle. 'It was impossible to check the confusion of the troops . . . There was one common feeling—despair.' About midday (after Bagration's departure) the Second Army (the entire left wing) was in such a state that certain units had to be moved back the space of a shot before order could be restored.

Promptly after the attack by the Second Army, thrown back by a French counter-attack, Fyodor Glinka saw the wounded General resting at the foot of a hill. His linen and garments were soaked in blood, his uniform was unbuttoned, one foot had been divested of its boot, his head was bespattered with blood, there was a large wound above his knee. 'His face, covered with dark patches of gun powder, was pale but calm.' Someone supported him from behind, holding him with both arms. Seemingly oblivious to his agonizing pain, he gazed silently into the distance, listening to the rumble and din of the battle. 'He wanted to know the outcome of the battle, but that was becoming more and more dubious. The terrible news of the second Commander-in-Chief's death spread down the lines, and the soldiers lost their courage.'

Bagration was carried away, and this was the most critical, the most fateful moment of the battle. His soldiers loved him, as they loved no other commander except Kutuzov. Moreover, they had believed in his invincibility. 'After his death,' witnesses tell us, 'the soul itself had departed from the entire left wing.'

A mad frenzy, a passionate desire to avenge their leader, seized the men who had fought directly under Bagration. While Bagration was being carried away, the cuirassier Adrianov, who had attended him in battle (handing him the spy-glass, and so forth), ran towards the stretcher and said: 'Your Excellency, you're being taken away to be cured. I'm of no more use to you!' Then, witnesses report, 'Adrianov, in the sight of thousands, sped like an arrow, cut his way among the enemy dealing blows at many, and dropped down dead.'

In his final report to Emperor Alexander, General Saint-Priest accounts for the capture of the *flèches* by the elimination of Bagration from the battle. At the beginnings of the attacks on Semenovskoye, the Russians had fifty guns in all, while the French employed over a hundred. As the battle went on, more guns were brought up on both sides. The points attacked by the French so quickly changed hands that the artillery on both sides often lacked time to modify its range and sometimes for a brief space shot down its own men. Just before Bagration's death, during the final storming of the *flèches,* this relatively small sector of the battlefield was the target of 400 French and 300 Russian guns. Napoleon now directed the same guns against Rayevsky's battery, stationed in the centre of the Russian position.

. . .

The left wing was broken. Bagration was dead. From various points, Kutuzov received reports of heavy losses. The brothers Tuchkov, both generals, Buksgevden, Kutaisov, Gorchakov had all been killed. The soldiers fought on with astonishing steadfastness and fell by the thousands.

'During this time,' writes General Nikitin, an eyewitness, 'cavalry attacks closely succeeded one another; they were so powerful that the troops clashed in whole masses, and the losses on both sides were tremendous; horses whose riders had been shot down ran about in droves.'

As at Smolensk, the wounded, despite inconceivable agonies, would not leave the ranks, and disobeyed the officers who ordered them to the field hospital. And the officers were as courageous as their men.

Prince Eugène of Württemberg, who fought in the Russian army at Borodino, relates an astounding incident. In the heat of battle, General Miloradovich ordered his adjutant Bibikov to find Eugène of Württemberg, whom he wanted to see. According to all evidence, the roar of artillery all through the day was dreadful, greater than at Eylau, Wagram, or any other battle of the Napoleonic epoch. Even the rifle fire was inaudible.

Apparently Bibikov could not shout loud enough to attract Eugène's attention; he raised an arm indicating where Miloradovich was to be found. At that moment a cannon-ball tore off his arm. Falling from his horse, Bibikov raised the other arm and again pointed.

After the capture of the *flèches*, the second great moment in the battle was the struggle for Rayevsky's so-called 'mound battery,' in the centre of the Russian front. After the capture of Borodino by the French, Russian chasseurs drove them out only to be driven out in their turn. Borodino remained in French hands. Eugène, Viceroy of Italy, crossed the River Koloch and began an attack on the big battery, which had been under constant attack since ten o'clock that morning.

General Bonamy seized the battery by a frontal assault, but was driven out by the Russians. He stormed it again, and was again driven out. Monakhtin, chief of staff of the Sixth Corps, received two bayonet wounds, but just as a third charge was on the way, he pointed to the battery and managed to shout to his soldiers: 'Imagine that's Russia, my boys, and defend her to the last!' At that moment a bullet entered his stomach, and Colonel Monakhtin was carried away. Though mortally wounded he lived a few days. On learning that Kutuzov had ordered Moscow abandoned to the enemy, Monakhtin tore the bandages from his wounds and soon gave up the ghost.

Ermolov dislodged Broussier's division from Rayevsky's battery and its approaches. Bonamy, with bayonet wounds all over him, was taken prisoner. Napoleon had given orders to take Rayevsky's battery at all cost.

At two o'clock in the afternoon, Napoleon ordered his artillery to move up to the positions round the Semenovsky *flèches,* which had been taken from the

French after Bagration's death. The deadly artillery fire mowed down the Russian troops. The cannon-balls dug holes in the ground, sweeping away men, horses, ammunition wagons, guns. Explosive shells smashed ten soldiers each. Simultaneously, from Bagration's *flèches* and from the right flank, the French artillery poured fire at Rayevsky's battery and at the Russian troops withdrawing from it. Never before had the Russian officers and men shown such complete indifference to danger, to the flaming death about them. Barclay, who was obviously seeking death on that day, rode forward to the spot where the fire was most intense and there halted. 'He wants to impress me!' shouted Miloradovich to his soldiers, and overtook Barclay, going even closer to the French batteries, stopping at the very spot where the French fire from the *flèches* on the left crossed the fire from the Viceroy's positions on the right. He dismounted, and seating himself on the ground announced that he would have his breakfast there. Such desperate courage was typical of Miloradovich.

The soldiers flung themselves forward, often without awaiting the command. An eyewitness writes: 'The men of the company [Second Light Artillery of the Guard] were far more cheerful under this strong fire than when kept in reserve and haphazardly shelled.' An enemy projectile struck off one of bombardier Kurochkin's hands and killed his comrade Usov. 'Ah, my poor little hand, my poor little hand!' exclaimed Kurochkin, waving a mangled arm. Another bombardier who stood at his side remarked: 'I'm sorry for your little hand, but there, look—Usov is gone altogether, and he can't say a word.'

The Russian artillery replied with deadly fire. But the French fire grew more and more savage; it was becoming evident that Napoleon had resolved to take Rayevsky's battery and then to disorganize the Russian army with artillery fire. But this came to nothing. The Russian army withdrew in perfect order.

By Kutuzov's command, Platov with his Cossacks and Uvarov with the First Cavalry Corps undertook a large-scale diversion almost in the very rear of Napoleon's army. This saved Rayevsky's battery for several hours. Platov and Uvarov crossed the Koloch and put to flight a French cavalry brigade which, stationed far from the centre of battle, did not expect an attack; they also attacked the infantry in the French rear, but were beaten off with losses. Uvarov was ordered to retire, Platov was thrown back. Nevertheless, this Russian cavalry raid delayed the final destruction of Rayevsky's battery and prevented Napoleon from even partly satisfying the second request of Ney, Murat, and Davout for reinforcements. Napoleon replied that he could not risk his Guard at such a distance from France and that he 'did not yet see the chessboard with sufficient clarity.' But there is no doubt that one cause of the Emperor's refusal was the insecurity of the rear, after the audacious raid of Platov and Uvarov.

Immediately after the raid had been beaten back, Napoleon ordered Viceroy Eugène and a part of Murat's cavalry to take Rayevsky's battery by storm at any cost. The Russians met the attack with desperate resistance. Wounded soldiers remained in the ranks, both sides fought with rage and ferocity; the battle was fought at the battery itself, and between the battery and the spot where Bagration had been that morning. Now the left Russian wing had been moved considerably back, first by Konovnitsin, who replaced the mortally wounded Bagration, then by Dokhturov, who replaced Konovnitsin. As the fourth hour began, three quarters of the Russian defenders had been slain and the remainder thrown back. The battery was captured by the French.

Yet the Russians did not abandon the field of battle, and their artillery did not cease firing. Russian cannon-balls began to fall close to the Emperor and to fly above his head. Napoleon then ordered several new batteries of the Guard artillery to be moved closer to the Russian lines. A short time passed, and again Russian cannon-balls began to fly above the heads of Napoleon and his suite. A few spent cannon-balls rolled towards Napoleon's feet. 'He quietly kicked them aside, as one kicks a stone when taking a walk,' says Bausset, the Court Prefect, who was with Napoleon at the time. The Emperor's sullen mood and ill-concealed anxiety did not pass; Bagration's death, the taking of the Semenovsky *flèches* and the victory over Rayevsky's redoubt did not improve his mood. He did not tell anyone how he felt when the bloody day had at last begun to wane and the sun to vanish behind the clouds.

'The Russians tried to recapture the redoubts,' wrote de la Flise, the regimental doctor attached to the Guard, 'but they only left piles of bodies, mowed down by our grapeshot. Not once during the entire battle did Napoleon mount his horse. He walked on foot with his suite of officers, and he did not cease to pace up and down, following the movement on the field of battle. Someone said that he did not mount his horse because he was not feeling well. A steady stream of adjutants received orders from him and rode away. Behind Napoleon stood the Guard and several corps of reserves. We were drawn up in battle formation, inactive and awaiting orders. The regimental band was playing military marches, reminiscent of the first triumphant marches of the Revolution: *Allons, enfants de la patrie!* when the fight was for freedom. Here, the same sounds did not inspire the warriors, and some of the older officers laughed, as they compared the two epochs. I left my horse with a soldier and went forward to join a group of officers who stood behind the Emperor. Before us the spectacle of the terrible battle unfolded. Nothing could be seen behind the smoke of a thousand ceaselessly thundering guns. Thick clouds, one after another, rose in the air, in the wake of the flashes from the cannon. From time to time, rockets went up among the Russians, signals no doubt, whose meaning eluded me. Bombs and grenades burst in the air, forming small white clouds; several ammunition wagons blew up among the enemy with a force which shook the earth. Such accidents occur more rarely among us than among the Russians, because their ammunition wagons are of poor construction. I moved a little closer to the Emperor, who had not ceased looking through the spy-glass at the field of battle. He wore his gray uniform, and spoke little. Sometimes a cannon-ball rolled towards his feet, but he merely stepped aside, as we did, standing behind him.'

Striving to hasten the rout and flight of the Russians, Napoleon ordered his cavalry—the Cuirassiers and the Uhlans—to strike at the Russian infantry corps commanded by Count Osterman. The latter had early been carried away because of a bad contusion, but his infantry met the attack of the French cavalry with such strong fire that the attackers wavered. At this moment, fresh regiments of the Guard hurried to the assistance of the infantry, and the French were repulsed. Then came the storm of Rayevsky's battery. The French cavalry (Saxons) broke into the battery from the rear, while Viceroy Eugène's infantry threw themselves headlong upon the battery in dense masses. A horrible slaughter ensued; the Russians met the charging infantrymen with bayonets, pushing them down into the ditch below. No prisoners were taken by either side. Once in possession of the battery, the French slaughtered all those whom they found alive.

This was the final great act of the battle. The artillery continued to thunder. Partial cavalry attacks were beaten off by the Russians. The Polish cavalry under Poniatowski was repulsed with heavy losses. There was no sign of a Russian flight; notwithstanding the greatly thinned ranks, there was no sign even of a retirement.

Evening came. The greatest of all Napoleon's battles was drawing to an end. The outcome was unclear both to Napoleon and to his Marshals. In their time they had seen more real, brilliant victories than anyone before them. Could this bloody action be called a victory? It was easy enough to write cheerful bulletins and letters. 'Ma bonne amie,' wrote Napoleon to Marie-Louise the day after the battle, 'I am writing to you on the field of Borodino where I defeated the Russians yesterday. Their entire army of 120,000 men was here. The battle was hotly contested. At two o'clock in the afternoon, the victory was ours. I have taken several thousand prisoners and 60 guns. Their losses may be counted at 30,000 men. I had many killed and wounded.'

In reality, Napoleon did not take 'thousands of prisoners.' All the prisoners he had taken numbered about 700 men. The letters to Marie-Louise were merely little 'bulletins,' calculated to attain a wide publicity; in them the truth could be treated as unceremoniously as in the official communiqués.

Actually, no one felt victorious. The marshals talked among themselves and were dissatisfied. Murat said he had not recognized the Emperor that whole day. Ney said the Emperor had forgotten his trade.

On both sides the artillery thundered until evening, and the bloodshed continued. The Russians stood their ground. It was quite dark now. A fine rain began to fall. 'What about the Russians?' Napoleon asked. 'They are holding, Your Majesty.' 'Intensify the fire, if that's what they want!' commanded the Emperor. 'Let them have it!'

Morose and uncommunicative, Napoleon made a tour of the battlefield. He gazed with inflamed eyes at the endless piles of corpses. His suite and his generals dared not interrupt his silence. That evening it was not yet known to the Emperor that of their 112,000 men the Russians had lost not 30,000 but about 58,000; or that out of his own 130,000 he had lost over 50,000. But he did learn that evening that among his killed and gravely wounded there were 47 of his best generals (not 43 as it has sometimes been stated). The French and Russian corpses were so closely pressed that the Emperor's horse had to seek a spot on which to set down his hoofs. The moans and groans of the wounded reached him from all sides. The behaviour of the Russian wounded struck the Emperor's suite with wonder: 'They did not let out a groan,' writes Ségur. 'It is possible, of course, that being far from their own, they counted less on compassion. Yet it is true that they seemed hardier in sustaining pain than the French.'

With 58,000 killed and gravely wounded, the Russians lost only 700 men as prisoners. 'The most terrible of all my battles was the one before Moscow. The

French showed themselves worthy of victory, and the Russians worthy of being invincible,' said Napoleon of Borodino a short time before his death.

. . .

In the final accounting, Borodino proved a great moral triumph of the Russian people over the all-European dictator.

That evening Napoleon led away his troops from the field of battle before Kutuzov gave the order to retire. The Russian army withdrew from Borodino in good order. And, most important, there was not even the shadow of discouragement among the Russian troops. Hatred and the desire for vengeance were stronger than before. These feelings, of course, did not possess everyone, but they were indisputably the prevailing mood. On this point witnesses agree. French historians borrowed the official version of 'the great victory over Moscow' from the Emperor's triumphant reports, intended for the French public. The Tsar and his intimates who hated Kutuzov readily accepted this version of the Russian defeat at Borodino. Accounts such as Wintzengerode's were the product of this court atmosphere. 'No matter what is being said,' wrote Wintzengerode to Alexander on 13 September 1812, from the village of Davydovka near Tarutino, 'the results are sufficient proof that the battle [Borodino] was lost. The army, and especially the left flank, have suffered extraordinarily heavy losses. One of the contributing causes of the defeat, I have been told, was the disorder in the artillery park following Count Kutaisov's death; there was also a shortage of ammunition, and no one knew where to get replenishments.' Robert Wilson, in a letter from Krasnaya Pakhra dated 13 September, expresses the same idea in fewer words. A similar tendency is reflected in the words of such military theoreticians as Clausewitz and Jomini. But it is interesting that this talk of 'defeat' did not arise until some time later, after the yielding of Moscow. On the evening after the battle, the participants in the battle did not consider themselves defeated. On the contrary! For a moment it was believed that Kutuzov would attack the enemy the following day.

Yet it is true that the losses were unprecedented and terrifying.

Darkness finally enveloped the battlefield and the unceasing moans of the wounded abandoned by French and Russians alike filled the night. And all night long fires were alight on all the hillocks to which Kutuzov's staff had withdrawn the surviving units of the Russian army. 'The gloomy night, following the bloody battle, was utilized to move our troops to another position with the help of camp fires lighted on the heights which served as gathering points,' wrote Barclay de Tolly. Throughout the night, exhausted wounded men walked and crawled to these signal fires, the entire night and the entire morning were spent in making a first, approximate count of the losses. Kutuzov had to make a quick decision, and it depended on the count.

In the morning, the general picture was clear. Reality exceeded the worst fears.

The bloodiest of all Napoleon's previous battles had been Eylau on 8 February 1807, and contemporaries never compared Borodino with any other battle. But eyewitnesses rejected even this comparison. The following lines were written three days after Borodino: 'Everyone says that the battle of Borodino cannot compare with it [Eylau], because the entire field was covered with corpses.'

'At Borodino,' writes Liprandi, 'the Russians lost about 58,000 men, half of the battling army. Of Vorontsov's Grenadier Division, 300 men remained at three in the afternoon out of the 4,000 who had gone into battle. In the Shirvansk Regiment 96 soldiers and 3 officers were all that was left of 1,300 men.' Some battalions and companies were destroyed almost to a man. There were whole divisions with only a few survivors. There were corps reduced to the size of battalions.

Yet despite all losses, the Russian army did not consider itself defeated. Nor did the Russian people feel defeated. In its memory Borodino lives not as a defeat, but as a symbol of determination and power to defend its national independence against the most overwhelming odds.

6

THE BURNING OF MOSCOW

THE French and the Russian armies withdrew a short distance from the battlefield and remained inactive for several hours while the results of the carnage were being computed.

One corps commander after another, one adjutant after another reported to Kutuzov, and what they had to say was so terrible that the old Field Marshal definitely decided to surrender Moscow without any further attempt to halt the invader. He realized that now he could surrender the capital without another battle. The Sixth, Seventh, and Eighth Corps had been destroyed almost in their entirety. Other units suffered considerable losses. At the same time, Kutuzov learned that Napoleon's Guard was intact because it had taken no part in the battle. On 8 September, Kutuzov also learned that Napoleon was moving his right wing round the Russian left wing. To stand without giving battle was becoming impossible, and to fight immediately was equally impossible. Kutuzov decided to retreat towards Moscow.

Supplementary reports came pouring in throughout the day.

On the morning of 8 September, the Field Marshal ordered his army to withdraw from Borodino on the direct road to Moscow. This was the beginning of the ingeniously conceived and brilliantly executed tactical march towards Tarutino, one of the Field Marshal's greatest achievements.

Kutuzov retreated from Borodino on the route that led through Mozhaisk, Zemlino, Luzhinskoye, Nara, Vyazma, and Mamonovo.

At noon of 8 September, the day following Borodino, Napoleon ordered Murat to pursue the Russians with his entire cavalry. To Murat's right, Poniatowski's corps marched towards Borisovo; to the left was Eugène, Viceroy of Italy, moving in the direction of Ruza; while almost directly behind Murat, upon that same Moscow trunk road, aiming straight for Mozhaisk, proceeded the corps of Ney and Davout, behind them the Young Guard, and finally the Old Guard with Napoleon himself. The remaining forces marched behind the Old Guard.

What happened to thousands of wounded in Smolensk was repeated on a much larger scale after Borodino. A great number of Russians and Frenchmen were left to the mercy of fate and burned alive. According to an officer of the Grand Army, 'the battlefield was a terrible sight. There was almost no sanitary service or activity. All the villages and habitations close to the Moscow road were packed to the full with wounded in the most helpless state. The villages were destroyed by ceaseless chronic conflagrations, which raged in the regions occupied or traversed by the French army. Those of the wounded who succeeded in saving themselves from the flames crawled by the thousands along the

great road, seeking means to prolong their pitiful existence.'

Armed peasants ruthlessly disposed of the lagging
Frenchmen. It goes without saying that the French sum-
marily executed Russian peasants suspected of such activities.

During these fateful days the bitterness of the people
grew by the hour, and the Field Marshal had to take
this into consideration. He decided not to reveal at
once his plan of surrendering Moscow.

During these six days, 8 to 14 September, between the
retreat from Borodino and the occupation of Moscow by
the French, Kutuzov pretended that he meant to give a
new battle and was only looking for a good position;
he did not cease uttering words to which he himself
attached no significance.

'Kutuzov never intended to give a battle on the second day, his words were only a matter of policy. At
night I and Toll made a tour of the position, on which
our exhausted warriors slept like dead, and he [Toll]
reported that it was impossible to think of going forward, much less of defending the position, previously
occupied by 96,000 men, with only 45,000, especially as
Napoleon still had his entire Guard which had not
fought at Borodino. Kutuzov knew all this, but he
awaited this report and gave the order for prompt retirement only after receiving it.' This statement was
made by Kutuzov's orderly, Prince Golitsin, who spent
the entire night after Borodino visiting the bloody
field.

Murat with his cavalry pressed hard on the Russian
rear-guard, 'throwing the rear-guard upon the army,'
said Wintzengerode. On the third day after Borodino,
9 September, word came that Napoleon had ordered

Viceroy Eugène to march with four infantry divisions and twelve cavalry regiments to Ruza. This move threatened to outflank the right wing of the retreating Russian army.

Apparently Kutuzov thought he had at least to give the impression that a battle was being waged for Moscow. On 13 September, as Miloradovich was retiring with his rear-guard under severe pressure of the main French forces, a paper from Ermolov reached him. It conveyed Kutuzov's order that Moscow be surrendered, but suggested to Miloradovich 'that he honour the ancient capital with a show of battle before its walls.' 'This expression aroused the indignation of Miloradovich,' says A. A. Shcherbinin, who was close to him at the time. He thought it a Machiavellian device and attributed it to Ermolov. If Miloradovich had engaged the mass of Napoleon's forces and had been defeated, as was inevitable, he would have been told: 'We ordered only a manœuvre, a show of battle.'

Contemporaries were at a complete loss when faced by this contradiction between Kutuzov's words and actions after Borodino. 'I cannot understand,' wrote M. I. Volkova to her friend V. I. Lanskaya, 'how this unfortunate battle could rejoice you even for an instant. Although, according to participants (I have met a few) the battle was not a defeat, on the following day its consequences were clear to everyone. The news has been published in Moscow, and has reached us, that after the terrible bloodshed on both sides, the weakened enemy retired a distance of eight versts, but that on the following day the Russians would victoriously conclude the battle by attacking the French and forcing them to a final retreat—this was the text of Kutuzov's official letter to Rostopchin, which appeared in print. But instead, our forces began to retire on the twenty-seventh, and to this moment no one knows the cause of this unexpected retirement. There is a mystery hidden here. We may one day learn it, or we may not; but what is true and beyond doubt is that there is some important reason which made Kutuzov change his plan, so solemnly announced on 26 September.'

The Russian army, all that remained of it after Borodino, was now fairly close to Moscow. The moment came to proclaim immediately and unequivocally that Moscow would be yielded to Napoleon without a new battle. Kutuzov was not very sure of his generals. Ever since Borodino, Bennigsen, who had been forced upon him by Alexander, had, with a great show of patriotic phrases, harped on the inadmissibility of surrendering Moscow. From Ermolov, who was insincere, double-dealing, always a sort of snake in the grass, never really sympathetic to the Field Marshal, it was difficult to expect much support. Konovnitsin and Dokhturov also sided with Bennigsen on this point. Barclay might have helped him, but during these days he was full of bitterness. After his replacement by Kutuzov, Barclay spoke sincerely only to his wife. But to his indignation, his letters were intercepted. 'I cannot understand why you have not received the letters I wrote you after the battle of the 26th [i.e. Borodino] and sent by the same courier who was bearing a letter from Kutuzov to his wife. I cannot understand how it is possible to detain family letters. It is an infamy, added to the others which have been heaped on me!'

In these letters to his wife, Barclay asserts that he alone had saved the army before Borodino, and that at the moment of his replacement he was in a particularly good position and stood ready to battle with the advancing French. The subsequent letters to his wife, which have come down to us, were sent through the English commissioner with Kutuzov; in them, he is less restrained. 'I ask of you one mercy; deliver me from here [from the army], I don't care by what means . . .' 'Should they make no effort to atone for the wrong done me, and a great wrong it was, I have decided not to risk my life, as it only brings further humiliation upon me.'

The Russians entered the village of Fili. At four o'clock in the afternoon of 13 September, in the house of the peasant Sevastyanov, Kutuzov called a conference of the most important generals: Bennigsen, Barclay de Tolly, Platov, Dokhturov, Uvarov, Rayevsky, Osterman, Konovnitsin, Ermolov, Toll, and Lanskoy were present. Miloradovich, however, never left his rear-guard, which was keeping an eye on the advancing French.

Kutuzov threw the question open to discussion: should the army fight another battle or retire beyond Moscow, giving up the city to Napoleon? At the very start he expressed the opinion he had hitherto concealed: 'As long as the army exists and is in condition to oppose the enemy, we preserve the hope of winning the war; but if the army is destroyed, Moscow and Russia will perish.'

Bennigsen expressed himself in favour of a battle, Barclay in favour of retirement. Dokhturov, Uvarov, and Konovnitsin supported Bennigsen. Ermolov also supported him with a few meaningless, purely verbal reservations. No minutes were kept, and it is not clear what opinions were expressed by Platov, Rayevsky, Osterman, and Lanskoy. The council lasted only a little over an hour. The Field Marshal apparently broke up the meeting in a manner surprising to all present; he suddenly rose and announced that his order was for retirement.

We have one other report of the meeting at Fili. England had been eagerly awaiting accurate news of Borodino. One of the first circumstantial reports to reach England was a letter received by Count S. P. Vorontsov, whose son had been wounded in the battle. 'The day of Borodino was not decisive for either army. The losses must have been about the same on both sides. The Russian losses are painful because the great number of officers killed and wounded must inevitably lead to disorganization of the regiments.' This letter also gives a few details of the military council at Fili: Osterman asked Bennigsen if he could guarantee success in the event of a new battle before Moscow; Bennigsen replied that only a madman would answer such a question with any positiveness. At this council, Kutuzov said among other things: 'You fear a retreat through Moscow, but I regard it as farsighted, because it will save the army. Napoleon is like a stormy torrent which we are as yet unable to stop. Moscow will be the sponge that will suck him in.'—'By the authority granted me by the Tsar and the Fatherland, I command retirement.' These were his final words and with them he left the house. But it was clear to all who observed him that he was depressed by what he had done.

During the remaining hours of that day, Kutuzov spoke to no one. He returned to the peasant's house for the night, but did not sleep. Several times in the night he was heard weeping. At this moment, no one supported him—Barclay's agreement with him was purely negative. Ermolov, who but a few hours before the council had been in favour of retirement, had switched to Bennigsen's side. Kutuzov understood that he was now regarded as a leper—like Barclay before Tsarevo-Zaimishche. Knowing men as he did, Kutuzov could scarcely count on anyone to support him before the most powerful of his enemies, who was in the Winter Palace in St. Petersburg. But not even his enemies ascribed his distress to personal fear or shame. His whole subsequent behaviour showed that he followed only the dictates of his conscience, that he acted far more independently than ever before in his life, and certainly had no fear of irritating the Tsar. His intimates explained his tears that night by his agony over Moscow and his fear for Russia. Against his one utterance that the loss of Moscow did not mean the loss of Russia, they recalled several earlier assertions that the loss of Moscow did mean the loss of Russia. On 30 August he had written to Rostopchin from Gzhatsk: 'In my opinion, the loss of Moscow means the loss of Russia.' And everyone knew these words. He had plenty to think about on this sleepless night.

At nightfall of 13 September the army learned of the Field Marshal's decision. 'The dejection was general,' writes a witness.

The officers and soldiers were completely confused after all Kutuzov's categorical announcements that Moscow would be defended to the last. 'I remember that when Lindel, my adjutant, brought the order for the surrender of Moscow, everyone was seized with consternation: many wept, others tore off their uniforms and threatened to resign from the service after this humiliating surrender, or abandonment, of Moscow. My General Borozdin definitely regarded the command as a piece of treason and did not move from the spot until General Dokhturov arrived to replace him. By daybreak we were in Moscow. Its inhabitants, as yet un-

aware of their imminent misfortune, received us as de-
liverers, but when they learned the truth, swept after
us almost in a body. This was no longer the march of
an army, but the transportation of whole nations from
one end of the world to the other.'

On 12 September, the vanguard of the Russian army
had halted at Poklonnaya Hill, about two versts from
Dorogomilov Gate. An endless stream of carriages
and carts, thousands upon thousands of riders and pedestrians were leaving Moscow, despite rumours that Kutuzov was preparing another battle—in fact, only a few
knew of the decision taken on 13 September at the
council of generals, which had met at Fili.

The authorities had learned that three basic opinions,
precise practical suggestions, had been expressed at the
council: Bennigsen had suggested a new battle to save
Moscow; Barclay had suggested retirement to the city
of Vladimir; and a few others favoured retirement to
Tver, to hinder Napoleon's advance on St. Petersburg.
They knew that Kutuzov had concluded the meeting
by announcing that he would give no battle, but withdraw, yielding Moscow to Napoleon. He decided, however, not to retreat northward, but towards the old
Kaluga road. In accordance with this plan, the Russian
troops were ordered to advance along the Moscow streets
towards Kolomna Gate. From the early morning of 14
September the Russian army marched through the capital. At daybreak the first formations of the retreating
army had entered Moscow and, by way of the Arbat
and a few parallel streets, went towards Yauza Bridge
in the southeastern part of the city.

Frightened, confused, silent throngs of those Muscovites who had not yet been able to leave crowded
the streets and public squares, watching the depart-

ing troops. The soldiers marched gloomily, silently, with their eyes downcast. Witnesses tell us that some among the rank-and-file were weeping.

The first units of the retreating Russian army were still crossing Yauza Bridge when General Miloradovich, in command of the rear-guard, received news that the French cavalry was entering Moscow through Dorogomilov Gate.

Miloradovich, and General Kaptsevich, whose regiment bore up the rear, had difficulty in eluding the advancing Murat. Miloradovich received one report after another that the enemy was striving to cut off the rear-guard from the city. In other words, two cavalry corps, ten Cossack regiments, and twelve guns of mounted artillery were threatened with capture. Miloradovich succeeded in communicating with Murat. He convinced him that the people of Moscow would fight desperately with the troops if the French did not allow the Russian army to pass unmolested through Moscow, and thus he managed to hold Murat for four hours at a spot seven versts from Moscow; the rear-guard entered Moscow and passed through without further hindrance.

All this enabled thousands upon thousands of inhabitants to evacuate Moscow, but it saved neither the arsenal, where 'fine new rifles fell into enemy hands,' nor the depots and stores of grain, cloth, and other army supplies.

Two battalions of the Moscow garrison, merging with the main army as it passed the Kremlin, left the city amidst martial music. 'What rascal told your band to play?' shouted Miloradovich to the commander of the garrison, Lieutenant-General Brozin. Brozin replied that according to a regulation made by Peter the Great, a garrison leaving a fortress must play music. 'But where do the regulations of Peter the Great provide for the surrender of Moscow?' shouted Miloradovich. 'Will you please order that music to stop!'

In an endless stream, the Russian army marched through Moscow. Kutuzov glanced at his taciturn suite and said: 'Who among you knows Moscow?' Only one man responded. It was his orderly, the 20-year-old Prince Golitsin. 'Lead me by a route where I won't meet anyone.' Kutuzov rode from the Arbat through the boulevards as far as Yauza Bridge, across which the army was retiring, followed by the countless mass of the inhabitants. And here he met the man he had been most anxious to avoid. Rostopchin was on the bridge, trying to maintain order. It was a dry encounter. Rostopchin began to speak, but Kutuzov did not reply. He ordered the bridge to be cleared as quickly as possible for the passage of troops. Then he dismounted and took his place in a *drozhky*. 'On leaving Moscow, the Prince turned his *drozhky* towards the city and leaned his head, grown gray in battle, on his elbows. He gazed coolly upon the capital and upon the troops that went past him with downcast eyes, and for the first time they did not cry "Hurrah!" when they saw him.'

That day and night and the following day, endless human streams poured out of Moscow across Yauza Bridge. Kutuzov ordered the Russian army to the south, towards Krasnaya Pakhra, and from Krasnaya Pakhra to the old Kaluga road. That evening in the village of Uopa he sat drinking tea, surrounded by peasants. Suddenly, in terror, they pointed to the distant glow of burning Moscow. 'Kutuzov, striking the cap upon his head, said: "Yes, it's a pity. But just wait. I'll smash his head" . . .'

The flight from Moscow, and it was a mass flight, continued for several days. All the gates of the city were jammed with the fleeing population; indeed, they had been jammed since the first reports of Borodino and the retirement of the Russian army towards Mozhaisk. Crowds of people, confused and shaken by the storm hanging over them, milled in the streets for days. Some thought that Moscow was lost, others believed to the last moment that Kutuzov would fight again before the walls of the capital. Tens upon tens of thousands were fleeing Moscow, surrounding, overtaking the army, streaming along all the roads, sometimes cutting straight across country. This endless flight went on for days. All the roads to the east of Moscow, for dozens of versts in all directions, were covered with fugitives. The population of the vast capital became a herd of shelterless nomads. On the morning of 20 September, the following scene took place a few versts from Ryazan:

'We had scarcely reached the plain when we were confronted by a unique and pitiful spectacle. As far as the eye could reach, the entire Moscow road was covered with lines of carriages and pedestrians, fleeing from the unhappy capital. They jostled and overtook one another and hurried, driven by fear, in carriages, cabriolets, *drozhkis,* and carts. Everyone carried what he could. All faces were dusty and tear-stained. Children of all ages crowded round the grown-ups. Most pitiful was the sight of well-dressed men and women trudging on foot, dragging after them their children and meagre provisions. The mother would lead the older children, while the father would push the babes, too young to walk, in a barrow, or carry them on his shoulders. All had left in haste, with no chance to make any preparation; misfortune had taken them unawares; they wandered without aim and, for the most part, without money or bread. Looking upon this picture of woe, it was impossible to restrain one's tears. The din raised by the multitude of riders and walkers was audible at a distance. The sounds mingled into a groan that stirred the soul . . . And upon the other highways—to Vladimir, Nizhegorod, and Yaroslavl—it was the same thing, if not worse . . .'

. . .

Fyodor Vasilyevich Rostopchin, Governor-General of Moscow, had long hated Kutuzov, but during the days of evacuation, his fury against the Field Marshal knew no bounds. He defamed him in every possible way, and wrote denunciations of him to the Tsar. On 14 September 1812, he fell into an impossible, humiliating, and absurd position, especially in the eyes of the unhappy fugitives. He had to find a scapegoat. On this day he murdered a man in order to save himself.

In 1812, when Rostopchin was appointed Commander-in-Chief of Moscow—or more simply Governor-General—he was nearly fifty years old. He had first gained some prominence during the reign of Tsar Paul. During the first ten years of Alexander's reign, Rostopchin was in retirement, but in 1810 he became Chamberlain, remaining in this position until he was chosen for his present office in Moscow. Rostopchin was a man of quick but undisciplined mind, a wit (though not always a successful one), a noisy jester, a braggart, self-centred and self-confident, without any special talents or calling. When the menace to Moscow became clear, he assumed the role of demagogue-patriot. He began to issue handbills, which were distributed, mailed, and posted in the streets. He wrote these in a pert language with dashing, pseudo-popular turns of speech. These compositions were trivial, obvious, artificial, and insincere. At home with his wife, a Frenchified Catholic, he conversed only in French. With his friends he also conversed in French; he was completely ignorant of Russian literature, and although he died in 1826, there are no indications that he ever suspected the existence of Pushkin or Zhukovsky. And this man of the world, this noble, conceived the idea of acting the lively Muscovite artisan, not just some fellow talking on an empty stomach, but one who knew how to take a stiff drink. His absurd handbills did not produce the slightest impression on the public.

He had other silly ideas. At that time, for example, he made a great fuss over a certain Leppich, a German adventurer who claimed that he could build a balloon in which he would rise above the French army. He had hinted that with luck Napoleon himself might be destroyed.

The Tsar, too, was interested in Leppich and his balloon. We have a late statement, supposedly originating with Arakcheyev, to the effect that the Tsar meant to use the idea only to quiet and distract the people, but that he himself had never believed in the charlatan's foolish prank. But it is certain that Rostopchin did believe in Leppich. A charlatan and an adventurer by temperament, Rostopchin showed great sympathy for the resourceful German, who most seriously assured him in day-to-day notes that with a little more patience and a little more money the balloon would—lo and behold!— go up in the air. And that would be the end of Bonaparte. Leppich disliked Napoleon not only for his invasion of Russia, but also because when in 1811 he had been offered the same balloon, he promptly ordered

Leppich deported beyond the frontiers of the French Empire. The charlatan had better luck in Moscow.

The French called this Leppich a 'charlatan-me-chanic.' They found in Rostopchin's house documents showing that the Count believed in Leppich and had apparently paid him well. Leppich, for example, in a brief note dated 30 July demands the sum of 12,000 roubles. A letter from Leppich is preserved, dated 24 August, two days before Borodino (the 'inventor' had as yet achieved absolutely nothing): 'Your Serene Highness, you cannot imagine what difficulties I have encountered in preparing the balloon for its journey. But tomorrow it should surely fly.' In a special handbill Rostopchin announced to the people of Moscow: 'The Tsar has commissioned me to make a big balloon, in which 50 persons shall be able to fly where they wish, with or against the wind, and when this happens— you will see and rejoice. If the weather is good, tomorrow or the day after tomorrow I shall have a small balloon for testing purposes. I am telling you this so that upon seeing it you shall not think it comes from the scoundrel for whose injury and destruction it was made.'

Having swindled enough Government money out of his patron, Leppich vanished into thin air—without the help of his non-existent balloon. The Moscow public was no more impressed by the affair of the balloon than by Rostopchin's other documents.

In the days before and after Borodino, Rostopchin developed a seething activity. Men were seized on the charge of being alien spies, and publicly thrashed with rods or a knout; proclamations were issued to assure the public that Bonaparte would never enter Moscow, but a portion of Government property was sent out of the city for safety. To be sure, Rostopchin later justi-

fied himself by Kutuzov's previous statements that he
was going to fight for Moscow to the last drop of blood.
Napoleon was not the sole cause of Rostopchin's worries. He was one of those higher Russian dignitaries for
whom the word 'Russia' and the word 'serfdom' merged
into one indivisible essence. Years before this, as early
as 1806, he had begun to warn Alexander that Napoleon
was a deadly enemy, for the very reason that the
'servile estate' in Russia associated certain hopes with
his name. In 1807 he had again warned his sovereign
that the basic aim of the Russian 'rabble' was the destruction of the nobility. And now in 1812 in Moscow
he feared a revolt. He sought out the leading agitators
and banished Post Office Director Kliucharev from Moscow; he suspected the Old Believers among the merchant class of secret sympathies with Napoleon. In the
end, he energetically took up the case of Vereshchagin.
To illustrate the lamentable state of historic investigations concerning 1812, we shall first quote here the
absurd version of events that has often been given out
as the established truth.

Vereshchagin (so the version runs) 'translated into the
Russian two newspaper items concerning Napoleon: a
letter from Napoleon to the King of Prussia and a
speech of Napoleon addressed to the Princes of the Confederation of the Rhine in Dresden.' Actually, Napoleon had written no such letter to the King of Prussia
and addressed no such speech to the Princes of the Confederation of the Rhine. Nor could he have spoken such
nonsense (in Dresden of all places!), or written such an
absurd collection of phrases to the Prussian monarch—
'I announce to you my intentions, I desire the restoration of the colony, I want to wrest away its political
existence, et cetera.' It goes without saying, these two

strange, curiously ungrammatical letters could never
have had anything to do with Napoleon; they were composed, as Vereshchagin admitted in the end, by Vereshchagin himself. He communicated these fabrications
to his comrade Meshkov, and, apparently, sent round
many copies of them.

The author of these forgeries was either criminal or
crazy; in either case his behaviour was perfectly senseless.

In the archives I have found a complete hand-written
copy of these two documents, and an interesting proof
that similar copies of this 'translation' by Vereshchagin
had found their way into the provinces. On 4 July 1812
—reports the public prosecutor of Saratov to the Minister of Justice on 15 July—there appeared in Saratov
'some copies of a letter allegedly written by the French
Emperor to the Princes of the Confederation of the
Rhine, in which, among other things, he promised to be
in both northern capitals within six months.' An investigation revealed that 'this libelous statement' had been
received on 2 July by Arkhip Sviridov, a Saratov merchant, from his son in Moscow, who was working for a
paper merchant by the name of Bikovsky. There were
several such copies: 'The police confiscated all these
copies and forbade anyone to have them in his possession.' When the *Moscow Vedomosti* later published
news of the arrest of Vereshchagin and Meshkov, the
inhabitants of the capital were apprised of the affair.
Vereshchagin and Meshkov were arrested and locked up
in the Moscow jail. The tragedy came to a head on 14
September, on the day when Rostopchin fled from his
Moscow palace.

The fuss about Leppich's balloon, the handbills, the
public indignation over the banishment of the utterly

guiltless Post Office Director Kliucharev—all this did
not conceal from Rostopchin's eyes the terror approaching along the Smolensk road. What was he to do? . . .
One day Rostopchin waxed indignant at the 'ladies'
who were fleeing Moscow, the next he encouraged evacuation. He seems to have been really convinced that
the Russian army would stop Napoleon. He was jubi-
lant when Kutuzov replaced Barclay. From time to
time, however, he said that if the worst came to the
worst, it would be better to burn Moscow than yield it
to Napoleon.

Exactly three weeks before the entry of the French
into Moscow, Count Rostopchin wrote to Bagration
(24 August): 'I cannot imagine the enemy coming to
Moscow. Should you be compelled to retire to Vyazma,
I shall evacuate all Government property and let everyone get away; but the people here are loyal to the Tsar
and the Fatherland, and they would surely die at the
walls of Moscow. But if God should not help them in
their noble undertaking, then, following the Russian
rule: *don't let the scoundrel get it,* they will burn the
city to ashes, and Napoleon, instead of booty, will get
only the spot where the capital had been. It might not
be a bad idea to let him know this; then he will not
count on millions in gold and stores of bread, for he
will find only coals and ashes.' To the people, however,
he said nothing about burning Moscow, but only that
the French would never see it.

Rostopchin wrote on his posters: 'I answer with my
life that the scoundrel will never come to Moscow, and
here is the reason: we have 130,000 fine soldiers, 1,800
guns, and Prince Kutuzov, the Tsar's own chosen warrior and commander over everyone, and with him behind the enemy are Generals Tormasov and Chichagov

with 85,000 fine troops, and General Miloradovich has
come from Kaluga to Mozhaisk with 36,000 infantry,
3,800 cavalry, and 84 guns, etc . . . And if this is not
enough to destroy the scoundrel, then I'll tell you:
"Well, militia of Moscow! We'll go, too, at the
head of 100,000 fine fellows, we'll take with us the
Iverian Mother of God and 150 guns and we'll finish
the job all together!" ' The Governor-General of Moscow must have felt that he had gone a little too far,
for he tacked on a few words at the end, as if in em-
barrassment: 'Read this through! It is all perfectly
clear. There is no need to comment!' The people did
not 'comment'; they simply did not believe a single
word of this circus talk. The good Count, who spoke
French more correctly than Russian, didn't quite come
off as a showman or Santa Claus.

Not content with his posters, Rostopchin began to
ape the good old Caliph Haroun-al-Raschid, and stroll
through the streets of Moscow talking with the 'people,'
that is, the merchants and persons wearing the old-
fashioned Russian attire. He made it his business to tell
them tall stories about the magnificent stand made by
the Russian armies and assure them that the scoundrel,
meaning Napoleon, would never see Moscow. He
learned then and there that the average Muscovite was
not to be fooled by the average General. 'My presence
attracted many merchants and people, with whom I
talked in simple language, telling them some good news
or other, which later they disseminated through the
city. You must be careful with these people,' adds
Rostopchin not without sadness, 'because no one pos-
sesses such a large store of common sense as the Russian, and they often made such observations and asked
such questions as would have embarrassed even a diplo-

mat versed in the arts of dispute.' No wonder. The
bearded Muscovites, whom Rostopchin praises so highly
for their patriotism and common sense, could not, of
course, accept his cock-and-bull stories as gospel truth.
He, who loathed the French, was in many respects closer
to the worst type of Marseillais, the babbler, the braggart, the cheerful liar, than to the average Muscovite,
who every day through a thousand channels received
reports of the terrible storm that was devastating his
homeland. Rostopchin's talk was a sheer waste of time
and breath. The Russian people genuinely loved their
homeland, and there could be nothing in common between them and this frivolous *grand seigneur,* this club
wit, who felt happier in Paris, whither he actually went
after the war—and remained till shortly before his
death.

In his absurd clownish placards Rostopchin categorically promised that the French would not come to Moscow. 'The Moscow citizen Karniushka Chikhirin,' a
character invented by him, 'drank a glass too many . . .
flew into a rage and cursed all Frenchmen in filthy language.' 'How will you manage to get here?' he shouted
at the (absent) scoundrel Bonaparte. 'No, you won't see
Ivan the Great, not even in a dream, and you won't
see the Poklonnaya either . . . ! Better not try, but
turn round and go home! And learn what the Russian
nation's like for all time to come!' And now Napoleon
with his suite stood on Poklonnaya Hill gazing at Moscow, while he, Rostopchin, had to flee from Moscow as
fast as he could, knowing that hundreds of thousands
of fugitives were cursing him because they had believed
him and had not run soon enough. The Governor-General's position was difficult indeed.

Rostopchin was beside himself with rage when he

heard of the council at Fili and Kutuzov's irrevocable decision.

A general flight from Moscow began. Rostopchin's last proclamation was interpreted as a signal for the entire people to take up arms and fight a battle at Poklonnaya Hill. When the news spread, however, that no battle would be fought, an angry crowd gathered round the Governor-General's house. Night came, the last night before the surrender of Moscow. But the night brought no peace.

On 13 September, at eleven o'clock on the eve of Napoleon's entry into Moscow, the Duke of Oldenburg and the Prince of Württemberg came to Rostopchin with a strange request. They wanted him to go to Kutuzov and persuade him not to yield Moscow. Quite reasonably, Rostopchin advised them to do it themselves, particularly as one of them was the Tsar's own cousin, and the other his uncle. 'The Princes informed me that they had gone to see Prince Kutuzov, but that he was asleep and they were not admitted to his presence. Expressing many regrets and severe censure of Prince Kutuzov they departed, leaving me full of bitterness and misery at the thought of Moscow's fate.'

At ten o'clock on the following day, Rostopchin ordered his carriage. But the people were already waiting for him; it was not so easy to run away from Moscow. An immense crowd had been waiting since early morning at the gates of his palace. The man who was now abandoning Moscow to her fate had for months been telling these people that in no circumstance would he allow the scoundrel to enter the city. The scoundrel was about to enter Moscow, and the same Rostopchin was cravenly running away!

The enraged rabble surged towards the Governor-

General's house, shouting that they had been deceived, that Moscow had been betrayed to the enemy. The crowd grew in numbers, and became more and more inflamed. It called for the Governor-General to explain himself. The loud cry went up: 'Let him come out to us! Or else we shall get to him!' Rostopchin went out before the people who 'greeted him with angry cries'—we know these details from Karolina Pavlova, who quotes the words of her father, K. Yanish, and other Muscovites who had lived through this time.

The crowd round the palace and his waiting carriage was out for blood. Rostopchin promptly realized whose blood could save him. He ordered Vereshchagin brought from jail, and invited the people to execute him. But the crowd was silent. Rostopchin then ordered two non-commissioned officers to *kill* Vereshchagin, and while the crowd's attention was turned to the corpse, sped from Moscow.

A month and a half later Rostopchin explained his deed to the Minister of Justice: 'As to Vereshchagin, this traitor and state criminal was, immediately before the entry of the scoundrels into Moscow, delivered by me to the crowd, which surrounded him and, seeing in him the voice of Napoleon and the herald of their misfortunes, sacrificed him to their just anger.' Rostopchin was lying, and he was to lie again and again about his crime. Only in his Memoirs did he tell the truth about the murder of Vereshchagin: 'Having ordered Vereshchagin and Muton brought to me, I turned to the first-named, and I began to reproach him for his crime, which was all the more odious because he alone among the entire Moscow population had conceived the desire to betray his Fatherland. I announced to him that he had been sentenced to death by the Senate and that he must suffer the sentence, and I ordered two non-commissioned officers of my convoy to kill him with their sabres. He fell without uttering a word. Then, turning to Muton, who awaited the same fate, and stood there praying, I said to him: "I grant you your life. Go to your own folk and tell them that the scoundrel whom I have just disposed of was the only Russian to betray his Fatherland." '

He was telling the truth on the main point: that it was not the people at all, but he, Rostopchin, who killed Vereshchagin. Yet even here he did not admit his real motive—his own personal cowardice.

The 'psychology' of this murder is not very complex: on the day of the French entry into Moscow, Rostopchin's position in the eyes of the inhabitants who had remained (and even of those who had left) was humiliating and ludicrous. Even aside from his absurd placards, he had up to the last hour given official assurance, in print and by word of mouth, that Moscow would not be yielded, 'come what may.' And all this noisy patriotic verbiage, all this bluster, aroused the just indignation of the Moscow public against their foolish, frivolous Governor-General. He had to pretend somehow that Moscow would not actually have been surrendered had it not at the last moment been betrayed from within, by Vereschagin.

While the crowd trampled and tore the body of Vereshchagin, Rostopchin made haste to get away from the city under the protection of Kutuzov's army.

It was then that Rostopchin ran into Kutuzov at Yauza Bridge.

Here Rostopchin, in his Memoirs, tells a most obvious falsehood. At this meeting he maintains Kutuzov said to him: 'I can assure you that I do not intend to leave Moscow without giving a battle.' Rostopchin, according to himself, 'made no reply to him, as any reply to such an absurdity would only have been nonsense.' No one—and particularly Prince Golitsin, who was on the spot—heard any such thing—and Prince Golitsin is a witness for whom it was just as natural to speak the truth as it was for Rostopchin to lie and to boast. And aside from that, the entire scene is absolutely implausible. In Kutuzov's eyes Rostopchin was a wholly insignificant personage; the Field Marshal could not possibly have tried to justify himself in his eyes, or make such absurd promises. Moreover, we know from other reports that Rostopchin did ask Kutuzov something, and that Kutuzov simply paid no attention to him. When irritated, Kutuzov was quite capable of putting Alexander Pavlovich himself in his place. And the moment had not yet come when Rostopchin could write Kutuzov letters charged with malice and affront.

The survivors of Borodino looked gloomily downwards as they passed the Field Marshal. Many had not fully recovered from their wounds, and could scarcely drag their feet. Others were weak from starvation. Towards evening, refugees from the city brought news that the French had occupied the Kremlin.

·   ·   ·

On 9 September, Napoleon was in Mozhaisk. He was still suffering from his cold and remained there until 12 September. He overtook his army on the thirteenth as the vanguard was approaching Poklonnaya Hill.

Napoleon spent the night of 13-14 September in the village of Vyazem. That night and morning, the French vanguard marched past Vyazem on the road to Mos-

cow. Would Kutuzov offer battle on the heights surrounding Moscow? The answer was not yet clear to the
Imperial Staff. As we have seen, the Russians themselves
did not know until the council of Fili.

On the morning of 14 September, Napoleon and his
suite rode slowly towards Poklonnaya Hill. The marshals followed at some distance. Their irritation and resentment at the Emperor's refusal to let his Guard complete the victory at Borodino had not yet passed. During these days, Napoleon rarely spoke to them and the
court etiquette forbade starting a conversation with
His Majesty on one's own initiative.

At two o'clock in the afternoon Napoleon with his
suite ascended Poklonnaya Hill, and Moscow unfolded
before their eyes. A bright sun shone down on the vast
city sparkling with innumerable golden domes. The Old
Guard, following Napoleon's suite, suddenly forgot
discipline. They broke ranks and rushed upon the hill.
Thousands of voices cried: 'Moscow! Moscow! Long
live the Emperor!' And again: 'Moscow! Moscow!' On
the peak of the hill, Napoleon stopped and, unable to
restrain his joy, also exclaimed: 'Moscow!' Count Ségur,
who was present, tells us that the marshals promptly
forgot their resentment and, 'drunken with the enthusiasm of glory,' rushed towards the Emperor with
congratulations: 'Here, at last, is the famous city!'
Napoleon said: 'It was time!' Even in this moment of
triumph Napoleon did not forget what it had cost him
to win the great Eurasian beauty.

Not Milan, or Venice, or Alexandria and Cairo, or
Jaffa, or Berlin, or Lisbon, or Madrid, or Warsaw, or
Amsterdam, or Rome, or Antwerp—not a single capital
his troops had entered as victors—had in his eyes and in
the eyes of his army such a tremendous political sig-

nificance as Moscow, the connecting link between
Europe and Asia, the key to world domination. In
Moscow the Emperor expected that Alexander would
sue for peace; the army expected warm apartments,
plentiful provisions, all the comforts and indulgences of
a big city after an agonizing campaign marked by starvation rations, absence of drinking water, sultry heat,
and constant clashes with a brave and stubborn foe.

Persons who experienced these hours on Poklonnaya
Hill, generals of the suite and the Old Guard, the
guards themselves, said later that for them this was the
culminating point of the campaign of 1812; they were
then ready to believe that the resistance of the Russian
people was broken, and that the signing of a truce, followed by peace, was but a matter of days.

The sun began to set in the west. Murat with his
cavalry had already entered the city, and, in a parallel
stream, somewhat to the left, the corps of Beauharnais.
Napoleon wished to receive a deputation from the city
here, on Poklonnaya Hill, and he knew that the first
thing Murat and Eugène would do on entering the
city would be to get in touch with the Moscow authorities and Moscow population, who would be directed to
send this deputation with the keys of the city.

But no deputation appeared. Suddenly an incredible
report began to spread, first among the Guard, then
among the suite, till it reached Napoleon: there would
be no deputation from the inhabitants of the city, because there were no inhabitants in Moscow. Moscow
had been abandoned by the entire population. This
news seemed to Napoleon so preposterous that at first
he simply refused to believe it. Finally he decided to
abandon Poklonnaya Hill and he rode up to Dorogomilov Gate. There he summoned Count Daru: 'Moscow is

empty! Incredible! We must enter. Go and bring me
some of the Boyars!' Napoleon, apparently, had received the impression from his spies that the higher
aristocrats in Russia bore the formal title of 'Boyars,'
as those in England were called Lords.

Daru rode into the city but soon returned without
any 'Boyars.' He merely confirmed that the city was
empty, that its inhabitants had vanished. 'But such was
Napoleon's stubbornness, that he insisted on waiting,'
wrote Ségur, the most truthful of Napoleon's worship-
pers. 'Finally, an officer, either anxious to please or
convinced that everything desired by the Emperor must
take place, penetrated the city, caught five or six va-
grants, and, pushing them forward with his horse,
brought them into the presence of the Emperor, imag-
ining that he had brought a deputation. From the very
first answer of these unfortunates, Napoleon saw that he
had before him but a few pitiful day-labourers.'

To Napoleon, this absurd masquerade was a bitter
insult: 'Oh, the Russians don't know yet what the capture of their city will do to them!' he exclaimed. He
waited for news from Murat, who had been ordered to
occupy the Kremlin.

Murat with his staff and cavalry entered Moscow
about midday. The previous day he had concluded an
agreement with Miloradovich. Murat, commander of
the French vanguard, pledged himself not to interfere
with the passage of the Russian army through the city,
while Miloradovich, commander of the Russian rear-
guard, pledged himself not to undertake any hostile
action against Murat. Hence, Murat did not fear to
stretch his cavalry along the narrow endless Arbat,
though if the Russians had chosen to attack they could

have inflicted heavy losses upon the thin file and held up its advance.

Everything was quiet, silent, dead. Here and there, at street intersections, a few persons lounged about. Later, the French spoke of their uncanny feeling as they moved past the vacant windows and doors of the great city. They realized that the people were not hiding, that these houses and yards were empty, that no one was in the city. Actually, a few thousand persons of all sorts remained—no exact count was possible. There were those who just hadn't managed to get away; there were foreigners—Frenchmen, Swiss, Italians, Poles, Germans—who hoped that the conqueror would show himself kind; and there were a few Russian soldiers who had deserted or who just happened to stray into the city. But these few thousand persons were lost in the vast emptiness.

The cavalry proceeded cautiously, fearing an ambush and expecting a surprise attack at every corner. But the silence persisted, while the French army poured into the city in endless streams. Only when the advance detachment of Murat's cavalry reached the Kremlin, several shots were fired from behind its locked gates. With a cannon shot, the French forced the gates and killed a few men within. To this day, no one knows who these men were. Their corpses were thrown away somewhere, and no one took the trouble to establish their identity. When the French broke into the fortress, one of the defenders furiously flung himself upon a French officer, trying to strangle him, and bit his hand. He was killed like the others.

Before sunset, Napoleon was informed by Murat, Poniatowski, and Eugène that the city had been occupied without opposition. Napoleon decided not to spend his first night (14-15 September) in the Kremlin, but in one of the abandoned houses near Dorogomilov Gate, where he had stopped with his suite after leaving Poklonnaya Hill. He was very gloomy. 'What a terrible desert!' he exclaimed, surveying the desolate streets. This was quite different from his entrance into the other European capitals, or Alexandria.

Even before he retired for the night several adjutants and orderlies came to report from various parts of the city. Each had one and the same story to tell: fires were breaking out everywhere.

Napoleon did not at once realize the full significance of this fact. At first he assumed that the soldiers of his army were looting the abandoned houses and that their carelessness was responsible for the fires. Actual reports of looting were coming in. He summoned Marshal Mortier, whom he had just appointed Military Governor of Moscow, and sternly commanded him to stop the pillaging. 'You will answer with your head for this!' the Emperor added.

He had not yet fallen asleep, when, at three o'clock in the morning, he was informed that the heart of the city was on fire. Gostinny Dvor, the centre of Moscow trade, was aflame; houses never entered by a French soldier, and situated in districts to which no French soldier had penetrated, were burning. The wind blew furiously, the sparks fell like a dense rain of fire and ignited the neighbouring buildings. The sun rose, and in the daylight dense clouds of smoke floated over the city.

On the morning of 15 September, Napoleon rode from Dorogomilov to the Kremlin, where he decided to take up residence. The spectacle of Moscow with its magnificent palaces and churches impressed him as

much as it had from Poklonnaya Hill. His emotions
seem to have been shared by his officers and men. An
officer of the French Commissariat, in a letter written on
15 October and later intercepted by the Cossacks, describes the entry of the French into Moscow: '. . . We
entered the city in the hope of finding inhabitants and
enjoying a rest from foul bivouacs, but no one was
there, save a few Frenchmen and foreigners who had
refused to follow the Russians. Everything was quiet
and nothing presaged the terrible happenings that followed. On entering Moscow I was seized with astonishment and enthusiasm, because I had expected to see a
wooden city, as many had told me, but on the contrary
nearly all the houses were of brick and in the most ele-
gant and most modern style. The homes of private persons are like palaces, and everything was rich and magnificent. We were quartered in a very good house.'

On his third day in the capital, Napoleon wrote to
Marie-Louise: 'The city is as big as Paris. There are
1,600 church towers here, and over a thousand beautiful palaces; the city is provided with everything. The
nobility has left, the merchants have also been forced to
depart, the people have remained . . . The enemy is
retreating, apparently towards Kazan. An excellent conquest this—the result of the battle near Moscow.'

Why Napoleon thought that the 'people' remained is
unknown. He soon realized, in any case, that there were
virtually no people in Moscow, save those few thousand
who hid themselves in various corners of the immense
city.

The French could scarcely believe their eyes as they
roamed about the vast capital and saw that it was
empty. The impression was eerie and sinister. 'Following the infantry,' writes a French artilleryman, 'I passed

through immense squares and broad streets. I glanced into the windows of every house and, not finding a soul within, I grew numb with horror. From time to time we passed cavalry regiments galloping along the streets and, like ourselves, meeting no one.' Few as yet grasped what had happened. 'I announced loudly that the city had been abandoned by its inhabitants; even today I cannot recall without laughter the admonitory tone in which Captain Lefrançais replied: "Big cities like this are not abandoned so easily. These rascals must have hidden. We'll find them, and they'll yet get down on their knees before us." '

But by the morning of 15 September, the full weight of the catastrophe was clear. The fires begun the night before had spread over half of the city and were increasing.

First of all, the Wine Arcade burned down, with the New Arcades and the Market Stalls, and a powder magazine blew up. Then, in several places simultaneously, houses and churches began to burn, 'in particular, all the factories . . .'—'These fires continued for six days on end, so that it was difficult to distinguish between night and day. During all this time, looting continued.' The French soldiers, followed by French marauders, entered the houses and dragged out everything that had not been burned. They took linens, fur coats, even women's capes. 'Often pedestrians in the streets were stripped of everything down to their shirts; others were deprived only of their boots or coats. If the victims resisted, they were frenziedly beaten, often to death.' Some of the soldiers applied torture, especially to church wardens, to make them surrender the church treasures which they had allegedly hidden. 'The French tortured even merchants and peasants, taking them for priests on account of their beards.' Those caught in the streets were forced to work, to carry the sacks of loot, to dig trenches and 'to drag the corpses of men and horses off the roads.'

According to a letter, dated 19 September, from General Tutolmin, who had remained in Moscow, to the Tsar, the fires began on the night of 14 September, a few hours after Murat's cavalry entered the city, and on the following day 'were greatly increased by the incendiaries.' On 16 September, 'the ferocity and horror of the conflagration grew so great that I cannot describe them to Your Imperial Majesty: all Moscow was enveloped in flames, which a strong wind helped to spread, and the city is badly ravaged.'

Rostopchin, of course, actively co-operated in starting the fires in Moscow, though towards the end of his life, while living in Paris, he published a pamphlet denying it. At other times, however, he boasted of his part in the fires, calling it an act of patriotism.

Here is Police Superintendent Voronenko's official report to the Moscow Administration: 'On 14 September, at five in the morning, Count Rostopchin ordered me to go to the Wine Arcade and the Custom House . . . and in the event of a sudden entry by enemy troops, to destroy everything with fire, which order I carried out in various places as far as it was possible in sight of the enemy until ten o'clock in the evening . . .'

It is more than probable that independently of Rostopchin's arrangements other persons left behind in Moscow risked their lives to destroy anything that might be useful to the enemy. Finally, many fires were doubtless started by the French, while looting. Large

stores of liquor fell into their hands, and from the very
first days, the drunkenness among the French troops
was unbelievable.

·   ·   ·

The whole day of 15 September the conflagration
spread, reaching menacing proportions. The entire
Kitai Gorod (China City) and the New Arcades at the
very walls of the Kremlin were wrapped in flames, and
there could be no question of saving them. The invading soldiers began to pillage the shops of the Commercial Rows and the New Arcades. On the banks of the
Moskva River, towards evening of the fifteenth, the
flour elevators caught fire and the flying sparks ex-
ploded a large store of grenades and bombs abandoned
by the garrison. Carriage Row and the Balchug, near
the Moskvoretsky Bridge, also caught fire. In some
quarters, the flames were so bright that it seemed like
day. The centre of the city and the Kremlin were as
yet virtually untouched. The large Old Arcades had
burned down. Then came the night of 15-16 September, dwarfing all previous disasters.

That night Napoleon was awakened by the bright
light which suddenly illumined his windows. Half
awakened by the glow, the officers of his suite thought
that morning had come. The Emperor went to one
window, then to another; he looked out on all sides,
and everywhere the spectacle was the same: an unen-
durably bright light, immense sheets of flame, streets
transformed into rivers of fire, palaces and large houses
all burning like vast bonfires. A powerful gale fanned
the flames and drove them straight on the Kremlin; the
moan of the wind was so strong that at times it inter-

rupted and drowned the crash of collapsing buildings and the howl of the raging flames.

Napoleon, his suite, and the Old Guard were staying in the Kremlin. The previous day the French artillery stores had been brought there, and the powder magazine, abandoned by the Russian garrison because of the lack of facilities to transport it, was still in the fortress. A raging wind bore the flames towards the Kremlin. One of its towers was already on fire. It was necessary to leave at once, without wasting a minute. Napoleon was very pale but had recovered self-possession. He gazed silently through the window of the palace and said: 'They themselves are setting it afire. What a people! They are Scythians!' Later he said: 'What resoluteness! The barbarians! What a terrible spectacle!'

The Emperor's suite surrounded him. Marshal Mortier, who was doing everything in his power to save the Kremlin, categorically announced that the Emperor must immediately leave; otherwise he was in danger of being burned alive. Napoleon hesitated. The previous day, as he entered the palace, he had turned to his suite and said: 'So at last I am in Moscow, in the ancient palace of the Tsars, in the Kremlin!' He knew the significance of the Kremlin in Russian history and he did not like to leave it. But this was no time for deliberation: at any moment the fire threatened to envelop the palace and cut off all exits. Dawn was breaking and the situation was growing worse. The smoke and dust which filled the palace made breathing difficult. 'This exceeds all imagination,' said Napoleon to Caulaincourt. 'This is a war of extermination. Such terrible tactics have no precedent in the history of civilization . . . To burn one's own cities! . . . A demon inspires these people!

What savage determination! What a people! What a people!'

The marshals and the suite unanimously renewed their entreaties, urging the Emperor to leave the palace immediately. The Russians, they said, having organized the systematic burning of Moscow, had decided to turn their efforts on the palace in order to do away with Napoleon. Viceroy Eugène, Napoleon's favourite and stepson, and Marshall Berthier fell on their knees, imploring the Emperor to abandon the Kremlin. From all sides came loud cries: 'The Kremlin is on fire!' The Emperor decided to move into the Petrovsky Palace, which was at that time situated beyond the city limits, in the midst of thickets and vacant lots.

He left the fortress accompanied by his suite and the Old Guard, but all of them nearly perished in this effort to save themselves. The Viceroy, Ségur, Berthier, and Murat walked with the Emperor. They never forgot this exit from the Kremlin. Count Ségur's well-known description follows:

'We were besieged by an ocean of flames: flames closed all our exits from the fortress before us and repulsed our first attempts to leave. We finally found a narrow path between the stone walls leading to the Moskva River. By this narrow passage, Napoleon, his officers, and his Guard managed to escape from the Kremlin. But what had they gained? Being closer to the fire, they could neither retreat nor remain where they were. But how could they advance, how plunge into the waves of this fiery sea? Those who ran about in the streets, stupefied by the gale, blinded by the ashes, could not recognize where they were, because the streets vanished in smoke and ruins. But haste was imperative. Every instant the roar of the flames grew louder. The

only street, winding and all in flames, seemed more like
an entrance into the inferno than an exit from it. Without wavering, the Emperor, on foot, dashed into the
dangerous passage. He strode forward through the flaming bonfires, to the crash of collapsing arches, falling
rafters, and melting iron roofs. The ruins hindered his
footsteps . . . We walked upon burning ground, between two walls of fire. The piercing heat burned our
eyes, but we had to keep them open and alert to the
danger. The stifling air, the flying sparks, and tongues
of flame scorched the air we breathed; our breath grew
dry, short, gasping and we almost choked from the
smoke . . .'

Napoleon and his suite were saved by marauding soldiers who happened to be in the neighbourhood.

The Emperor moved to the Petrovsky Palace. For two
days longer, the seventeenth and eighteenth, the fire
raged, destroying three fourths of the city. Sporadic fires
continued after that, and during the entire stay of the
French in Moscow there was scarcely any day without
its fire. Napoleon was in the gloomiest state of mind.
'This presages great misfortunes for us,' he said, looking at the ruins and smoking debris into which the
wealthiest parts of the city had been turned. What mattered was not merely the unexpected loss of the conquered booty. The Emperor clearly realized that peace
with Alexander would now be even more difficult than
before. He did not yet understand that a peace with
Russia was not only difficult but impossible, that for
the Russian people the war which he considered ended
by the capture of Moscow was only beginning.

Napoleon's suite and those detachments of the army
which had left the Kremlin for the Petrovsky Palace
gazed for hours at burning Moscow. 'The flaming city

was a terrifying spectacle,' says a French witness. 'By
night we could see the line of fire, over a mile long. It
looked like a volcano with many craters. For three days,
while the conflagration continued, we remained in the
Petrovsky Palace. On the fourth day we returned to the
city and saw only ruins and ashes. The Kremlin was
preserved . . .'

During these and the following days, the wholesale
looting of houses and shops continued. It was impossible to restrain the soldiers, and many perished in the
flames—not all managed to leave the burning buildings
in time. Nevertheless, a certain number of stores of
flour and other provisions escaped the blaze. The
French soldiers were struck by the luxury of the interi-
ors, the furniture of exquisite craftsmanship in a few
private houses which accidentally remained intact. 'It
is very sad to walk among the streets, piled with debris,
and never meet a single inhabitant.'

'The devastation and fires continue,' wrote a Russian
who remained in Moscow, on 30 September. 'Afterwards, the buildings are demolished by cannon fire as
though they were fortresses . . . The abuses are great
and some have been punished, but now Sébastiani himself says he is unable to stop them. The Frenchmen are
drunk every day after dinner, and the inhabitants kill
them, and bury them in the night. The number of
these victims, however, is small . . . The French are
sad and resentful because the Russians have not sued
for peace, as Napoleon had promised they would;
hence, the French soldiers hope that by devastation and
pillage they will force us to make a peace . . . The
inhabitants are stripped of their shirts and boots, and
forced to perform all sorts of labour; they are not fed.
Sometimes they die of hunger and exhaustion, where-

upon others are taken in the houses and in the streets to replace them. Oddly enough, many of the French themselves flee daily, perhaps a hundred soldiers or more; there is no way to control them, and they refuse to obey their commanders. Every day some are shot for insubordination.'

The shooting of incendiaries, or, more exactly, of those whom the French chose to regard as incendiaries, began on the second day of the fires. On 24 September, in the house of Prince Dolgorukov, a court martial began to function under the chairmanship of General Michel, commander of the First Grenadier Regiment of the Guard. This court was called the Military Committee. At the first sitting, 26 men were tried and 10 sentenced to be shot; as for the remaining 16, the verdict was rather curious: 'The Military Committee, having taken into consideration that the evidence against these persons is insufficient, hereby sentences them to confinement in prison.' There was no more evidence against the first ten, and why any distinction was made is incomprehensible. Among those tried were black-smiths, tailors, painters, lackeys, and soldiers. Others were Kassianov, a sexton, and Ignatiev, a lieutenant in a Moscow regiment, who was shot. The executions continued for several days. There were many cases of outright murder, committed by pillaging soldiers on pretext of self-defence against arrested 'incendiaries.' Napoleon himself, in a letter to Alexander written on 20 September, acknowledged that he had shot 400 'incendiaries.' Here is a little picture: 'The streets are littered with dead men and horses; on the Tver boulevard lie many who have been hanged or shot. Beside them stands a placard reading: "Incendiaries of Moscow." '

Napoleon received reports of the outrageous looting

carried on by his army, particularly the Bavarians,
Westphalians, and Italians. He knew that even soldiers
belonging to French units were engaged in pillaging.
He also realized that instead of the promised winter
quarters his army had only the charred remnants of a
large city, a smoking ruin. What would Europe think
of the burning of Moscow? What would it say to this
success of the Russians, who had literally snatched the
prize from Napoleon's hands?

Napoleon's letter to Empress Marie-Louise gives as
usual a 'stylized' version of the facts. It was written on
18 September while the fire was raging. '*Mon amie,* I
have written you about Moscow. I had no real conception of this city. It contained five hundred palaces as
handsome as the Elysée, furnished in French style with
incredible luxury; a few Imperial palaces; barracks;
magnificent hospitals. All this has vanished, the fire has
been consuming everything for the last four days. As
all the small houses of citizens are made of wood, they
go up in flames like matches. The governor of the city
and the Russians themselves burned down this beautiful city, because of their rage at their defeat. Twelve
thousand inhabitants are in misery and despair in the
streets. But enough is left for the army, which has found
all sorts of riches; the disorder encourages much looting. For Russia the loss is enormous, her trade will be
greatly affected. These wretches have been thorough to
the point of removing or destroying all the fire pumps.'
On the same day, about eight o'clock in the evening,
the Emperor added a few lines: 'Only a third of the
houses remain. The soldiers have found plenty of goods
and provisions, they have ample stores, and a considerable quantity of French liquor.' This artificial optimism, the constant reiteration of the phrase 'My affairs

are going well' were intended for the Paris Court and for Europe. The Emperor knew perfectly well that his affairs were not going at all as he had expected.

Peace! Immediate peace with Alexander—this became Napoleon's first and chief aim after the Moscow fire. And in this he was to meet the greatest disappointment of his entire career.

.   .   .

About 11 September St. Petersburg heard the first rumours about Borodino and Kutuzov's 'great victory.' The cheerful tidings arrived on the Tsar's birthday and held the capital in a state of joyous excitement for about two days. Then, however, a messenger from Rostopchin to the Tsar brought news of the surrender of Moscow; three days later a courier came with a brief report from Kutuzov himself.

It was not until 16 September, nine days after Borodino and two days after the fall of Moscow, that Kutuzov informed Alexander of these developments. He explained the abandonment of Moscow by the weakening of his army after Borodino. 'I take the liberty and humbly report, Most Gracious Majesty, that the enemy's entry into Moscow does not mean his conquest of Russia.'

After this laconic message the Field Marshal lapsed into silence.

From 16 to 26 September, Kutuzov did not send a single line to Alexander, who 'without concealing his alarm and dismay,' wrote Kutuzov bidding him to communicate with him at least once every two days. In the interval, however, Kutuzov sent Colonel Michaud, a Frenchman and Sardinian noble who had entered the

Russian service after the Kingdom of Sardinia was conquered by Bonaparte, to Alexander with detailed reports. On 20 September, Michaud appeared before Alexander and had a conversation with him, the substance of which he communicated seven years later to Mikhailovsky-Danilevsky, who was at that time commissioned to write a history of the War of 1812 and was collecting materials for the purpose.

Michaud relates his conversation with Alexander in the sugared style which was then regarded as the correct way to speak about Alexander, whom he even calls 'our angel.' In reading Michaud's statement we must discount the courtly excesses of his style, the author's inventions intended to stress his wit, and the limits of the human memory.

'You have brought me some sad news, Colonel?'— 'Alas, very sad: the abandonment of Moscow.'—'How did it happen? Did we lose the battle? Or was my ancient capital given up without a battle?'—'Sire, as the environs of Moscow, unfortunately, did not offer a position from which it was possible to risk a battle with forces smaller than the enemy's, Field Marshal Kutuzov deemed it best to preserve Your Majesty's army, the loss of which would not have saved Moscow, but would have had the gravest consequences . . .'—'Has the enemy entered the city?'—'Yes, Sire, and the city has been turned into ashes. When I left, it was all in flames.'

At these words, writes Michaud, tears ran down Alexander's face. Then the Tsar asked about the mood of the army, and how it had been affected by the abandonment of Moscow. Here Michaud, authentic Frenchman of the *ancien régime,* typical court punster and wit, recounts the fanciful turn of phrase which he promptly devised in reply to Alexander's question about the spirit of the army. Of course he invented all this seven years later at his leisure. Could an unimportant émigré colonel, in the Russian pay, have dared to twist words at such a tragic moment?

'Sire,' Michaud quotes himself as saying, 'will you allow me to speak quite frankly, as an honest military man?'—'I always demand that, and especially at this moment. I beg you, hide nothing from me, speak quite frankly!'—'Sire, my heart bleeds but I must admit to you that when I left, the entire army, from its head to the lowliest soldier, was in a state of terrible fear, in a state of fright . . .'—'What are you saying, Michaud? How could that be? How could such a fear have arisen? Have my Russians fallen into dejection after their misfortune?'—'Never that, Sire. They only fear that Your Majesty, in the goodness of your heart, might be persuaded to conclude peace. They ardently desire to fight and prove to you, with the sacrifice of their lives, how brave they are and how devoted to you!'—'Ah, Colonel, you have taken a load off my soul! Well, return to the army, and tell my valiant soldiers, and my good subjects everywhere you happen to pass, that when there is not a single soldier left, I shall put myself at the head of my beloved nobility and my good peasants, and utilize all the resources of my Empire—there are more of these than my enemies think—but if it be God's will that my dynasty cease to reign on the ancestral throne, then, having used up all the means in my power, I shall grow a beard as long as that'—he pointed to his breast—'and shall eat potatoes with the lowliest of my peasants in the depths of Siberia, rather than put my signature to the shame of my Fatherland and my good subjects, whose sacrifices I know how to value. Providence is putting us to the test. Let us hope that it

will not abandon us.' The Tsar added: 'Colonel
Michaud, don't forget what I am now telling you. Perhaps we shall some day recall this with pleasure. It is
Napoleon or I, either he or I—we can no longer reign
at the same time! I have found him out, and he will
not deceive me again.'

If we exclude the unlikely phrases suggestive of inti-
macy, such words as 'we (i.e. the Tsar and Michaud)
shall recall this,' and so forth, there remains a kernel of
truth in the conversation, confirmed by many analogous
statements. This truth was that Alexander was firmly
resolved to continue the war against Napoleon to the
utmost.

Michaud's unreliability as a witness is clearly demonstrated by his assertion that he had been the first to ap-
prise Alexander of the surrender of Moscow. A document unknown to Michaud—otherwise he would have
refrained from the lie—informs us that Alexander received the first news of Moscow's surrender from Rostopchin by a courier sent on 13 September by way of
Yaroslavl. This document is the reproachful message
brought to Kutuzov's headquarters by Prince Volkonsky. 'I send . . . Prince Volkonsky to learn about the
situation of the army and the causes that have prompted
you to make so unhappy a decision.' These words with
which the message concludes well illustrate the Tsar's
attitude towards the Commander-in-Chief.

The Court of St. Petersburg, the Tsar's family, the
nobles, and the merchants were in a state of extreme
confusion. Would Napoleon advance from Moscow on
St. Petersburg?

The Tsar's sister, Ekaterina Pavlovna, who was at
this time in Yaroslavl, adjured her brother not to make
peace. 'Moscow has been taken . . . Inexplicable

things have happened. But do not forget your resolve:
no peace of any kind—there is still hope of restoring
your honour . . . My dear friend, no peace of any
kind, and even if you had to go to Kazan, no peace of
any kind'—wrote the Tsar's sister on receiving the first
news of Napoleon's entry into the ancient capital.

Alexander promptly answered his sister that he did
not even think of peace. 'Remain assured that my resolve to go on fighting is more unshakable than ever.
I should rather cease to be what I am than to compromise with the monster who is the misfortune of the
entire world . . . I put my trust in God, in the ad-
mirable character of our nation, and in my staunch resolve not to submit to the yoke.'

Of course, Alexander, too, may have been swept by a
natural feeling of offended vanity, irritation, and anger.
But the cause of the Tsar's firm behaviour after such a
terrible blow as the loss of Moscow must above all be
sought in his position with regard to the higher aristocracy and nobility, the broad circles of generals and officers (especially, those of the Guard) and the merchants
who had a stake in the export trade. He knew that a
new Tilsit would not be forgiven him; even before the
war he clearly understood that if war came he would
have to emerge from it with honour or lose the throne.
And he knew only too well, by the fate of his father
and grandfather, that in St. Petersburg those who lose
their throne do not long survive.

At about the time when Alexander was assuring
Colonel Michaud and his sister that he would never
compromise with Napoleon, Caulaincourt was explaining to Napoleon why it was impossible for the Tsar to
conclude peace. In 1811, Alexander had given Caulaincourt, then ambassador in St. Petersburg, a message to

his sovereign: 'Tell Emperor Napoleon that the ground is shaking beneath me, that in my own empire my situation has become unbearable through Napoleon's violation of his agreements. Convey to him in my name this honest and final notice: that once the war has begun, then—one of us, either he, Napoleon, or I, Alexander, must lose his crown.' This was no mere phrase; it fully expressed the Tsar's deep conviction, which in this case only reflected the objective truth.

And now, after the loss of Moscow, Alexander's own sister wrote him exactly what he himself had declared to Napoleon. There was no need of convincing the Tsar. He knew that the destruction of the Russian army on the field of Borodino, the loss of Smolensk, the loss of Moscow, the loss of half of Russia would be forgiven him, but a peace with Napoleon, never. The moment had come to decide which of the two was to lose his crown: Napoleon or Alexander.

The Tsar's determination was only intensified by what he saw happening round him. The temper of the nation had become much more frank, direct, impassioned.

On leaving Epiphani at three o'clock in the morning of 17 September, the merchant Marakuyev saw 'from the direction of Moscow a strong glow, very different from the ordinary glow; on the horizon the sky was like a burning pillar which seemed to be wavering or trembling . . . I beheld it, speechless, numbed with fear, pity, and dreadful uncertainty.'

'Fear' and 'pity' do not adequately describe the impression that the conflagration produced on the peasants: on this point all the existing documents are unanimous.

In October, General Lauriston, Napoleon's ambassa-

dor, complained to Kutuzov about the 'barbaric' conduct of the Russian peasants towards the French. The
old Field Marshal by way of apology and explanation
said that the Russian peasants treated the French as
their ancestors had treated the Mongols. Lauriston was
not satisfied with this comparison between His Majesty's civilized army and the hordes of Genghis Khan, but
it accurately illustrates the psychology of the Russian
peasant, who saw a colossal armed horde invading his
homeland, looting, burning, killing, and torturing. For
many years after the event, peasants living round Moscow described the Napoleonic invasion as the 'Tartar
devastation.'

After Borodino and the loss of Moscow, the will to
destroy the intruders became national in the full sense
of the word. Napoleon had gambled on terrorizing
Russia, and lost.

.   .   .

Ekaterina Pavlovna, however, was not reassured by
Alexander's letter. On 19 September, she again wrote
her brother: 'I cannot restrain myself any longer, notwithstanding the pain which I am forced to inflict on
you. The capture of Moscow has caused extreme irritation. Dissatisfaction has reached the highest point, and
your person is far from being spared. If such things
reach even me, you may judge the rest for yourself.
You are loudly blamed for the misfortune which has
overtaken our Empire, for the general devastation and
the ruin of private persons, and, finally, for having dis-
honoured the country and yourself. It is not one class
that brings these charges against you, but all classes.
Not to mention what is being said about the way we
are carrying on the war. You are chiefly attacked for

violating your word to Moscow . . . abandoning the
city. It looks as though you had betrayed the city. You
need not fear a catastrophe of a revolutionary kind. But
you can judge for yourself the state of affairs in a country whose head is despised. There is nothing that people
would not do to restore our honour, but, considering
their desire to sacrifice everything for the Fatherland,
they ask: "What good will that do if everything is destroyed, spoiled, by the incapacity of our leaders?" The
desire for peace is, fortunately, far from universal, because the feeling of shame caused by the loss of Moscow
engenders a desire for revenge. People are blaming you,
and blaming you loudly. I think it is my duty to tell
you this, dear friend, because it is extremely important.
What you should do is not for me to say, but do save
your honour, which is being attacked. Your presence
may incline minds toward you; do not neglect any
means to achieve this end, and please do not think that
I exaggerate. No, unfortunately, I speak the truth, and
my heart bleeds for you; I owe you a great deal, and I
would give my life a thousand times to save you from
the situation in which you now find yourself.'

In his answer, dated 30 September, Alexander tries to
rehabilitate himself, at least in his sister's eyes. Her
letter offended and distressed him. In the course of his
entire life no one had so directly insulted him, except
perhaps for Napoleon in 1804, when he had transpar-
ently hinted that the Tsar had killed his father.

'It is quite common,' wrote Alexander, 'for those who
are stricken by misfortune to be unjustly treated, accused, and tormented. I have never entertained any
kind of illusions in this respect. I have known that this
would happen to me, if fate did not favour me . . .
Despite my reluctance to weary anyone with personal

details, a reluctance which is vastly intensified when I find myself in misfortune, my sincere attachment to you impels me to overcome this feeling, and I shall set the matter down as I see it.

'What more can a man do than follow his best conviction? That alone has guided me. It made me appoint Barclay commander of the First Army on the basis of the reputation he won in previous wars with the French and the Swedes. This conviction made me think that his abilities were higher than those of Bagration. When this conviction was further intensified by Bagration's major errors committed in the present campaign, errors which are partly responsible for our defeats, I considered him even less capable of commanding both armies which had united at Smolensk. Although I was rather dissatisfied with Barclay's actions, I regarded him as less inadequate than Bagration in the matter of strategy, of which Bagration hadn't the slightest idea. In a word, it was my conviction at that time that there was no better man . . .'

The Tsar had been advised that army men considered Barclay and Bagration equally incapable of commanding such large masses and wanted Peter Pahlen for the job. 'I shall not go into the untrustworthy and perfidious character and crimes of this man, but just remember that he has not seen an enemy for 18 to 20 years . . . How could I depend on him, and where is the proof of his military talent? In St. Petersburg I found that everyone favoured the appointment of old Kutuzov as Commander-in-Chief. This was the general clamour. What I knew personally of the man at first repelled me, but when in a letter of 5 August Rostopchin informed me that all Moscow wanted Kutuzov to command, because, in their opinion, Barclay and Bagra-

tion were incompetent; and, as Barclay was committing
one stupidity after another at Smolensk, I could not
help yielding to the general wish. I appointed Kutuzov.
I still think that in the circumstances I could not have
acted otherwise; from among three generals, equally un-
fitted for the supreme command, I had to choose the
one who was universally favoured.

'Now I shall pass to the point which concerns me
most directly: my personal honour . . . I cannot think
that your letter refers to the personal courage which
every soldier has, and to which I attach no special value.
If I must humiliate myself to discuss this matter, I will
tell you this: the grenadiers of the Malorossiysky and
Kievsky Regiments can assure you that I am quite capable of behaving under fire as calmly as anyone else. But,
again, I do not think that your letter refers to that kind
of courage, and I assume you meant moral courage, the
only kind that matters in critical situations. If I had
remained with the army, I might have been able to
convince you that I have a share of that, too. What I
cannot understand is that you, who, in your letter of
5 August, delivered by Velyashev, pleaded with me,
"For God's sake, don't take the command upon yourself . . . ," thus establishing the fact that I cannot inspire any confidence—I cannot understand what you
mean by saying in your last letter: "Save your honour
. . . Your presence may incline minds towards you."
Do you refer to my presence in the army? How can you
reconcile two such contradictory opinions?'

The Tsar goes on to say that having appointed
Kutuzov, he rejected the idea of joining the army,
partly because of his sister's advice, and partly because
he recalled what this man 'had done at Austerlitz.' The
Tsar, of course, is referring to Kutuzov's conduct before

the fatal battle of 2 December 1805. At that time, the Tsar was neither intelligent nor cunning enough to recognize the game of Napoleon, who pretended to be frightened, in order to lure the Russians to attack him and be destroyed. Napoleon had duped the Tsar; but the Tsar understood Kutuzov's game. He understood that Kutuzov alone had guessed Napoleon's intention, and although he had advised against giving battle, he had not done it with sufficient emphasis; he had yielded too easily, without a strong warning. Alexander had never forgiven Kutuzov, who had so patently revealed his military incompetence—when it was Alexander's dream to be a great military captain. Then, passing to his position after Borodino, the Tsar says that not being with the army, he could not prevent the 'ruinous retreat' and abandonment of Moscow.

Here Alexander again reveals his profound ignorance of military affairs. He thinks (or perhaps merely pretends to) that if not for the 'incapable' Kutuzov, it might have been possible to defeat Napoleon in a new battle immediately after Borodino.

The letter concludes with the assurance that he was serving the Fatherland with all his strength. 'As to talents, perhaps I lack them, but talents cannot be acquired: they are a gift of nature, and no one ever obtained them by his own effort. Served as poorly as I am, lacking necessary weapons in all fields, directing such an enormous machine in such a critical situation, facing an infernal enemy who unites a most extraordinary talent with the most criminal nature, who has all Europe at his command and the most gifted personnel, trained in 20 years of revolution and war—it is not surprising that I should suffer defeats.'

In no other letter to his sister or to anyone else does

the Tsar so fully express his feelings at this time. In his whole life he had not experienced a more critical period than that between Borodino and Tarutino.

In this letter, Alexander gives a fully negative evaluation of the three best generals of his army—Barclay, Bagration, and Kutuzov—and, incidentally, preserves complete silence about a fourth perennial candidate for the supreme command—Bennigsen. And yet if we take seriously Alexander's view about the 'perilous consequences' of the retreat after Borodino, it is clear that Alexander would have preferred Bennigsen to the 'incapable' Kutuzov. During the war of 1807, he had appointed Bennigsen Commander-in-Chief. Only bitter necessity, only the sense of his own helplessness could have compelled Alexander to appoint Kutuzov, whom he hated.

'You are accused of incompetence,' wrote his shrewd and sharp-tongued sister in reply to these outpourings. In the Tsar's helpless situation, a struggle against the loathed one-eyed *vieux satyr*, camped in Tarutino with his army, was out of the question. He had to submit and to wait. Alexander submitted.

The fate of the army and of Russia had passed into Kutuzov's hands.

7

THE RUSSIAN PEOPLE AND THE
INVASION

IN this brief analysis a complete picture of internal conditions in Russia during the invasion is impossible. We shall, however, devote a few pages to the attitude of the various classes among the Russian people towards the event. Let us begin with the peasant serfs.

At first glance, we are confronted by a paradox; the peasants who loathed their servitude, who protested by murders of landowners recorded in annual statistics, and by revolts, which had, only 37 years before, imperiled the entire feudal order by the Pugachev insurrection—the same peasants met Napoleon as a fierce enemy, fighting with all their strength, as no other peasants had fought him except those of Spain. They refused to trade with the enemy, burned their grain and hay, even their huts, particularly if there were any French foragers inside; and actively assisted the guerrillas.

And yet there is definite evidence that as early as 1805-7, and at the beginning of the invasion of 1812,

rumours associating Napoleon with dreams of emanci-
pation circulated among the Russian peasantry (above
all, among servants and near the cities). There was talk
of a letter Napoleon had allegedly sent to the Tsar,
warning him that until he liberated the peasants, there
would be war and no peace. How then shall we account
for so decisive a change in the peasant outlook?

It must be remembered that Napoleon burst upon
Russia as a conqueror, a beast of prey, a ruthless de-
stroyer, and that he never had the slightest intention of
liberating the serfs. For the Russian peasants, the defence of Russia from the invading enemy was a defence
of their lives, their families, their property.

At the beginning of the war, when the French army
occupied Lithuania and White Russia, the White Russian peasants revolted, hoping to liberate themselves
from the *Pani*, their tyrannical White Russian masters.
In July and August 1812, White Russia was swept by
stormy peasant agitation, which in places passed into
open rebellion. In panic, landowners fled to the cities—
to the Duke of Bassano in Vilna, to Marshal Davout in
Moghilev, to General Dombrowski in Minsk, to the
Emperor himself in Vitebsk. They asked for armed
help against the peasants, pleaded for punitive expeditions, since the newly established Polish and Lithuanian gendarmery was not strong enough to maintain
order. The French command promptly crushed the
peasants and restored all the feudal rights. Napoleon's
actions in Lithuania and White Russia had thus shown
that he had no intention of helping the peasants in
their efforts to throw off their chains, and would use
his might to uphold the serf-owning nobles. This was in
accord with his policy: he considered the Polish and
Lithuanian nobles the basic political force in these

places and had no desire to frighten them away by
inspiring their peasants with the idea of liberation.

'The nobles of these Governments of White Russia,'
writes Colonel A. Benckendorf, who served under Wintzengerode, 'paid dearly for their desire to be free of
Russian rule. Their peasants considered themselves free
from the terrible servitude and poverty in which the
greed and dissoluteness of the nobles had kept them.
They revolted in almost all the villages, demolishing
the furniture in the houses of their masters, destroying
the factories, and taking savage pleasure in destroying
the dwellings of their petty tyrants, who had employed
so much cunning to impoverish them. The French
guard, obtained by the nobles for protection from their
peasants, only increased the people's fury; the gendarmes either remained indifferent witnesses of the dis-
orders or had no means of stopping them.' There are
many similar statements.

Marshal Saint-Cyr, who fought in the campaign of
1812, tells in his memoirs that a peasant movement in
Lithuania had begun, and that the peasants were driving the landowners from their estates. 'Faithful to his
new system, Napoleon began to protect the landowners
from their serfs; he returned the landowners to their
estates, from which they had been driven,' and gave
them his soldiers to protect them from the serfs. The
peasant movement, which in some places (chiefly in
western governments) was taking on a distinct character, was ruthlessly crushed by Napoleon.

·   ·   ·

The Russian serf peasantry soon realized that no
liberation could be expected from Napoleon, but it by

no means follows that in 1812 there was no peasant movement against serfdom. Without a doubt, there was such a movement, but with insignificant exceptions it had no connection with the invasion. In the archives and printed sources, we often find deliberately vague and casual hints, statements, and notes on the subject. I shall try to present a few facts, based on concrete data. This aspect of the history of 1812 has been greatly neglected and stands in great need of specialized study.

In 1812, now in one place, now in another, the peasants rose against the landowners, as they did before and after. However, the presence of the enemy army did not strengthen but weakened the anti-landowner movement. The ruthless enemy deflected the peasants' attention from the landowners. The threat that hung over Russia, the enslavement of the entire Russian nation by the alien conqueror, became the first consideration.

We must add that the landowners themselves grew much milder in 1812, and tried to appease the peasants. Numerous landowners fled from their villages to the capitals and district towns; little was heard of them in their estates, and in their absence their stewards conducted themselves better than usual. The people in the villages and in Moscow were often indignant at the gentry for running away from the enemy instead of showing resistance. Patriotic feeling flamed up in the nation, especially after the destruction of Smolensk. Nowhere, not even in Egypt or Syria, did Napoleon's army behave so savagely, nowhere did it kill and torture the population with such cruel cynicism as in Russia. The French took revenge for the firing of the villages and towns, for the burning of Moscow, for the irreconcilable hostility of the Russian people.

The wholesale pillaging by the conquering army, by

countless marauders, and sometimes by criminal bands
of French deserters, caused the peasants' hatred of the
enemy to grow from day to day.

The successive recruiting levies evoked no complaints; on the contrary, they were greeted with unprecedented enthusiasm.

On 12 December 1812, the order went out to choose
8 recruits from every 500 men throughout the country.
This, counting the militia levies, was the third general
levy—at least, for some of the governments.

In ordinary times, recruiting was viewed with loathing and horror. But now, after the loss of Moscow, it
aroused quite other feelings. 'In Tambov everything is
quiet . . .' wrote M. I. Volkova to her friend V. I.
Lanskaya on 30 September. 'Only the noise of the recruits reaches us. We live opposite a recruiting centre.
Every morning we are awakened by thousands of peasants: they weep until their heads are shaved, but as soon
as they are inducted, they begin to sing and to dance.
They say there is nothing to grieve over, for such is
God's will. The better I learn to know this people, the
more I am convinced that there is none better . . .'
Tambov and the Government of Tambov were at this
time threatened with no danger, but patriotic wrath
and indignation outweighed the misery of the peasants. Contemporaries find it hard to restrain their
astonishment, but categorically confirm the fact itself.
We know how these recruits conducted themselves at
Smolensk, at Borodino, at Maloyaroslavets. It was they
who caused Napoleon to set the Russians above any
of his other foes, in regard to their courage and
fortitude.

Napoleon, of course, exaggerated and lied when he
spoke of the 'numerous villages' which entreated him

to liberate them. But isolated attempts to obtain his aid for that purpose were no doubt made, and inevitably so, until it had become clear to all the peasants that Napoleon had never even thought of abrogating the landowners' rule, that he had come as a conqueror and pillager, and not at all as a liberator of peasants. I know of only one document of this kind. It has never been published or even utilized. It exists in the form of a copy among the Schilder papers, in the manuscript division of the Leningrad Public Library.

During the entire existence of serfdom, scarcely a year passed without some peasant disturbance. The invasion year is characterized by their comparative rarity. Those revolts which did take place, including the gravest (in the Government of Tver and in the Penza militia camp), were in temper patriotic and anti-French. And in any case, the unrest among the peasants in 1812 was a drop in the sea, compared with the immense surge of anger against the alien beast of prey.

Writing to her friend, Lanskaya, M. I. Volkova tells of the days preceding the loss of Moscow. She regrets that everyone is abusing Rostopchin; in her eyes he had performed a great service—he had 'preserved the rabble, which is thoughtless everywhere,' from 'Napoleon's perfidious designs.' How had he done this? Precisely by insisting to the last moment that Moscow would not be surrendered. The people had no opportunity to revolt, because the news of Moscow's surrender came simultaneously with the entry of the French vanguard through Dorogomilov Gate. For this beneficent lie, many nobles of Volkova's type forgave Rostopchin all his sins.

The peasant unrest did not crystallize into any strong and organized movement. After Smolensk, and especially after the occupation of Moscow, when it became clear that the conqueror had not the least intention of liberating the serfs, even isolated manifestations of the peasant movement ceased almost entirely. The peasant movement in Lithuania and White Russia, aroused by illusory hopes in Napoleon, was far stormier and far more extensive than in the governments of Russia proper.

In the spring of 1812, in the Government of Vologda, the courts took up the case of some peasants sold by landowner Shcherbinina to Councillor Yakovlev. The peasants refused to obey Yakovlev, on the ground that the deal had been illegal, since they were inalienably attached to the Vorontsov family (Shcherbinina was born a Dashkov and was a niece of S. P. Vorontsov). Moreover, the peasants complained that Yakovlev forced them to work in his Vyatsk and Perm factories. The trial lasted throughout 1812 and well into 1813; the authorities had been reluctant to resort to armed intervention while Napoleon was still in Russia. It was not until June 1813 that a Bashkir regiment was sent to the 'rebellious district'; it fired on the peasants and killed 24 men, wounded a larger number, and restored 'order.' Some of the peasants hid in the Vologda woods and returned home only gradually. A few ringleaders were brought to court and sentenced to 200 lashes with the knout. Unfortunately, the documents do not state the number of those sentenced, or how many survived their punishment. It is well known that even 100 lashes were more than sufficient to kill a man. The peasants of the Cherepovetsy district in the Government of Novgorod refused to obey Yakovlev for similar reasons.

Only from a few obscure words in the brief record of a cabinet council do we learn that in June 1812 the 'insubordination' of the factory peasants (assigned to factories) in the Perm Government had 'ceased entirely'; that this 'insubordination' involved 20,000 men; that troops were sent, et cetera. The leaders were arrested. What happened to them later is unknown.

Unfortunately, reports on peasant unrest were particularly brief in the autumn of 1812. Here is a sample: 'In the Belsky district, the peasants have revolted against their landowner Likoshin, and killed him. The commander of a detachment, Debich, having investigated the case, ordered two persons shot; the village was burnt, and this restored obedience.' All this happened near the town of Rzhev.

There was also unrest in the Government of Tver, and on 24 September the Ministerial Council examined the case 'of the rebellious peasants in the Volokolamsk district and of a priest who sympathized with them.' The peasants had 'refused obedience,' had 'pillaged their master's estate, taking his grain, cattle, horses, and killed a peasant of the village of Petrakovo with a pistol.' The peasants of the entire region revolted, and the governor was forced to request assistance from General Wintzengerode, commanding the forces in the Tver district. The Ministerial Council, having heard the case, decided: 'Baron Wintzengerode is ordered to send a sufficient number of troops to the place of the peasant revolt, to find the instigators, and hang them as a warning to the others.' Fortunately, Wintzengerode handled the case intelligently and, far from hanging anyone, revealed the criminal behaviour of the landowners and their stewards, who deliberately framed the peasants on a charge of high treason. He sent Major-General Benckendorf to the scene, and Benckendorf submitted a report in French, as Wintzen-

gerode did not know Russian: 'Permit me to speak without mincing words. The peasants, whom the Governor
and other authorities call mutineers, have not mutinied
at all. Some are refusing to obey their arrogant stewards,
who like their masters, abandon the peasants on the
appearance of the enemy, instead of utilizing their good
intentions and leading them against the enemy . . .
They have the baseness to maintain that some of the
peasants call themselves Frenchmen. The peasants wipe
out enemy detachments whenever possible, they send
their prisoners to the nearest towns, arm themselves
with captured rifles and defend their homes . . . No,
General, the peasants must not be punished, but the
public officials should be replaced, and imbued with
the good spirit prevailing in the nation.' The report
of the peasant mutiny was a pure invention: '*I will answer for this with my head.* I am using the peasants to
get information about the enemy.'

The peasant temper in 1812 was reflected in the out-
breaks among peasants drafted into the militia. Despite
their new attire, they did not cease to be peasants.

In the autumn of that year, four infantry regiments,
one company of cavalry, and one of artillery were
formed in the Penza Government. Each regiment numbered 4,000 men. Here, as everywhere else during that
year, the militiamen surprised their commanders by
their rapid progress in learning the soldier's trade. 'Patriotic zeal' worked wonders, writes Shishkin, an officer
of the militia, in his *Revolt of the Militia in 1812.* The
militia was not ready to fight until 22 December, after
Russia had been cleared of the enemy and the campaign
beyond the frontiers was beginning. Unexpectedly, a
revolt broke out among the militia. The militiamen
demanded to be sworn in. Among the myriads of ru-

mours going round in 1812, there was one to the effect
that sworn militiamen would be emancipated from
serfdom at the end of the war. More than likely, this
rumour was responsible for the demand to be sworn in.
The Third Regiment of militia revolted and, fully
armed, appeared in the square of the little town of Insar,
where it was stationed. The regiment destroyed the
apartments of the colonel and of the officers, locked up
the officers, and manhandled the colonel, a major, and
some of the others. After choosing a leader from their
own midst, they prepared to put their officers to death.
The inhabitants of Insar were also attacked by the infuriated militiamen, and some of them fled precipitately
from the town. The militiamen took possession of the
town, and transferred the officers to the town jail. The
officers were accused of concealing the Tsar's decree
about the oath of allegiance and of forcing peasants to
serve in the militia when the Tsar had ordered that
the nobles should serve. The militiamen erected three
gallows in front of the prison and announced their intention of hanging all the officers. On the fourth day,
troops with artillery arrived from Penza and forced the
rebels to surrender. Simultaneously, lesser revolts took
place among other regiments of the Penza militia.

The court martial sentenced over 300 of the mutineers
to run the gauntlet, to be beaten with knouts, to forced
labour, to deportation, to perpetual servitude as soldiers
in Siberian garrisons. 'For three days the blood of the
guilty militiamen flowed, and many of them lost their
lives under the lashes of their executioners,' writes
Shishkin. The rest of the participants were given
marching orders, and in the course of their march received an 'all-gracious pardon.'

Characteristic of the entire political atmosphere of

1812 was the aim of this conspiracy—for it was, in fact, a conspiracy, all the regiments having agreed to act on the same day, 9 December. 'The purpose of the mutineers involved the foolhardy design of men steeped in ignorance: they intended, after killing their officers, to march in full force to join the active army, to head straight for the battlefield, to fall upon the enemy and defeat him, then to appear before the Tsar confessing their guilt, and implore his forgiveness and perpetual freedom from the domination of the landowners.' Despite the ferocious repressions, despite the tortures ('the strongest measures were used during the questioning,' the well-intentioned Shishkin assures us), the militiamen refused to divulge the name of the chief instigator: 'In whose mind had such an absurd thought been born; who had first agreed to carry out such an insolent intention?—This, the most rigid inquisition, the sternest measures, failed to reveal. It remained a deep mystery to the end.'

These militiamen from Penza were moved by thoughts and aspirations typical of the serf masses in the year of the invasion, and more particularly during the second half of the war, when the peasants had finally ceased to believe in the myth of liberation by the invading enemy. Now the peasants hoped to drive the enemy from the homeland, and, in return, to receive their freedom from the Tsar, who, they imagined, was separated from the nation by the landowning nobles who concealed his beneficent decrees from the people. Vengefulness towards the foreign conqueror, hatred of the landowning class, the monarchistic legend about the Little Father Tsar—all mingled in the Insar movement of 1812.

A secret report of the public prosecutor of the Penza

Government to the Minister of Justice informs us about the uprising of another militia regiment. In Saransk, the movement did not assume such decisive forms as in Insar. The militiamen 'rashly cried out' that it was not the Tsar who was sending them, but the nobles, and that they were being starved. There was also a similar revolt at Chembar, where the militiamen submitted only after a special military detachment had fired on them. Five men were killed and twenty-three wounded, and on 24 December the court martial began operations.

In the archives we find more details of this repression: of those sentenced to the knout and running the gauntlet, 34 died at Insar, 2 in Chembar, later 4 more died from the same causes at Insar and 2 in Chembar; 43 were sentenced to hard labour, but the dossiers do not indicate the length of the terms.

We see that the militiamen indissolubly associated their liberation from serfdom with the liberation of their Fatherland from the invading enemy.

After the burning of Moscow, the bitterness of the peasants was intense. Despite appeals and enticements, the peasants round Moscow refused to trade with the French, and they savagely killed the alien foragers and marauders who fell into their hands. They even attacked French prisoners convoyed by Cossacks. When the foraging parties were escorted by large convoys, the peasants burned their provisions, sometimes entire villages, and fled to the woods. Those caught resisted desperately and perished. The French took no prisoners among the peasants, and sometimes on approaching a village would open fire to crush the possibility of resistance.

The guerrilla movement, which began immediately after Borodino, achieved its tremendous success only through the active, voluntary, and zealous assistance of the Russian peasantry. But this unquenchable hatred of the despoilers, destroyers, murderers, and ravishers manifested itself, above all, in the enthusiasm with which peasants joined the army and fought. The national character of this war was at once revealed in organized forms—in the army. In Spain, the national war assumed quite other forms, because in that country much time passed before military units could be organized. But in their indomitable hatred of the foreign ravishers and pillagers, in their thirst to give their lives for the destruction of a cruel and predatory foe, in their firm consciousness of their inner right, the Russian people was not a whit behind the Spanish people.

In describing the retreat of the Grand Army, I shall speak in detail about the guerrilla war. But it must be noted here that the peasants had begun partisan warfare during the first half of the war, before the chief pioneer of the movement, Denis Davydov, had come forward with his plan. Stepan Eremenko, a private of the Moscow infantry regiment, wounded and abandoned at Smolensk, escaped from prison and organized a peasant guerrilla detachment of 300 men. Samus collected about 2,000 peasants and made bold attacks on the French. The peasant Ermolai Vasilyev gathered a force of about 600 men, arming them with rifles and sabres seized from the French.

These national heroes did not chase after glory, and their deeds have not been systematically recorded. A peasant woman of a Sokolovo village, in the Government of Smolensk, alone defended herself against six Frenchmen, slew three of them, including a colonel, with a pitchfork, and put the remaining three to flight. She is known to us only by her first name, Praskovya.

This Praskovya, at the head of a small group of peasants of both sexes, energetically attacked detachments sent out by the French to requisition grain and hay in the Dukhovshchin district of Smolensk Government.

On entering Smolensk in November, Napoleon was apprised of the lack of provisions. In his rage, he ordered Siaufat, the commissary officer, to be shot, and another commissary officer, Villeblanche, to be put on trial. Siaufat was shot; the other was saved, when Jomini informed the Emperor that he was not so much to blame, as the peasants of the region had attacked the French foragers with particular ferocity and destroyed them; in his report he mentioned Praskovya and her astonishing feats. As a result, Napoleon stopped the proceedings against Villeblanche.

'The National War' is not a mere chapter in the history of the year 1812. The entire war against the invader was from start to finish a national war. Napoleon's strategy had counted his own troops and Alexander's troops, but he had to fight the Russian people, whom he had not counted. It was the hand of the Russian people that inflicted the irreparable, mortal blow.

Nikolai Ivanovich Turgenev and others of the Decembrist generation have shown that the Russian peasants, after the expulsion of the enemy from Russia, thought that by their heroic struggle against Napoleon they had 'earned their freedom' and that they would receive it from the Tsar. They received not their freedom, but instead a single line in Alexander's manifesto of 1814, in which the Tsar 'most graciously' thanked all classes and granted them various privileges. This single line ran: 'The peasants, our loyal people, will be recompensed by God.'

The national minorities were not a whit behind the

Russian population in their desire to defend their Fatherland.

The Cossacks of the Don, the Bashkirs, the Tartars, the Cossacks of the Urals, the peoples of the Caucasus, all fought sturdily and courageously. The heroic Bagration worthily represented Georgia. The Kalmuks, composing the Stavropol Kalmuk Regiment, distinguished themselves by their bravery: their 'flying detachments' achieved glory, especially during the pursuit of the retreating enemy in the second half of the war. Platov was so enchanted with the Bashkirs that he formed a special detachment of 200 of them who had particularly distinguished themselves, and on 27 July at Molevo-Boloto this detachment executed its first brilliant attack on the French.

Denis Davydov often speaks of the Jews as a fully reliable element in the western governments. A symposium of recollections of the National War says the same: 'We must acknowledge that the Jews do not deserve those reproaches to which they have been subjected the world over . . . because, notwithstanding all the devices of the godless Napoleon, who had proclaimed himself the jealous defender of Jews and their religious worship, they remained loyal to their [Russian] Government, and never let an opportunity slip to prove their hatred and contempt for the proud and inhuman oppressor of nations, and their genuine love, their gratitude for Russia . . .' Denis Davydov was greatly hurt when one brave man of his detachment, recommended by him for the Cross of St. George, was rejected on the sole ground of his Jewish faith.

· · ·

Passing from the exploited class to the exploiters, from the peasant serfs to the soul-owning nobility, we see that they met the invasion of Napoleon with diverse feelings.

In the first chapter of this work I have described the hostility shown by the nobility, and particularly by its aristocratic upper-crust, towards Napoleon. Even aside from the Continental blockade, the Russian land-owning class had great cause for alarm. After Tilsit, King Frederick-William III had been forced to modify and partly even to abolish serfdom. Would not the Tsar do the same thing in Russia, which was also defeated at Friedland and humiliated at Tilsit? When it became clear that no such plans were afoot, when even as modest a reformer as Speransky was deported to Siberia, the serf owners were reassured.

They were satisfied with the state of affairs in 1811 and the first half of 1812; they relished the quarrel between the two emperors. But their feelings changed radically when Napoleon's armies advanced deep into Russia. The Dowager Empress, Maria Feodorovna, a savage hater of Napoleon, was constantly in tears; every day she made preparations to leave the capital. She asked the Tsar to 'bow to God's will' and make peace with Napoleon. A considerable section of the Court and most of the nobility were panic-stricken. Suppose Napoleon issues a decree liberating the peasants? Suppose he arouses the peasant masses to a new revolt, a hundred times more terrifying than Pugachev's in 1773-4? They knew that the peasants had long been talking of Napoleon.

As early as December 1806, when another bloody and unhappy war with Napoleon had begun, Count Rostopchin reminded Alexander that the nobility was 'the sole prop of the Fatherland.' 'This distinguished estate,' continued Rostopchin, 'sacrifices everything to the Fatherland and takes its only pride in the title of Russian . . . But all this unprecedented zeal, activity, and arming will instantly turn into nothing, if the talk of so-called freedom arouses the populace, impatient to obtain it, to destroy the nobility, which in all revolts and mutinies is the sole aim of the rabble. Today, following the example of the French, the rabble is more impatient than ever to achieve this aim, as a result of the unfortunate Era of Enlightenment, which leads inevitably to the destruction of the laws and the Tsars . . .' Rostopchin points out to the Tsar that 'the servile estate is awaiting Bonaparte, in hopes of freedom.'

Suppose this 'servile estate' should revolt? In 1812 this thought kept all the nobility in a state of alarm.

'The troops are few, the leaders are moving backward; what they know they've learned at parades, and beyond that they know nothing . . .' wrote Pozdeyev, an old landowner. 'The French are spreading everywhere, preaching freedom for the peasants, so you may expect a general uprising. Considering such frequent and severe levies of recruits, you may expect a general insurrection against the Tsar and the nobles and their stewards . . . All you can do is keep quiet and await the general massacre.' Pozdeyev had fled to Vologda, as far as possible from the French. From there he poured out his grief in letters to Razumovsky (21 September) and S. S. Lansky (19 September). He refused to believe that the war would pass without a great peasant revolt; 'For where is it safe? Our muzhiks, aroused by Pugachev and other hotheads, are hankering for so-called freedom. Despite all the devastation, the magic word "freedom" turns their heads, because they have no sense.'

Pozdeyev was not alone in his apprehensions.

". . . But it seems that the close and trusted advisers of the Tsar have decided to wage a defensive war and allow the enemy to enter our borders,' wrote a woman landowner. 'Those who do not know German scientific tactics and judge by common sense are aggrieved by this . . . they are also afraid that when they get near to the Russian governments and proclaim the peasants free, an uprising may easily follow, but what's that to Phull, Armfeldt, and the rest of them?' This fear grew immeasurably among the nobility as the 'German' Barclay 'gave away' one government after another to Napoleon.

But these apprehensions soon began to vanish. 'Here is new evidence that the word "freedom," upon which Napoleon had based his plan of conquering Russia, does not do him any good. There are no Russian preachers of freedom, for I don't count the mad or the inebriate, whose words remain without consequences,' wrote Rostopchin to Balashov, Minister of the Police, on 12 July 1812.

'It is needless to conceal from oneself,' we read in a letter received by S. P. Vorontsov in England after Borodino and the occupation of Moscow, 'that the enemy, in advancing upon Moscow, had two aims. One of them was to call forth a movement among the peasants, and the other—to compel a peace by threatening the capital. He was disappointed on both counts. Everywhere the people manifested an extraordinary national spirit. They destroyed their own property rather than yield it to the enemy, against whom they have armed.' Similarly, peace was absolutely impossible.

Marakuyev, a big merchant, and mayor of Rostov, gives in his *Memoirs* a characteristic picture of the attitudes among nobles and peasants in the southern governments: 'Towards the close of a market fair in Kharkov, the painful news of the fall of Smolensk was received. Some military personages then in Kharkov asserted that, with Smolensk's fall, the position of Moscow had become untenable. This only deepened the general depression. As for Rostopchin's stupid handbills, they completely killed the hopes of the public . . . The Ukrainian rabble received news of French successes with inward satisfaction; the seditious spirit of the Poles had not yet died in them. But the nobles did not detach themselves from us, they thought and acted like true sons of the Fatherland.' It is absurd here to speak of the Polish spirit. The 'rabble,' that is the Ukrainian serfs, but recently enslaved by Catherine, loathed the Polish gentry no less than the Russians, and they associated the invasion in its first stages not with the restoration of Poland but with the destruction of serfdom.

'The landowners and district police officers armed the peasants and began systematically and skilfully to operate against the common foe. The events which had occurred in White Russia were not repeated here. We entered the heart of Russia proper. Nobles, priests, merchants, peasants—all were animated by the same spirit . . . Everywhere we met only with the most heroic self-sacrifice . . .'

There were many progressive and enlightened nobles who did not think like the serf-owners Rostopchin and

Pozdeyev. This class is represented by such a man as Nikolai Ivanovich Turgenev.

According to the Decembrists, who belonged to this and the following generation of nobles, the triumph of 1812 made not only serfdom but also the continuance of autocratic despotism morally intolerable.

After Napoleon had left Russia, the struggle, far from ending, became even more intense. No one knew the final outcome of the foreign campaign undertaken by Alexander, but as a result of the recent storm, some of the progressive nobles began to advocate the alleviation of the conditions of serfdom. 'I am no Jacobin,' writes one great noble, who seems to be close to the highest circles, 'but I confess I think that something, little by little, should be done about the liberation of the serfs. There is a good opportunity to begin in Poland, by confiscating the property of those who served against us, and by distributing their estates to our poor or crippled generals and officers; then we could determine the maximum tax which may be imposed on the peasants, and make them free. No one looks a gift horse in the mouth; the new landowners would be satisfied and a considerable number of peasants would be freed from their present unfortunate condition.'

The author of the letter compares Prussia, where after the destruction wrought by Napoleon in 1806-7 serfdom had fallen into desuetude, with the position of the peasants in Russia and Russian Poland: 'Here in Prussia, the muzhiks are no longer serfs, and their general condition is much better than in our Poland. It has been said that the part of Poland which has come into our hands is more fortunate than the parts which belong to Prussia and Austria. This is an unadulterated

lie. It is true that the landowners and the nobles are
better off (they are worthless ingrates), because they rob
the muzhiks . . . but the peasants are worse off.'

·   ·   ·

The merchants, that 'middle class' which Napoleon
hoped to find in Moscow, showed themselves absolutely
irreconcilable towards the conqueror, though Rostopchin regarded the merchant-dissenters with suspicion
and imagined that in the depth of their hearts they
expected something from Napoleon. In any case, the
merchants, despite all wooing, carried on no trade with
the enemy; and, whenever possible, they abandoned the
occupied towns with the rest of the population, leaving
their homes, shops, stores, to the mercy of fate. The
Moscow merchants contributed ten million roubles for
defence—an enormous sum for those days. Merchants of
other governments also gave considerable sums of
money.

The contribution of the merchant class was considerable. But though a part of this class suffered great losses
as a result of the devastation, another part made considerable profit. Many firms 'began to live after the
French arrived'—not to mention such favourites of
fortune as Kremer and Berd (later a famous manufac-
turer), who enriched themselves by selling rifles, gunpowder, and munitions to the Government.

On 9 September, the Ministerial Council decided to
order 40,000 poods of gunpowder and 50,000 rifles from
England. Commercial Councillor Kremer and factory-
owner Berd undertook to import these supplies. They
fixed the price of gunpowder at 29 silver roubles a pood

and 25 roubles per rifle. These prices were very, very good—not for the treasury but for the contractors.

But even the 'average' contractors, who supplied the army with hay, oats, grain, cloth, and hides, were no fools and lived in friendship, love, and connivance with commissary officials. We recall Ermolov's rage at a commissary officer whom he had caught red-handed. But few contractors were ever prosecuted, and those only long after the war was over.

There was a flood of justified complaints against the merchants, over the sudden rise in prices of all goods, particularly necessities. 'As soon as our trade with England was interrupted,' ran a popular rhyme, 'our enemy at home began to run after profits; our true foes are those brazen fools who sell us goods—merchants without honour who rob the people.'

These verses were composed not during the war with Napoleon, but in the preceding years of the Continental blockade. They achieved their real popularity, however, in 1812, when prices soared to unheard-of heights. The cessation of imports and the immense purchases for the army gave rise to an orgy of speculation. The devastation of occupied territory, the destruction of industrial enterprises and crops made matters worse. In Smolensk, Vyazma, Gzhatsk, and Mozhaisk, all factories without exception were destroyed by fire or completely stripped by looters. There were about 150,000 factory workers in Russia at that time (in 1814 there were 160,000). Most of the workers were serfs working in the factories of their masters, or in enterprises belonging to merchants who hired them for definite periods; a part of the workers were freemen. Most of them had close ties with the peasants, and, when the storm of 1812 broke, those in occupied towns scattered to the villages.

There was much speculation in arms, and it received a new impetus after the Tsar's visit to Moscow. Before the Tsar's arrival, his patriotic proclamations, and the calls for militia, a sabre in Moscow brought 6 roubles or even less, but afterward, it fetched 30 to 40 roubles; the price of a Tula rifle rose from 11 to 15 roubles to 80 roubles; pistols were sold for five or six times their customary price. The merchants realized that the enemy would not be repulsed with bare hands, and they shamelessly took advantage of the opportunity to enrich themselves.

As early as December the Moscow merchants began to declare their invasion losses to the authorities, attaching detailed inventories. Many of these declarations began with one and the same curious formula, apparently originating with some scribe employed by the merchants: 'The well-known enemy has broken into Moscow and burned its houses and shops, among which various of my goods worth several thousand of roubles.' As a rule, these petitions remained unanswered.

There is some evidence of financial sacrifices on the part of the nobility, but most of the landowners' stories of sacrifice to the Fatherland cannot be taken at their face value. For example, the landowners of the Nevelsky district in the Government of Vitebsk announced (after the war) that they had supplied provisions to the Russian forces out of pure patriotism, and that they had no desire to be paid. But von Herzfeld, the sceptical Governor of Vitebsk, reported to the Senate: 'They [the landowners] claim to have acted out of sheer loyalty, but strongly hint that they should receive payment for the oats and other products they provided;

they also ask to be relieved of taxes, the amount of which is probably higher than what the treasury would owe them for the provisions they supplied. In other words, they are asking a twofold reward while pretending loyal sacrifices.'

Often we find a strange mixture of patriotism and material interest. On 30 September, after the burning of Moscow, General Lavrov wrote from Tarutino to Arakcheyev: 'One must, at last, give justice to the Russians, that they do not lose heart in the worst of situations; their zeal is invariably ardent. In truth, I'll tell you that I haven't heard a single soul complain of his loss. Every man aspires to one object, to free Russia from the invader. The minds are inflamed to such a degree that generals, officers, soldiers, and muzhiks would sooner be buried beneath the ruins of their Fatherland than hear of peace . . . With the help of the All-Highest, we shall avenge ourselves on the enemy —such is the goal of all our desires—and then we shall go somewhere for a rest. In the meantime, do me a favour, my most gracious benefactor: tell Guryev to order the Kaluga State Chamber to give me the title to the land granted me by his Majesty in the Kozelsk district; it seems that the Chamber has not yet been notified.'

Arakcheyev himself during the whole war was never within a hundred versts of the front, though he was a general on active service. He was distinguished by his exceptional cowardice and even more by his extraordinary cupidity; he constantly bothered the authorities with complaints and petty requests to release him 'as a landowner of Novgorod' from any unusual expenses and taxes caused by the war.

Of course, the thieving commissary officials and land-

owners who robbed the State Treasury found Arakcheyev a staunch protector. Sergey Grigoryevich Volkonsky, the future Decembrist, who served in 1812 under
General Wintzengerode, tells us a characteristic episode
in his *Recollections*. 'The laments of the officials, whom
Wintzengerode hindered from making purchases at
fabulous prices, and similar laments from the landowning gentry . . . found a response in St. Petersburg,
and Count Arakcheyev sent a politely couched inquiry
to Wintzengerode. The chivalrous Wintzengerode was
furious; he made no reply to Arakcheyev, but wrote a
letter direct to the Tsar, and commanded me to take it
immediately to St. Petersburg.' Prince Volkonsky was
received by the Tsar in October. Alexander asked him
three questions: '(1) "What is the spirit of the army?"
I answered: "Sire! From the Commander-in-Chief to
the lowest private, everyone is ready to lay down his life
in defence of his Fatherland and Your Imperial Majesty." (2) "And the spirit of the people?" To this I answered: "Sire, You should be proud of it. Every peasant
is a hero, devoted to the Fatherland and to you." (3)
"And the nobility?" "Sire," I answered him, "I am
ashamed to belong to it. They have talked much, but
done nothing." '

Alexander I, who understood only too well that
Wintzengerode was wholly in the right and that Arakcheyev was the patron of thieves and official embezzlers,
took the side of Arakcheyev. 'Here is a letter to Wintzengerode. He'll understand me and will be convinced
that he has my full confidence and esteem, but that
in administrative matters it is necessary to let them
have their way . . .' What is the meaning of this deliberately obscure phrase? Simply this: Wintzengerode
need not bother about any unpleasant papers sent him

by Arakcheyev. That is one side of it. On the other—
the Tsar promptly added, concluding his conversation
with Prince Volkonsky: 'In a few hours, Aleksey An-
dreyevich [Arakcheyev] will ask to see you—*do not tell
him that I have asked to see you and that I gave you
an envelope to be delivered to Wintzengerode.*' These
words are underlined by S. G. Volkonsky himself, who
adds: 'These last words indicate the strange double-
faced game which the Tsar played with Arakcheyev, as
well as Arakcheyev's influence over the Emperor.'

Volkonsky was not fated to convey this strange interview with the Tsar to General Wintzengerode. On
his journey from St. Petersburg to the active army,
Wintzengerode was taken prisoner. It is clear that
neither Wintzengerode nor any of his brother warriors who fought in the interest of the Treasury received the slightest support from the Tsar; the landowners could calmly sell their products at 'fabulous
prices,' knowing that they had a substantial protector in
Arakcheyev, the 'Novgorod landowner.' Neither with
Arakcheyev nor with the other landowners did the Tsar
consider it wise to quarrel . . .

Arakcheyev had a highly placed model. The Tsar's
brother, Constantine Pavlovich, who had fled to St.
Petersburg to escape the war, did not waste his time
there. He offered 126 horses to the Ekaterinovsky Regiment, asking 225 roubles for each. 'The Economic Committee of the Militia hesitated about assigning money
for the purchase, finding that the horses were not worth
it.' But the Tsar gave the order, Constantine received
28,350 roubles, and the horses were accepted: '45 horses
had glanders and were shot at once lest they infect the
others, 55 were unusable and ordered sold at any cost;
the remaining 26 were incorporated into the regiment.'

This was Constantine Pavlovich's sole contribution to
the War of 1812. In her Recollections, V. I. Bakunina
says that 'words are inadequate' to describe Constantine's behaviour.

• • •

Though the people's hatred of the invader was gradually increasing, and no serious discontent was notice-
able among the nobility, the Government felt insecure. The disastrous beginning of the war, the absurd
camp at Drissa in which the entire Russian army
came close to destruction, the French pursuit of Barclay and Bagration, the loss of Smolensk—all this greatly
perturbed the nobles, the merchants, and the peasants
in governments directly affected by the invasion. Rumours that Bagration himself considered Barclay a
traitor, that Vollzogen and Wintzengerode and other
Germans held important posts in the army, suggested
a sinister explanation of Barclay's endless retreat and
his generous surrender of nearly half the Russian Empire. The surrender and destruction of Moscow dan-
gerously increased the public irritation.

Alexander and his closest collaborators were in a state
of great anxiety. Balashov, Minister of Police, had long
been worried by certain manifestations of 'excessive'
patriotism. 'Who gave you permission, gentlemen?' he
greeted a delegation of nobles who had arrived at the
capital to prostrate themselves 'at the foot of the throne.'
Rostopchin, we recall, had prepared fast *troikas* for the
over-active Moscow patriots in July 1812. At that time,
the gendarmes' corps did not yet exist; political surveillance was in a primitive stage, and carried on chiefly
by amateurs and volunteers. The Ministry of Police
under Balashov; the St. Petersburg police under the

Frenchman, Jacques de Sanglen; Kozodavlev, the Minister of the Interior; Rostopchin, whom they all hated, and who could not endure them—all these agencies were engaged primarily in intriguing against each other; their other activities were collecting Court and upper-class gossip, and intercepting other people's letters.

Russia was full of Napoleon's spies of both sexes and all colours. They lived absolutely unmolested in St. Petersburg, Moscow, Odessa, Riga, and Kronstadt. Even after the invasion, many remained and zealously served Napoleon when he was in Moscow. The Russian bloodhounds did not track down a single one of them, despite much fuss and pother.

The owner of a cloth and wool-carding factory in the village of Bondari, in Tambov District, a Frenchman by the name of Lionnes, was suspected of spying for Napoleon. Fearful of the indignation of patriotically inclined workers, the central and local authorities made every effort not so much to render the spy harmless as to conceal the fact of espionage from the workers. The Minister of the Interior wrote to the Governor of Tambov: 'Publicity would be highly dangerous, for it might induce the peasant factory workers to revolt and interrupt work in the factory.'

After the loss of Moscow, when the authorities were particularly uneasy, they committed rash acts, which aroused the greatest misgivings on the part of all who had any serious ideas about police work.

Take the case of Dmitry Pavlovich Runich, assistant-director of the Moscow Post Office, who arrived in Nizhni-Novgorod from occupied Moscow—this was the same Runich who later suppressed atheism in the University of St. Petersburg. One day he received news from St. Petersburg of a circular which had been sent to all provincial governors requesting them to ask all postmasters for suspicious letters and subject them to examination by a censor. This news upset him. The experienced Runich knew that the opening of letters was not a trade which could be learned overnight, but one of the fine arts, which had to be cultivated lovingly. It was, in his view, inadmissible to let any old governor dabble in it, as that might have the most perilous consequences.

'. . . The inspection of correspondence and the supervision thereof,' wrote Runich to his Minister Kozodavlev, 'was always carried out at one central post-office by specially trained officials, and this done so secretly and with such care that other postal employees did not know whose correspondence was under surveillance, and what letters were censored.' This procedure had always secured good results: 'As a proof of the great secrecy that attended this operation, one may adduce the fact that in the course of many years, recipients of censored letters did not harbour the least suspicion; and the authorities, because of the trust inspired in the public by the post-office department, disposed of a fact-finding apparatus which, despite the most zealous investigations, often remained secret. In view of these truths, I am convinced that if post offices are entrusted with the surveillance of correspondence, the long-established confidence of the public in the postal department may be undermined, because provincial offices are not equipped for this work. Moreover, the execution by the postmasters of the orders of the governors may give rise to publicity, and as a result the persons under observation will be on their guard. I also have reason to think that inadmissible abuses will be committed under this pretext.'

This public 'confidence' in the post office did actually—to judge from his later complaints—begin to vanish; it was replaced by the most 'vicious' caution on the
part of letter writers.

Although the temper of the people rendered unnecessary any artificial measures to create hostility to the
enemy, the authorities made every effort to mobilize the
priesthood for patriotic propaganda. The invading army
removed church plate, billeted troops in church buildings, and often used them for stables. This was the chief
content of the anti-French sermons from the Russian
pulpits.

Napoleon ordered his spies to spread far and wide
the tidings that he had no intention of persecuting the
Orthodox faith. One of the bulletins ran: 'What do
the priests say about the arrival of the French? Do
they know that Napoleon is not making war upon faith,
but only upon his enemies? Do you know that the
Caesar [Polish translator's version of Emperor] has
given strict orders to respect churches, monasteries,
archimandrites, and priests?' This Napoleonic counter-
agitation had extraordinarily small success, and the prof-
anation of the churches was mentioned with indignation many years after the invasion.

It must be said that the priesthood that remained in
occupied localities entered into relations with the enemy
authorities to obtain the right to worship. The priest
Murzakevich in Smolensk even went so far as to meet
Napoleon 'with the cross,' and for this and like activities he was prosecuted after the departure of the French.
There were similar cases in other places, but in the end
the priesthood was cleared of the charge of treachery.
The position of the Orthodox priesthood in Lithuania
and White Russia was more complex; during the en-

tire war it was commonly believed that these lands would forever remain with Poland, which Napoleon intended to restore.

On 25 July 1812, Marshal Davout ordered Varlaam, Archbishop of Moghilev, to induce the population to swear an oath of allegiance to Napoleon. Appearing with his retinue in the Cathedral, the Archbishop brought the people to swear the required oath, and he performed a *Te Deum,* mentioning 'the powerful French Emperor and King of Italy, the great Napoleon, and his wife the Empress and Queen Marie-Louise.' The same ceremony was repeated in all the churches of Moghilev Diocese. Oddly enough, the Secretary of the Consistory, Demyanovich, who later testified against Varlaam, advised him against the oath of allegiance, on the reasonable ground that 'The French have not yet occupied all of White Russia.' Another accuser of Varlaam, the priest Orest, not only brought his flock to swear allegiance to Napoleon but even denounced those churchmen who refused to do so.

Varlaam, Orest, and many others were fully convinced that Napoleon would win and that the Western Governments would be permanently severed from Russia. They hoped, by full submission to the stern conqueror, to save the Orthodox diocese from the menace of Roman Catholicism. They preferred Davout to the Roman Catholic priest Mayevski, who uttered threats against the Orthodox archbishop; they preferred Napoleon to the Pope.

As early as 1807, the Synod had deemed it politic to pronounce Napoleon a forerunner of the Antichrist. The masses, finding the Slavonic word *predtecha* (forerunner) difficult and unintelligible, began to call Napoleon simply Antichrist. After the battle of Fried-

land, when peace was suddenly concluded followed by
the closest, friendly alliance between the Orthodox Tsar
and this same Antichrist, when the two publicly embraced on the raft at Tilsit, and the Tsar bestowed the
Ribbon of St. Andrew upon the Antichrist, receiving in
return the Cross of the Legion of Honour, the Synod
ordered the clergy to stop all talk about forerunners at
once. And now, in 1812, Napoleon was behaving in
the most authentic Antichrist-like style, profaning the
churches, devastating Russia, burning Smolensk, burning and pillaging Moscow. It was most tempting to dig
up the old slogan. And by the end of summer the talk
about the Antichrist actually did revive in some places.
But the clergy were definitely unlucky in this slogan,
and were forced to abandon it once more. In Russia at
this time there were not a few among the peasantry,
the petty bourgeoisie, and the merchants—Orthodox as
well as Dissenters—who were well read in the Scriptures.
These *Nachiotchiks* (well-read persons, especially in
biblical lore) knew the Old and New Testaments well
and were especially interested in the Apocalypse. In
religious debates they quite often got the better of
priests and even bishops. They forced the clergy to
think out to the end this teaching about the appearance
of the Antichrist, showing them that the matter was unreasonable, absurd, and even harmful.

For if the Russian people actually believed Napoleon
to be the Antichrist, what was the good of resisting
him? Had it not been foretold that the Antichrist would
triumph and rule for a thousand years? In that case the
Antichrist would collapse in 2812—and all you could do
was wait until that lucky year. The slander could only
benefit Napoleon. 'Let not your hearts be confused,'
wrote the Synod, 'be not downcast, and do not allow

yourselves to think that this was Antichrist, a particular
being of sin, foretold in the sacred writings as one who
would appear in the end of days . . . There have been
many in times past who were thought to be Antichrists,
but it was all without reason . . . Hence, cease to oppose Holy Writ and common sense, cease thinking that
Napoleon Bonaparte is Antichrist, and, therefore, invincible. He is only an impostor, who fights not with
strength but with cunning . . .'

After the battle of Tarutino and Napoleon's departure from Moscow, all patriotic agitation and police
measures became unnecessary. Once it became clear
that Russia was not lost, that the enemy was on the
defensive, Alexander was forgiven his obvious incompetence, his retreat to the safety of St. Petersburg—in a
word, everything. He had not made peace with Napoleon—and that was all that mattered. All murmurs
against him ceased.

8

TARUTINO AND NAPOLEON'S DEPARTURE FROM MOSCOW

IMMEDIATELY after the burning of Moscow, Napoleon was faced with two principal tasks. First and foremost was to obtain a peace, here in Moscow. Second, to restore discipline in his motley army and to preserve the provisions and clothing that had been saved from the fire and from pillaging. Both tasks proved entirely beyond his powers.

The conflagration was dying down in the centre of the city, but it still raged on the outskirts, when Napoleon returned from Petrovsky Palace to the Kremlin. On the very day of his return he was informed that Major-General Tutolmin, the director of the Foundling Hospital, had asked for a guard to insure the safety of his wards. Quite unexpectedly, Napoleon complied with the request, and invited him to the Kremlin on 18 September.

'I should have desired,' said Napoleon to Tutolmin, 'to deal with your city as I dealt with Vienna and Berlin, which to this day have not been demolished. But the Russians have left this city nearly empty, and have committed an unprecedented act. They have delib-

erately set their capital on fire to cause me temporary
inconvenience, they have destroyed the work of many
centuries . . . I have never waged war in this manner.
My warriors are capable of fighting, but they do not
burn cities. Beginning with Smolensk, I have found
nothing but ashes . . .'

In this conversation Napoleon was very gracious. He
spoke of Rostopchin's criminal behaviour and blamed
him alone for the fires. The Governor-General had
given orders to remove all the fire pumps, and to Napoleon this proved that the crime had been premedi-
tated. There were other proofs: the real or fictitious
statements of persons tried as incendiaries. When the
Emperor asked if he wished to make another request,
Tutolmin requested permission to write a report to
Maria Feodorovna, at the head of all Foundling Hospitals in Russia. Napoleon not only assented, but suggested that Tutolmin should add that he, Napoleon,
still held Alexander in esteem and wished to make
peace. Tutolmin wrote all this the same day and sent
his message with an official of his department who, by
special orders of the Emperor, was permitted to pass
through the advance lines of the French army.

Even this first attempt was quite unlike Napoleon's
customary procedure, and showed that Napoleon felt
none too sure of himself.

Actually, Napoleon had gambled on the Tsar's weakness and low morale; he had expected that sooner or
later Kutuzov would sue for a truce, as Bennigsen had
after Friedland. But Borodino was not Friedland. No
emissary came.

If Alexander could have been induced to sign a peace
now, Napoleon's prestige would have been marvellously
enhanced in the eyes of all Europe. What sort of peace

would he have dictated at this time? There is documentary proof that he would have demanded the cession of Lithuania, the resumption of the Continental blockade, an alliance with France. Later Napoleon would have been content with saving his honour.

Napoleon sent a second message to the Tsar even before Alexander's reply to his first feeler could have arrived: exactly two days after his conversation with Tutolmin. This second message was conveyed by Ivan Alekseyevich Yakovlev, A. I. Herzen's father. It is mentioned in French sources and in the first pages of Herzen's *My Past and My Thoughts*. We also have the complete text of Napoleon's letter to Alexander, sent through Yakovlev. This Yakovlev, a rich Muscovite noble and an original character, had accidentally remained behind in Moscow—he had moved too slowly in preparing to get away. His family found itself in a difficult situation, and Yakovlev turned to Marshal Mortier for protection. The Marshal had made the acquaintance of Yakovlev in Paris, and he reported the matter to Napoleon, who ordered Yakovlev to appear before him. According to Herzen: '. . . Napoleon upbraided Rostopchin for the fire. He called it vandalism, and insisted, as always, on his oft-tested love of peace. He argued that his war was with England, and not Russia, and he boasted of having placed a guard at the Foundling Hospital and the Uspensky Cathedral, and he complained of Alexander, saying that he had surrounded himself with stupid advisers and that his own peaceful intentions were unknown to the Tsar. My father remarked that it was up to the conqueror to offer peace. "I have done what I could. I have sent someone to Kutuzov, but he simply refuses to enter into any negotiations or bring my proposals to the attention of the

Tsar. If they want war, it is not my fault—they shall
have war." '

Yakovlev, to be sure, had mixed his dates in recount-
ing the interview to his son. Napoleon had not yet sent
anyone to Kutuzov. Lauriston was sent after the conversation with Yakovlev.

Napoleon first refused to give Yakovlev a pass. When,
however, Yakovlev persisted in his plea, 'Napoleon
thought a moment and suddenly asked: "Will you undertake to deliver a letter to the Emperor from me? If
you do, I will have a pass given you and your house-
hold." "I should be glad to accept Your Majesty's proposal, but I cannot give a guarantee." "Will you give
your word of honour that you will do everything you
can to deliver the letter?" "I will, Sire." '

On 20 September, Napoleon wrote a letter to Alexander, and Yakovlev took it with him. It was delivered
to Alexander. Its full text is published in the official
edition of the correspondence of Napoleon.

This letter is interesting both politically and psycho-
logically. Napoleon wants to maintain the pose of the
indisputable but magnanimous conqueror. To make it
easier to enter into negotiations, he points out his almost complete innocence in the devastation of half of
Russia and the destruction of Moscow. His desire to
appease the Tsar is transparent, especially towards the
end of the letter. But even the beginning is characteristic: 'The proud and magnificent city of Moscow is no
more. Rostopchin has burned it. Four hundred incendiaries were arrested on the spot of the crime. They all
declared that they set fire to the city by order of the
Governor and the Director of Police. They have been
shot. The fire seems to have died down at last. Three
quarters of the houses have burned down, only a quar-

ter remain. Such conduct is atrocious and useless. Was the intent to deprive me of supplies? But they were in cellars that the fires could not reach. Besides, what a petty object for which to destroy one of the most beautiful cities in the entire world, the work of centuries! This conduct, pursued since Smolensk, has only served to reduce 600,000 families to beggars. The fire pumps of Moscow had either been broken or carried away . . .' His reception had been different in well-ordered capitals, where the administration, the police, the guard were usually left behind, and then everything went well. He does not suspect Alexander himself of having encouraged the incendiaries; otherwise 'I should not have written you this letter.' 'Alexander's principles, heart, and the rightness of his ideas are not in keeping with these excesses, unworthy of a great Tsar and a great nation.' And yet, Napoleon adds, though in Moscow they had not forgotten to remove the fire pumps, they had left 150 field guns, 60,000 new rifles, 1,600,000 cartridges, a quantity of gunpowder, et cetera.

The last lines of the letter are curious, revealing as they do Napoleon's astonishing blindness, his complete unwillingness to see his opponent's point of view. After all he had done in Russia, from the crossing of the Niemen to the occupation of Moscow, he writes: 'I am waging a war against Your Majesty without animosity.' He is so 'magnanimous'; 'a single note from Your Majesty, either before or after the last battle, would have stopped my campaign. I even wish I had been able to sacrifice the advantages of occupying Moscow. If Your Majesty preserves a remnant of your former feelings towards me, you will accept this letter as it is intended. In any case, you can be only grateful to me for the report on what is taking place in Moscow.' The letter bears the signature, 'Napoleon.'

This letter contains no direct proposal of peace, but in reality every word of it proposes peace.

To this personal letter, as to Tutolmin's report, Alexander made no reply.

The anxiety among the marshals grew. How long would they go on sitting in Moscow? The cold weather was approaching. The 'supplies' in the Moscow cellars, of which Napoleon had written to Alexander, were fictitious except for great quantities of liquor—brandy, vodka, liqueur, and wine. Drunkenness among the soldiers was rampant, but bread was as scarce as before; there was practically no oats or hay, the horses fell by the thousands. Neither the counterfeit Russian banknotes brought by the French nor even genuine Russian banknotes were of any avail. The Russian peasants simply refused to deal with the invaders. And, the main thing, the discipline in the French army was shattered beyond repair. The soldiers—and not only the German, Polish, and Italian, but also some of the French—were degenerating into a looting rabble.

'The most cruel tormentors and barbarians of the peoples composing Napoleon's horde were the Poles and the Bavarians,' writes A. N. Olenin in his Notebook, published in *The Russian Archives* in 1868.

Such reports are by no means rare. There were numerous complaints against the Prussians, Westphalians, and Italians. The number of complaints against native Frenchmen is decidedly smaller.

The inhabitants of Moscow distinguished the French from the other peoples in Napoleon's army. 'The *genuine* French are good,' says an eyewitness. 'You can recognize them by their uniforms and their speech; they

are mostly polite. But the people they recruited elsewhere, and all the Germans, are real trash.' The Old
Guard refrained almost completely from pillaging.

There were no deserters from the army stationed in
Moscow for the simple reason that French soldiers who
went beyond their outposts were caught and slain by the
peasants. But from the flanks, especially the northern,
came disturbing reports. In September, soon after Borodino, Marèt, the Duke of Bassano, sent Napoleon a
coded message from Vilna: 'Marshal Saint-Cyr . . . can
no longer rely on the Bavarians: the few remaining with
him are afflicted with illness or low spirits, or *pos-
sessed with the mania of desertion.*'

From the southern flank came reports of the dubious
conduct of the Austrian 'allies.' Their double game was
becoming clear.

Matters were going none too well along the entire
line of communications, even in Moghilev, Minsk, and
Vitebsk, though Napoleon had enormously weakened
the Grand Army by the establishment of garrisons.

In an unofficial letter, dated 26 October, Pastoret, the
French commissary official in Vitebsk, wrote to his col-
league, Bignon, in Vilna: 'The French Emperor has put
me in charge of 12 districts, but the Russian Emperor
has thought it proper to govern 8 of them personally
or through his generals, and, still worse, he does not
leave me in peace even in the remaining districts.
Wittgenstein is about 6 leagues from me, and within the
past few days the Cossacks have appeared for the third
time to breakfast in the suburbs of Vitebsk . . .'

Napoleon also had to give thought to a conquered
Europe, which loathed him and knew that its fate
was being decided in Russia and Spain.

For four years Spain had been an open wound in the

body of the great French Empire and remained a source of constant worry to Napoleon. On 16 October he ordered two million francs sent to Portugal, two million francs to the French army fighting in the north of Spain, half a million to the army fighting in the centre of Spain, and half a million to Catalonia. The order never reached its destination: it was intercepted by the Cossacks, who found the portfolio with the documents in a captured baggage train.

Napoleon organized an administration for Moscow with Marshal Mortier as military governor, Duronnel as commander of the fortress and the city, and Lesseps—'as Commissary Chief [civil commander] of the city and province.' Lesseps 'selected' twenty-two persons of the Russian population, who were called 'municipality,' and Napoleon confirmed them in their office. These persons were appointed against their will, and were afraid of becoming known as traitors; they had no authority whatsoever. Lesseps addressed a proclamation in French and Russian to the inhabitants of Moscow.

'Proclamation. Inhabitants of Moscow!' it began. 'Your misfortunes are cruel, but His Majesty the Emperor and King wishes to put an end to them. Terrible examples have taught you how he punishes disobedience and crime. Strong measures have been taken to put an end to disorder and to restore common safety. A native administration, chosen from among you, will serve as your municipality or city government. It will minister to your needs and well-being . . .' Lesseps promised to protect the lives and property of all citizens 'because such is the will of the greatest and most just of all monarchs.' At the end of this curious document he suggested that they obey the authorities and

promised that if they did so, the 'tears' of the Muscovites 'shall cease to run.'

The harassed, penniless Russians were subjected to
violence at every step, and found shelter where they
could. Not a night passed without a few murders, and
the murderers remained unpunished. The stench of
rotting bodies infected the air. But the corpses were not
all Russian. From later evidence we learn that the bitterness of the Russians remaining in Moscow repeatedly
expressed itself in ambushes against French inebriates,
whom they killed whenever they could safely do so.

All this strongly worried and distracted the Emperor
during the five weeks of his stay in Moscow.

As the results of the Moscow fires grew clearer, Napoleon was faced with the urgent need of finding winter
quarters for his army in any place but Moscow.

According to the computations made after the departure of the French, 'scarcely 5,000' of Moscow's
30,000 houses remained intact.

A count made by Napoleon's officials tallied more or
less with the Russian figures.

But Moscow was still politically necessary to Napoleon. Europe must know that Napoleon had compelled
Alexander to sign the peace *in Moscow*. It was essential
to retain the attitude of the conqueror, and for this it
was necessary to await the answer to the letter sent to
the Tsar through Yakovlev.

The cares about order in the city and in the army,
the reception of couriers with papers from Europe and
occupied places in Russia—these could not deflect Napoleon's thoughts from his main concern. Why had
there been no answer? Had Yakovlev duped him? And
if the letter had been delivered, why was there no reply
from Alexander? Enough time had passed for an answer.

But there was no answer. Napoleon was losing days, the golden days of the beautiful, sunny, warm autumn, which prevailed that year through the entire central zone of Russia; and we have evidence that he understood as well as his marshals the danger of tarrying in Moscow *if* he had to continue the war. Something had to be done. The simplest explanation of Alexander's silence was that Yakovlev had been unable or unwilling to deliver the letter. Napoleon decided on a new step, incomparably more important than his two previous messages. This step was taken after a serious conference with the marshals. For several days Napoleon had been in a state of irritation, flying into a rage over trifles and taking it out on his suite.

On 3 October, after a sleepless night, he ordered his marshals to appear at the Kremlin, and announced to them: 'We must burn what is left of Moscow, then proceed by way of Tver to St. Petersburg, where Macdonald could join us . . .' But the marshals remained stubbornly silent: 'What glory shall be ours, and what shall the whole world say when it learns that within three months we have conquered the two great northern capitals!' The marshals raised objections. They considered the plan unfeasible. 'To go northward, towards the winter,' with a diminished army, with Kutuzov at the rear, was unthinkable. Napoleon fell silent. He did not insist.

On the same day, Napoleon summoned Caulaincourt. At first, he repeated his morning proposal of a campaign against St. Petersburg. Caulaincourt persisted in his objections. Then Napoleon suggested that he should journey to the Tsar with a proposal of peace. Caulaincourt again protested, pointing out that this would lead to nothing, but, on the contrary, would be harmful, because it would reveal the difficult position of the French to Alexander. 'Very well,' said the Emperor abruptly, 'in that case, I shall send Lauriston.' Lauriston respectfully repeated what Caulaincourt had said. But Napoleon cut the argument short by ordering him to go to Kutuzov at once and ask him for a pass to the Tsar in St. Petersburg. 'I must have peace, I need it absolutely. I must have it at all costs, save my honour.' The Imperial command put an end to all conversations and objections. Lauriston set out on his journey to Kutuzov.

. . .

On the morning of 5 October, a French officer bearing a white flag appeared at the Russian outposts, with the announcement that General Marquis Lauriston had arrived, asking for an interview with Field Marshal Kutuzov. The news gave rise to an extraordinary commotion at Russian headquarters.

Kutuzov's staff and entourage were divided into two hopelessly irreconcilable camps. This is perhaps an inaccurate way of putting it, for one man is not a 'camp,' and actually Kutuzov stood alone. His executive generals, Dokhturov, Konovnitsin, and Mayevsky cannot be taken into account; Bennigsen and Wilson were openly against him, and Ermolov, Platov, and Toll, secretly. And behind the back of this hostile camp Kutuzov always felt the invisible presence of the Tsar himself.

The surrender of Moscow had been skilfully exploited by Kutuzov's enemies. Bennigsen informed St. Petersburg by various channels that the Russian army had had a good chance to defend the capital but that His Serene Highness the Prince, in his weakness and

meekness, had decided otherwise. Barclay, whose tactics
Kutuzov continued, felt humiliated and vexed that
Kutuzov had replaced him, and he had no intention of
supporting the Field Marshal. Ermolov, gifted, shrewd,
but profoundly insincere, had shifted his position to
the side of Kutuzov's enemies, but he proceeded
shrewdly and cautiously.

During the first days after Borodino they still feared
Kutuzov and kept silent. Then, by roundabout channels they heard of Alexander's indignation, of his hostility towards Kutuzov. They grew bolder.

And yet Kutuzov's strategic talents never shone with
a brighter light than after Borodino. Taking counsel of
no one—he trusted neither Bennigsen nor Barclay—he
ordered the army to retire from Moscow along the
Ryazan road. Entering upon the Ryazan road, he
wheeled sharply southward and emerged on the old
Kaluga road, proceeding to Krasnaya Pakhra. Simultaneously he ordered Prince Vasilchikov to proceed
with his two regiments of Cossack cavalry towards
Ryazan. His purpose was to baffle Murat, who was engaged in the pursuit of the Russian army. For several
days, extremely precious days for Kutuzov, these Cossacks magnificently fulfilled their task, and it was not
until 22 September that the French became convinced
that they were following the wrong trail and reversed
their course. By the nineteenth, Kutuzov's entire army
was in Podolsk, and on the following day, having rested,
it continued straight southward, towards Krasnaya
Pakhra, along the old Kaluga road. And here ended
the skilful, profoundly conceived flanking movement.

By this bold movement Kutuzov had protected
Kaluga and the southern governments from a possible
invasion by Napoleon.

Kutuzov's dispositions were subjected to unfriendly criticism by Bennigsen, who had been imposed on him as Chief of Staff. Later on, matters grew worse. Murat, after a considerable delay, finally discovered Kutuzov's ruse, which had kept the French cavalry engaged in a futile advance along the Ryazan road, and rushed his forces to the Kaluga road, hot on the heels of Kutuzov's rear-guard. Kutuzov had no desire to engage the French at Krasnaya Pakhra or in its environs. Bennigsen and his adherents sharply protested against a further withdrawal to the south. At this time, no one except two or three persons on Kutuzov's staff understood the tremendous significance of his manœuvres; the Field Marshal stood quite alone. Bennigsen, Buksgevden, Platov, and, of course, their partisans had not the slightest idea of the purpose of Kutuzov's flanking operation, and they loudly talked of the old Field Marshal's 'senseless see-sawing.' This did not prevent them later from telling the public that they too had advocated the plan.

Kutuzov explained that it was essential to retire further south, to the village of Tarutino, because the nearer he would be to Kaluga, the easier it would be to control the three roads leading from Moscow to Kaluga, along any of which Napoleon might decide to advance. Despite the great clarity and expedience of this plan, Bennigsen began to insist so heatedly on the necessity of halting and accepting battle with Murat at Krasnaya Pakhra that Kutuzov, in sudden irritation, announced that this time he would divest himself of his authority and let Bennigsen manage as he would, putting his entire staff, all his adjutants, his entire army, in his charge. 'You are in command of the army, and I am only a volunteer,' he told Bennigsen and suggested to him that he immediately seek a position for battle with Murat here, at Krasnaya Pakhra.

From nine o'clock in the morning until midday, Bennigsen, accompanied by Kutuzov's entire staff, reconnoitred the countryside, found nothing, and upon his return admitted that it would be impossible to join battle here. 'In that case I shall resume command. Follow me, gentlemen, as before,' said Kutuzov, turning to his generals. 'Pyotr Petrovich, order the disposition for retirement,' he said to his orderly, General Konovnitsin. At once the Russian army moved southward, towards Tarutino, and took up positions in the village and its environs. Kutuzov with his entire staff set up quarters in the village of Letashevka, about five versts to the south of Tarutino. This occurred on 4 October.

This entire episode clearly showed that Bennigsen and his numerous partisans on the staff hostile to Kutuzov did not know how to correct Kutuzov's 'mistakes,' but they shouted about these 'mistakes' with the sole purpose of having the Commander-in-Chief replaced at the earliest possible moment. At the same time, Kutuzov's device—the cession of his authority for a day to his enemy Bennigsen—shows that the Field Marshal did not feel sufficiently strong to use severe measures and to exercise his legally absolute authority.

Now Rostopchin, too, grew bold. For over two weeks he had loafed about among the members of Kutuzov's staff. Kutuzov refused to receive him even once. The Governor-General finally decided to leave, but before leaving he wrote to the Field Marshal a brief letter in which he tried to include as many poisoned barbs as possible. The capital, he said in his letter, 'had been abruptly yielded to the scoundrel.' Moreover, Kutuzov had given orders to confiscate two poods of bread from every inhabitant of the Moscow Government, and all the hay and all the cattle without exception, 'something I have learned only yesterday from private sources, although I have spent over two weeks at headquarters, where, like the army, I have been deprived of the honour of beholding the face of Your Serene Highness.' He willingly stressed the fact that he was staying with Kutuzov not by his own choice but exclusively because the Tsar had commissioned him to do so. 'As soon as I have carried out his will, I shall join the Tsar, leaving those unhappy regions where the fortune of the army and of the Fatherland depend on your signature.' Having written all this, Rostopchin seems to have been disappointed with the feebleness of the result, and added a postscript: 'Your Serene Highness, judging it to be a blessing to abandon the Moscow Government as you abandoned Moscow, my duties in connection with the departure of the troops have come to an end, and, not wishing to be idle, or to witness the ruin of Kaluga Government, or to hear all day that you are engaged in sleep, I am departing for Yaroslavl and St. Petersburg. As a loyal subject and true son of my Fatherland, I wish you would concern yourself more with Russia, with the troops entrusted to you, and with the enemy. I, for my part, thank you for the fact that I have no need to yield to anyone either the Capital or the Government, and that you have not considered me worthy of your trust.' Kutuzov made no reply; nor did he receive Rostopchin.

Rostopchin vanished, but others equally hostile to the old Field Marshal remained at headquarters.

Kutuzov's plan—he did not conceal this even from his young orderly, Prince Golitsin—consisted in 'playing for time and in lulling Napoleon as much as possible, and in not disturbing him in Moscow . . . Everything that contributed to this purpose was preferable to the empty glory' of a successful attack on Napoleon's vanguard marching out of Moscow. Accordingly, Kutuzov made arrangements to take up a position south of that proposed by Bennigsen. He was sitting on a bench and dictating orders, when Bennigsen suddenly arrived from the left flank of the retiring Russian army. A discussion began which could have no positive issue; the two men loathed one another, and moreover Bennigsen had been waiting for the attack on the French advance posts previously promised by Kutuzov, and, from this point of view, Bennigsen was in the right when he announced that the position chosen by Kutuzov was not advantageous. But Kutuzov was not at all contemplating an attack, and from his point of view, tending to wait calmly, he too was in the right. 'The conversation continued for a long time,' recalls Golitsin. 'At first they discussed the matter with composure. Then, Kutuzov, growing heated and having no ready reply to contradict Bennigsen, said: "You thought that your position at Friedland was good. As for me, I am satisfied with this position, and we shall remain here, because it is I who command, and I am responsible for everything." ' This cruel reminder of Bennigsen's terrible defeat at Friedland was received as a mortal insult.

In his brief essay on Bennigsen, written in 1858 for the *American Encyclopedia,* Marx dedicates to his conduct in 1812 exactly three lines, which characterize him excellently: 'During the campaign of 1812 his main activity was at Alexander's headquarters, where he intrigued against Barclay de Tolly with the object of replacing him.' To this another line might be added:

From September 1812 he intrigued at Kutuzov's head-quarters with the object of replacing Kutuzov.

Kutuzov's greatest difficulties did not, however, arise from his differences with Rostopchin, Buksgevden, or even Bennigsen, who, surely, could not have hoped to force the Tsar to replace Kutuzov. Despite everything, the civilians and soldiers continued to trust the old Field Marshal.

Kutuzov's most influential enemy to whom the Tsar listened with the greatest attention was also attached to his staff and had a mighty power behind him—the British Empire. This was General Sir Robert Wilson, the English Commissioner with the Russian army. For Wilson; for Lord Cathcart, British Ambassador in St. Petersburg, who supported Wilson; for the British Cabinet, which supported Cathcart, the differences between Bennigsen and Kutuzov were not a mere 'Generals' quarrel.' They realized before everyone else that Kutuzov's strategy went against the interests of Great Britain.

Wilson, who secretly watched Kutuzov and sent reports about him to the Tsar, enjoyed Alexander's confidence, all the more so because the Tsar disliked the old Field Marshal for personal reasons, and was in full agreement with the English emissary.

Moreover, it would have been difficult for Alexander to quarrel with Wilson. 'Fifty thousand English rifles have arrived at Kronstadt. Please make arrangements for their immediate acceptance by the Artillery office,' wrote the Tsar to Gorchakov on 3 October. From England, of course, came not only rifles but also gold pounds, and they came in generous amounts—the English have always been generous when trying to defeat a strong enemy with the help of a foreign army. Robert

Wilson knew that he could get away with anything, and he took advantage of his position.

Having settled at headquarters, Robert Wilson promptly began to take part in the intrigues seething round Kutuzov. 'Your Majesty, of course, is aware that, considering Kutuzov's age and health, it is impossible to expect any active leadership, and that General Bennigsen is eager for the supreme command,' he wrote the Tsar on 27 September. In his correspondence with Alexander, he assumed a special tone. 'I am billeted in the same house as General Platov. I had hoped that he would be given a detachment of four thousand Cossacks and four squadrons of Hussars with six light guns, and, if possible, a few chasseurs.' Wilson was dissatisfied with Platov's position: 'But I find him after 42 years of excellent service . . . without a command . . . He strongly feels his humiliation, and I must confess that I share his feelings and hope that an order will be issued entrusting him with at least those Cossacks of the Ataman regiment who are coming to reinforce our army.'

Generally, he behaved as the master. He spoke to the Commander-in-Chief of the Russian Army as though he were a decrepit old man who had lost his wits and would commit some folly if not treated sternly. His arrogance was sustained by the knowledge that the Tsar detested Kutuzov.

Would the Continental blockade, causing poverty and unemployment in England, remain in force?—this was the Englishmen's greatest worry.

Semyon Romanovich Vorontsov's aristocratic English friends did not conceal from him the fact that the workers were irritated and restless. 'The workers of Birmingham complain bitterly that they have no work'—says a

letter written in September. This was one source of un-
happiness among Vorontsov's English friends, but there
was still another: their anxiety lest 'the insidious Corse'
should succeed in making peace with Alexander. One
was intimately connected with the other.

Such was the situation when Lauriston arrived in the
Russian camp.

. . .

General Lauriston's first appearance at the Russian
outposts on the evening of 5 October caused immense
excitement in Kutuzov's staff.

Robert Wilson, the English Commissioner and spy,
had been agitated since the morning of that day. With
his characteristic lack of ceremony he protested to
Kutuzov against the reception of Lauriston; and he did
not fail to bring the matter to the attention of Alexander. The form in which he did this shows that he
thought he could get away with every sort of arrogance:
'I have the honour to report to Your Majesty that Field
Marshal Kutuzov informed me this morning of his intention to grant an interview to Bonaparte's aide-de-
camp. I deemed it my duty to make the firmest and
most decisive representations against such an intention,
the execution of which would be incompatible with
Your Majesty's dignity and might have injurious consequences, adverse to the interests of Your Majesty, because it would serve to encourage the enemy, create
dissatisfaction in the army, and spread distrust among
foreign governments.'

In his note, Robert Wilson did not conceal his distrust of Alexander himself and threatened him with
British anger if he agreed to a truce, or, still worse,
to a peace with Napoleon. The same day Wilson also

reported to Lord Cathcart. This report bears a curious note in Arakcheyev's hand: 'Received from the Tsar on 16 October.' The letter had been written on 5 October; within eleven days it had been delivered to the Tsar, read, and turned over to Arakcheyev. Had it been intercepted? Had Cathcart himself delivered it to the Tsar? In any event, the Tsar learned that the reception of Lauriston was 'a measure fraught with impropriety and general harm' and that Wilson, in his capacity of general of an allied nation, had insisted that Kutuzov himself should not ride to the outpost to see Lauriston, but that Prince Volkonsky should go. Alexander also learned from this letter that Kutuzov did not harbour in his soul such hostile feelings towards Bonaparte as seemed desirable in Wilson's eyes, and that Kutuzov's 'decrepitude would always more or less incline him to desire peace.' Wilson was seconded by Prince Oldenburg and the Duke of Württemberg. Kutuzov was irritated no end by the meddling insolence of these foreign parasites, but could do nothing to stop it.

Kutuzov was compelled to receive Lauriston, if not in the direct presence of Robert Wilson and the Duke of Württemberg, who had tried hard to be present, at least in such a way that Lauriston could not help noticing them and the Duke of Oldenburg who was with them, on his way to the Field Marshal's study. The private conversation between Lauriston and Kutuzov lasted about half an hour, after which Prince Volkonsky was summoned and shortly afterwards was dispatched to Alexander in St. Petersburg.

After Lauriston's departure, the Field Marshal informed Wilson of the substance of the conversation. Lauriston had begun by complaining of 'the barbarous behaviour of the peasants towards those Frenchmen who fell into their hands.' The Field Marshal replied: 'It is impossible to civilize a whole nation within three months, and, in any case, to tell the truth, it is merely paying the French in the coin deserved by an invading horde of Tartars under Genghis Khan.' Lauriston proposed a truce on the basis of some sort of agreement. The Field Marshal replied that he lacked plenipotentiary powers. Lauriston then announced that it was not the French who had burned Moscow. Kutuzov answered that he knew this, and that it had been done by Russians who valued Moscow no more than any other city in the Empire. Lauriston said: 'You must not think that our affairs are in a desperate condition: our armies are almost equal. You are nearer your own reinforcements and provisions, but we, too, are receiving reinforcements. Perhaps you have received some news not very propitious for us from Spain?' To this, the Field Marshal replied that, actually, he had heard about it from Sir Robert Wilson, who had just left the room. Lauriston said that Wilson had his own reasons for exaggerating. Kutuzov did not agree with this. 'Actually, we did suffer a setback, which we owe to General Marmont's stupidities, and Madrid is temporarily occupied by the English, but our position will improve soon, as large bodies of troops are already on the way to Spain.' Kutuzov told Lauriston that the Russian people looked upon the French as they had looked upon the Tartars, who invaded Russia under Genghis Khan. Lauriston replied: 'Nevertheless, there is a difference,' and the Field Marshal retorted that the Russian people did not recognize any difference. With a realization of the complete futility of his journey, Lauriston returned to Napoleon in the Kremlin.

Desertions from the multi-national Napoleonic army

continued to increase. They assumed epidemic proportions in the Spanish regiments which, despite their fierce hatred of Napoleon, had been forcibly recruited in the occupied parts of Spain and forced to accompany him to Russia. In most cases they regarded desertion as a service to their distant Fatherland, devastated by Napoleon. The French did not succeed in their attempts at foraging. In some places the foragers were taken prisoner by the Cossacks, who infested the environs of Tarutino and the roads leading to Moscow; in others, they were exterminated by the peasants, whom they had come to rob; in still other places, they succeeded in obtaining hay only after slaying the peasants or driving them off into the woods.

General Baron Korf met the French General Armand at an outpost. Both the meeting and the conversation were accidental. 'We are really tired of this war; give us a passport and we shall leave,' said Armand. 'Oh, no, General,' retorted Korf, 'you have come to us as unbidden guests, and you shall have to leave us in the French manner [à la française], without saying farewell.' 'But, actually,' went on Armand, 'is it not a pity that two nations which respect one another should wage a relentless war? We shall apologize for having started it, and shall be glad to make a peace preserving the original frontiers.' 'Yes,' said Korf, 'we believe that you have lately learned to respect us, but could you respect us in the future if we allowed you to depart with your arms?' Armand's proposal expressed, of course, Napoleon's desire 'to conclude peace on the basis of previous frontiers,' but now, after the devastation of Russia's vast expanses, after the ruin of cities and countless villages, after the destruction of Moscow, such a proposal sounded like a new insult.

In Kutuzov's first account of his tête-à-tête with Lauriston, Kutuzov quite definitely makes no reference to the curses of posterity that would fall upon his head if he consented to a truce. All these rhetorical embellishments were later devised at leisure.

At all events, Napoleon saw that his third attempt at negotiations with Alexander was as much a failure as the first two. Such 'chance' meetings as that of General Armand with General Korf or that of Murat with Bennigsen, and later with Miloradovich (6 October), reinforced this conviction. 'Our people are terrible in their anger, they would instantly kill anyone who should venture to speak of peace proposals,' said Miloradovich to Murat.

Yet, foreseeing that he would soon have to abandon Moscow, and ardently desiring to sign a peace before leaving Moscow, in order to preserve his pose of conqueror, he decided to prod Alexander for an answer: he knew that Volkonsky, promptly after the interview between Lauriston and Kutuzov, had been dispatched with a report to the Tsar, yet no answer had arrived. On 20 October, that is, two weeks after Lauriston's interview with Kutuzov, Colonel Bertemi brought a letter from Marshal Berthier, Napoleon's Chief of Staff, to the Field Marshal. Berthier asked whether an answer had been received, and again spoke of 'establishing a better order,' meaning peace. Kutuzov replied to Berthier by a letter in his own hand, pointing out the distance and the difficulties of the autumnal roads, which doubtless delayed Alexander's reply. Kutuzov added: 'It is hard to stop a people angered by everything it has seen, a people which for three hundred years has not known a war within its borders, which is ready to sacrifice itself for the Fatherland and makes no distinction between what is accepted and what is not accepted in ordinary wars.'

Wilson was again infuriated and perturbed that Kutuzov should have entered into relations with the French. 'I know that the Field Marshal,' Robert Wilson wrote to Lord Cathcart on the evening of 20 October, from Tarusa, 'apprehensive of subjecting his life to danger, does not dare to begin any kind of negotiations, and is convinced that the Emperor would regard as a traitor any man who could propose such a thing to him; but the impressions which are produced by such relations are injurious internally and externally, politically and militarily, so much so that they might engender great misfortune; all estates are irritated, and the most thinking are disturbed.' Wilson did not trust Kutuzov, and he wrote with the obvious purpose of inducing Lord Cathcart to bring the matter to the Tsar's attention, suggesting that there was the threat of a revolution and a separatist movement on the Don. Wilson had apparently got wind of the fact that Napoleon actually contemplated entering into negotiations with the Cossacks. But the main thing was that Kutuzov was not averse to peace: 'There is no doubt that the Field Marshal is strongly disposed to pay attention to the enemy; French compliments please him immensely, and he respects these beasts of prey who have come to split Poland from Russia, to bring about a revolution in Russia itself, and to cause a rebellion of the people of the Don, for whom they profess a special respect and whom they desire to ingratiate by bestowing favours upon them.' Wilson expressed his desire to leave headquarters, 'if the Field Marshal retains control over the army and if the Tsar does not forbid him [Kutuzov] to have such personal relations,' so greatly was he, Wilson, 'vexed with such conduct.'

This was the end of Napoleon's attempts to obtain peace negotiations. Alexander made no answer to Kutuzov's report.

.   .   .

After listening to Lauriston's report, Napoleon could deceive himself no longer about prospects of negotiations. The single fact that Kutuzov had not allowed Lauriston to proceed to St. Petersburg revealed that the Russians had not the shadow of a desire to make peace. Nevertheless, Napoleon waited and made no further move. Actually, during these days—from 6 October, when Lauriston returned to Moscow, to 14 October, when Napoleon began to make preparations clearly indicative of approaching evacuation—he had relinquished hope of receiving an answer from St. Petersburg; at any event, an answer could scarcely have reached him sooner than the eighteenth. His condition was one of constant irritation. He spent whole nights pacing up and down in the Kremlin; he spoke of all possible plans, and confessed to Count Daru the real cause of his hesitation. How could he leave? How could he begin a retreat, when he had always been accustomed to attack and conquer? 'It will look like flight! What an effect it will have in Europe!' A retreat might bring on the most dangerous wars from all sides. 'Moscow is not a military position; it is a political position.' And, evidently recalling that this same Count Daru had told him long before, at Vitebsk, that he regarded this war as unnecessary, Napoleon added: 'In politics one should never retreat, one should never admit mistakes —to do so is to lose respect.'

That the whole war had been a mistake from beginning to end he now clearly recognized, though he did not yet suspect how fatal this mistake would prove to himself and to his army.

Daru was of the opinion that Moscow should be transformed into a fortified camp, that the French army should settle there for the winter, then resume active operations with spring, when it would be possible to bring up reinforcements from France and the Continent. The marshals, however, were opposed to this plan, as was Napoleon. The Emperor knew better than Daru how dangerous it was 'to bury himself in the Russian snows' for six or seven months, and how precarious was his hold on Europe, based exclusively on force. He had to retreat, because he could neither achieve peace nor safely winter in Moscow. He said nothing definite as yet, but began to make preparations for evacuating Moscow.

On 14 October, Napoleon gave the command to Berthier to *reiterate* a previous order: not a single French artillery park, no matter from where it had been dispatched for incorporation into the Grand Army, should be allowed to proceed beyond Smolensk; and that after 17 October not a single artillery or cavalry detachment should proceed to Moscow, but should remain in Mozhaisk, Gzhatsk, or Vyazma. 'The army will occupy another position.' Other significant orders followed fast. The Emperor issued the order to move as many wounded as possible from the Moscow district to Smolensk. He informed the Duke of Bassano in Vilna of this on 16 October, and added that he might take up winter quarters between the Dnieper and the Dvina.

On 16 October Napoleon wrote to Marie-Louise from Moscow: 'If I should be unable to return to Paris this winter, I shall invite you to come and see me in Poland.'

Napoleon tried to frighten Alexander with big new reinforcements, which were to pour in from all sides to the Grand Army. On 16 October he wrote to the Duke of Bassano, asking him to bid the King of Prussia, the Emperor of Austria, the King of Bavaria, and the King of Württemberg to send fresh reinforcements, and to recommend that all these 'allied' monarchs publish reports of these reinforcements in their newspapers, doubling the actual figures. All this was intended to show 'how great were the possibilities of recruiting at the Emperor's command not only in his own possessions but also in the possessions of his allies.' On the same day he ordered that oxen should be sent to Smolensk and, above all, warm clothing, as the cold season was approaching. 'Give orders to stop all other undertakings, and to concentrate all efforts on sending clothes to Smolensk.'

On the same 16 October, Napoleon wrote to Paris, to the Duke of Rovigo, Minister of Police: 'It is likely that the war will be prolonged through the entire winter, and only the occupation of St. Petersburg will open the Emperor's [Alexander's] eyes. Moscow is no more. It is actually a great loss for the Russian Empire. The city was justifiably called the centre and pride of the Empire. All the officers of the Russian army, it seems, are in despair over the Moscow catastrophe. They ascribe it to the insane and savage passions of Rostopchin, a kind of Marat, who was the city's governor. I have evacuated all my hospitals, which were situated here in houses amidst the ruins. I have fortified only the Kremlin, which is now immune to the danger of unexpected attack. From two to three thousand persons could hold out in it for a considerable period. I have placed here all my military supplies and provisions.'

In this letter, Napoleon speaks for the first time of the evacuation: 'I shall soon move from here, to prepare winter quarters and my operations for the coming year . . . All reports state that the enemy infantry is negligible. I am being assured that it hasn't as many as 15,000 veterans. The second and third lines consist only of militiamen. The enemy, however, has strengthened his cavalry. He has quadrupled the number of his Cossacks; the land is overflowing with them, and this gives rise to many annoying minor clashes.' This sentence, which says a great deal for all its deliberate obscurity, ends Napoleon's remarkable letter. Aside from hinting at the imminent evacuation of Moscow, it acknowledges the rapidly increasing audacity of the Cossack attacks on the couriers and conveyances bound for Moscow.

We have indirect proof that as late as 15 October, shortly before the battle of Tarutino, Napoleon did not yet contemplate so early a departure. On that day he wrote to Maret, the Duke of Bassano: 'Until now, relay messages have reached me; no incidents have marred their journeys. But it is difficult to expect this good luck to continue.' For that reason he asks that Bassano send important information by two or three separate couriers. It is clear that Napoleon's extended line of communications was increasingly imperiled by Cossacks and partisans. Yet the Emperor's request to repeat important messages and his instructions concerning the means of sending him newspaper clippings prove that on 15 October he did not yet foresee that four days later, on 19 October, he would leave the Russian capital forever.

It is true that an evacuation of the wounded from Moscow and Mozhaisk had begun a few days earlier, but it appears that Napoleon needed some sort of final jolt to end his last hesitations. That jolt came. On 18 October 1812, Napoleon was reviewing Marshal Ney's divisions, when he suddenly heard a distant thunder of artillery. Shortly afterward, an adjutant galloped in to report that Kutuzov had suddenly marched out of Tarutino, attacked Murat, and defeated him.

.   .   .

The thunder of guns that startled Napoleon came from the advance forces of the French army posted near the little river of Chernishna and commanded by Murat, King of Naples. These advance forces had been encamped there a long time, since 24 September, and had been completely inactive. They comprised from twenty to twenty-two thousand effectives. Kutuzov did not molest them, nor did Murat march against Tarutino. Since Lauriston's visit, which was interpreted as a sign of French weakness, Bennigsen, Ermolov, Baggovut, and Platov had not ceased asking Kutuzov for permission to attack Murat. They became particularly insistent after a thorough reconnaissance made by Quartermaster-General Toll brought in the information that Murat's detachment was careless, that his system of alarms was badly organized, and that his scouting service was inadequate because his horses were weak from insufficient fodder. Kutuzov wanted no battle, not even a minor one, but he gave in to his generals, having decided to prevent the clash from developing into a major engagement. On 16 October, Kutuzov examined the disposition proposed by Toll, and confirmed it. The attack had been fixed for 17 October, but Ermolov could not be found, and was not given his disposition in time.

The following day, on the morning of 17 October, Kutuzov found no one at the designated places. Irritated to begin with at having to undertake an action which in his opinion served no purpose, Kutuzov fell into a rage. He abused in the strongest words two officers he happened to encounter. One of them, Lieutenant-Colonel Eichen, resigned from Kutuzov's army as a result, but the other, Captain Brodin, whom Kutuzov called 'merely' a scoundrel, remained. Kutuzov gave orders to expel Ermolov from the army, but when his anger subsided he countermanded them.

This was the prelude. On 18 October, General Baggovut attacked Murat's left flank, and Orlov-Denisov his right flank. Bennigsen undertook to direct the battle —Kutuzov did not show up. Orlov-Denisov's first cavalry raid was successful: the French were knocked over, and several cannon were captured. At this point, the Cossacks spoiled the affair: they began to loot the part of the French camp which they had overrun, and the entreaties and threats of their superiors failed to stop them. The French had time to rally and they met two regiments of infantry chasseurs with a withering fire. Their commander, General Baggovut, was killed. The French retreated but in order. Bennigsen, assuming that his effectives were insufficient to pursue the French with any hope of success, asked Kutuzov's assistance, but the Field Marshal refused, and remained unmoved by the entreaties of Ermolov, Konovnitsin, and Miloradovich. Murat retreated slowly and in good order beyond the river Chernishna, to Spas-Kupla, exchanging fire with Orlov-Denisov, who followed him.

The engagement ended without any decisive result, except for the initial Russian success. Murat lost 2,500 men (3,000 according to some), the Russians from 1,000

to 1,200 men. The Russians were of course victorious:
they forced Murat to retreat, took 36 guns, 50 caissons,
and a flag. Claparède and Latour-Maubourg repulsed
Platov, who tried to cut Murat's retreat to Spas-Kupla.
Bennigsen later insisted that Murat's entire detachment
would have been destroyed if Kutuzov, by a malicious
whim, had not refused to give reinforcements at the
right moment. Kutuzov not only refused reinforcements; he even ordered his forces to withdraw from
Chernishna and return to their positions at Tarutino.

Bennigsen was beside himself with rage. Why had
Kutuzov failed to help him, permitting Murat to get
away with little loss and to retire in complete order?
'I can hardly control myself! What results might have
been achieved by that magnificent, brilliant engagement, if I had only received reinforcements . . . Instead, before the eyes of the entire army, Kutuzov forbade sending a single man to assist me; those were his
own words. General Miloradovich, who commanded
the left flank, burned with the desire to assist me, but
Kutuzov forbade him . . . You can imagine at what
distance our old man was from the battlefield! His
cowardice exceeds the proportions permissible even for
cowards, he gave the greatest proof of it at Borodino,
and for that reason he has covered himself with contempt and become ridiculous in the eyes of the whole
army,' wrote Bennigsen to his wife shortly after
Tarutino, on 22 October. What particularly revolted
Bennigsen was the Field Marshal's order to withdraw
12 versts immediately after the battle and reoccupy the
original positions. 'Do you realize my position? I must
quarrel with him every time a step has to be taken
against the enemy, and I am forced to listen to this
man's crudities!'

Kutuzov, whom Suvorov had embraced before the army, could neglect the charge of 'cowardice.' He never had the slightest intention of justifying his conduct on the day of Tarutino. He had his own firm plan, and at that time he had ceased paying attention to anything but his plan.

Bennigsen's indignation mounted by the day. He realized that Kutuzov's refusal to help him had been deliberate and that he had not permitted the battle of Tarutino to develop into a serious victory. The relations between Bennigsen and Kutuzov became tense in the extreme. This is what Bennigsen wrote to Kutuzov after the battle: 'His Majesty's armies achieved this victory with a correctness and order which are seen only at exercises. It is regrettable, very regrettable, that Your Serene Highness should have been too far from the place of action to get a complete view of the beautiful spectacle of the battle.' Kutuzov did not leave these jibes unanswered. 'Where is that imbecile? That red-headed one? That coward?' he cried one day, pretending he could not remember the name of the person he was looking for. When someone finally ventured to ask him whether he meant Bennigsen, the Field Marshal answered: 'Yes, yes, yes!' This incident occurred on the day of Tarutino. The army was confronted with a repetition of the struggle between Bagration and Barclay. But Bennigsen's reputation, strength, talents did not measure up to Bagration's; and Kutuzov, by virtue of all his past, by his military and moral authority, by his wide popularity, was much stronger than Barclay. To cope with Bagration's opposition had been beyond Barclay's strength; Kutuzov had no difficulty in getting rid of Bennigsen. Bennigsen was known as a most unscrupulous taker of bribes. In 1807, as Commander-in-

Chief, he took bribes from contractors, patronized thieves in the commissary department, and was responsible for the terrible defeat at Friedland (14 June 1807). It was said that his soldiers were starving to death, that he had begun his career as a poor man, and had grown wealthy by stealing from his army. With such a reputation he was no match for Kutuzov.

He was unable to control his fierce hatred of the Field Marshal. Finally he sent a report to the Tsar, which in violence surpassed all bounds.* It was said in the army that the Tsar transmitted the report to the Field Marshal. As a result of this report, Kutuzov ordered Bennigsen to leave the army.

The battle of October 18 somehow came to be known as the battle of Tarutino (actually Tarutino is far south of the battlefield). Though its military results were insignificant, it had considerable political and moral consequences. It raised the spirit of the Russian army: for it was the first purely offensive operation in the war, and it was successful. And it was the final, decisive jolt that roused Napoleon to leave Moscow.

.   .   .

Napoleon interpreted the engagement at Tarutino as follows: Kutuzov feels sufficiently strong to attack; therefore, we must march southward before the Russian Commander-in-Chief bars the way.

* 'Soon after the battle of Tarutino, Kutuzov received a letter from the Tsar, which had been sent to His Majesty by Bennigsen. This letter accused Kutuzov of keeping the army inactive and of indulging in luxury. Immediately after the reception of this letter, Kutuzov ordered Bennigsen to leave the army.' (Shcherbinin's Notebooks, in 'Materials of the Military-Scientific Archives of the General Staff,' 1812, number 1, p. 43.)

When Napoleon set out from Moscow he had nearly
110,000 men. In Tarutino and near Tarutino, Kutuzov
had 97,112. Napoleon's artillery had considerably de-
creased since Borodino; many pieces had to be abandoned because of the impossibility of transporting them
—even the cavalry had very few horses left, and entire
units had long been dismounted. Kutuzov had 622
guns. Napoleon did not know the exact strength of the
Russians, but he felt sure that in the event of a clash
on open ground the superiority would be on his side.

To save his face, Napoleon first intended to leave a
garrison of 8,000 men in Moscow and he had even appointed General Mortier to command it. In retaliation
for Alexander's failure to answer his three messages,
Napoleon decided to blow up the Kremlin before leaving. Mortier was not accustomed to question orders. He
immediately gave orders to seize the Russians remaining
in Moscow, and used their labour to mine the Kremlin
with its palaces, temples, et cetera. The mining went on
for three days and nights. Those Russians who refused
to dig were cruelly beaten.

On the night of 19 October, the French army began
to move out of Moscow. The 100,000 troops were accompanied by an interminable file of wagons and carts
filled to the brim with loot. Thousands of people followed in carriages or on foot—foreigners with their
wives and children, who had remained in Moscow and
were now leaving in fear of reprisals by the Russians.
The baggage train was so immense, the army so extended, that Napoleon said at once that nothing could
be more dangerous than this movement. But he could
not yet decide to make his men abandon the loot—he
gave that order later.

The Emperor marched towards Kaluga; he led his

army straight to Krasnaya Pakhra, picking up the remnants of Murat's detachment on his way. He ordered Mortier to join the army immediately after the Kremlin was blown up. Mortier had been left in Moscow for two days for the obvious purpose of temporarily concealing from the army the real meaning of the evacuation, and preserving, despite everything, the attitude of conqueror.

This was also necessary for Europe.

Napoleon had long ceased writing to his wife about Moscow. In his last letters from Moscow, he betrayed an interest chiefly in his little son. He praises the fine sunny weather, sends instructions to reward the author of a new opera which the Empress had liked, mentions the 'panorama' that was being shown in Paris, and so on. *'Ma bonne amie Louise* . . . I am glad to hear that you like the panorama of Antwerp. It might be a good idea to make one showing the burning of Moscow . . . Write often to your father, urge him to strengthen Schwarzenberg's corps . . .' The Emperor did not place too much confidence in the fighting zeal of his involuntary Austrian ally.

The day before his departure from Moscow, he again speaks of the fire and the madness of the Russians who had devastated their capital 'for centuries to come.' 'Moscow was a city all the more beautiful and marvellous because it was almost the only city of this size in all this immense country.' At 7 o'clock in the morning of 19 October, Napoleon followed his army out of Moscow. *'Mon amie,* I am on my way to my winter quarters. The weather is superb, but it cannot last. Moscow is entirely burned, and, as it is not a military position required for my ultimate purposes, I am leaving it and will remove the garrison that still remains.

My health is splendid, and my affairs are going well.' The same letter casually mentions Tarutino: 'There was a clash with the Cossacks.'

As soon as the Emperor and the army were out of Moscow, the explosions began.

On 19 October, the Wine Arcades were blown up and the Simonov Monastery, which had hitherto escaped destruction, was burned. Among the French army a movement at first incomprehensible to the uninitiated was observed. All night long, baggage trains, laden carts, troops moved in an uninterrupted stream. The movement continued with greater intensity on 20 and 21 October.

On 21 October, explosions in the Kremlin shook all Moscow. The Arsenal building, a part of the Kremlin walls were blown up; fires broke out in the Granitova building and in the cathedrals; the Nikolska tower and other towers overlooking the river were partly demolished. Fortunately, rain moistened the fuses, and the explosions proved less destructive than Napoleon had expected. The successful ones were so powerful that walls collapsed even outside the Kremlin. Ivan the Great escaped destruction by an accident: the slow-match of the mine beneath it was affected by water.

After each explosion the moans of wounded, half-crushed, frightened people were heard in the Kremlin and on the adjoining square. Napoleon's army was leaving the ruins of Moscow. On the night of the twenty-second, new deafening explosions suddenly rent the air. The remaining population was in a state of complete panic. The explosions were so powerful that buildings crashed in Kitai Gorod; a considerable distance away glass was shattered and window frames collapsed.

The last (fifth) explosion of the Kremlin walls occurred at daybreak on 23 October. A few hours later, Marshal Mortier's last detachments left the city. A state of anarchy marked by intensified looting continued for a few hours after the departure of the army.

'I left Moscow, having given orders to blow up the Kremlin,' wrote Napoleon from the village of Fomin-skoye, where he arrived on 22 October. 'I would have needed 20,000 men to keep the city. As the city was in ruins, it only handicapped my operations.'

The explosions were not heard in the distant Russian camp, but they were heard by Cossack patrols who had long been scouring the environs of Moscow.

.   .   .

On 22 October, Ensign Iazikov was reconnoitring near Moscow with a detachment of Cossacks, when the troops were startled by a terrible roar coming from the city. Iazikov decided to find out the cause of the explosion. It was a risky thing to do, but he entered the city at the head of his small detachment.

A dead silence reigned in the streets. Meeting no Frenchmen or anyone else, the Cossacks gradually made their way to the Kremlin. They were the first in Russia to learn the stunning news: Napoleon was gone.

9

THE RETREAT AND THE BEGINNING
OF PARTISAN WARFARE

LIKE an endless river, Napoleon's army flowed out of Moscow with its artillery and caissons, its colossal baggage trains, carriages, carts, wagons full of loot belonging to marshals, generals, officers, and privates. Once again the army unrolled its multi-coloured ribbon on the roads. The soldiers knew that Napoleon was displeased that they had burdened themselves with so much loot. They tried to cover the rugs, precious fabrics, the gold and silver plate, with baskets, bags of bread, flour, et cetera. But these very objects were the rarest of all. Napoleon saw through the subterfuge, but at that stage of the retreat he had not yet decided to make his half-starved soldiers abandon their looted valuables, thus depriving them of the comforting thought that they would later be rewarded for all their sufferings. They did not yet know that most of them would leave their very lives in Russia, along with the booty of Moscow.

Napoleon marched on Kaluga, intending from there to turn towards Smolensk. Why did he regard Smolensk as an indispensable halting point in his march? Why did he not advance towards the southern provinces, which were rich and intact?

Clausewitz was the first military writer to explode the widespread opinion that this was a blunder. 'Where could Napoleon have found provisions for his army,' writes Clausewitz, 'if not in the stores he had prepared in advance? What good was an "untapped region" to an army which had no time to lose and was constantly forced to bivouac in large masses? What Commissary official would have agreed to travel ahead of that army to requisition supplies, and what Russian organization would have executed his orders? His whole army would have been starving within a week.'

On the Smolensk-Minsk-Vilna road, Napoleon had garrisons, supply stores, and provisions; that road had been prepared, while nothing at all had been prepared in southern Russia. No matter how 'rich,' 'bread-producing,' and the like, these regions may have been, it was impossible to improvise the supply of an army of 100,000 men moving rapidly in a compact mass. 'A retreating army in enemy territory,' Clausewitz explains, 'needs, as a rule, a previously prepared route . . . By "prepared route" we understand a route secured by garrisons along which stores required by the army have been organized.' Clausewitz here reveals the strict realism of his thinking. No one was more adept than this greatest military thinker at unmasking empty clichés. The southern governments may have been ten times richer than Smolensk, but in Smolensk Napoleon had prepared stores, and in the south he had nothing at all. That settled the matter.

But leaving Moscow, he firmly resolved to reach Smolensk not by the old road, but by a new one, via Kaluga, because he had no stores before Smolensk anyway, and the old road was completely devastated. Having to choose between two roads, with no stores on either of them, but along one of which (Moscow-Kaluga-Smolensk) there were still 'intact villages' (the expression is Marshal Davout's), while the other was one scorched desert, Napoleon naturally preferred the Kaluga road. 'Let us march to Kaluga! And woe betide him who tries to stop me!' he said on 19 October, as he led his army out of Moscow.

This circumstance stresses the significance of Kutuzov's famous march on Tarutino: without this manœuvre Kutuzov could never have established an impassable obstacle south of Maloyaroslavets to bar the French from reaching Kaluga.

As soon as Kutuzov heard the news that Napoleon had left Moscow, he regarded Russia as saved, and said so. His army was increasing through levies and reinforcements—and by the middle of October it amounted to 85,000 men, not counting the Cossacks. Napoleon's army received some replenishments, but far less than this. The Russian cavalry had enough fodder, but the French horses were falling by the thousands; French foragers obtained no hay or oats; instead, they were hunted and killed by the peasants. From the moment of Napoleon's departure from Moscow, Kutuzov had no doubt that the French would leave Russia and that they would do so even without any battles—consequently he thought battle unnecessary.

For the remainder of the war, Alexander waged an unsuccessful struggle against Kutuzov's strategy and tactics. On the side of the Tsar was almost all of Kutuzov's staff; moreover, Wilson (that is, England) and all Europe conquered by Napoleon were thirsting for revenge.

Alexander had strongly disapproved the abandonment of Moscow, and showed his dissatisfaction in cold letters to Kutuzov. On 14 October, the Tsar again reproached Kutuzov for his inactivity. 'The responsibility will be yours,' he wrote to the Field Marshal, 'if the enemy is able to detach a considerable number of troops to threaten St. Petersburg, in which only a small force remains, because in the army entrusted to you, if you act with resolution and energy, you dispose of all the means necessary for averting that new misfortune. Remember that you still owe your injured Fatherland an explanation for the loss of Moscow.' One week later, on 21 October, another courier hastened to Kutuzov bearing new reproaches. This time, the Tsar was extremely displeased by Lauriston's meeting with Kutuzov; he reminds the Field Marshal that no enemy proposals whatsoever will induce him 'to interrupt the struggle and thereby to betray my sacred obligation to avenge the injured Fatherland.'

The Tsar's old dislike of Kutuzov rapidly grew to hatred. He accused him of inactivity, negligence, gross blunders. 'To my extreme regret,' he wrote on 11 November, 'I see that the hope of erasing the general sorrow over the loss of Moscow by cutting the enemy's road of retreat has completely vanished. Your incomprehensible passivity after the fortunate engagement of Tarutino has cost us the gains it promised; your unnecessary and pernicious retreat to Goncharov after the battle of Maloyaroslavets destroyed all the advantages of your position; you could have forced the enemy to hasten his retreat near Vyazma, and thereby cut off at least three of his army corps: those of Davout, Ney, and the Viceroy, which were fighting near that city.' The Tsar is further indignant that Kutuzov should have been so badly informed about the enemy's movement, despite the excellent light cavalry of the Russians.

He scented a deliberate design in Kutuzov's slowness and apathy. Kutuzov did not want to overtake Napoleon and give him battle—that was why he talked of the 'golden bridge' he had built for the enemy. Retreating freely without energetic pursuit by Kutuzov, Napoleon had attacked and defeated Chichagov and Wittgenstein who were waiting for him. 'By this negligence of yours you subjected Count Wittgenstein's corps to an obvious danger, for Napoleon had left the three above-mentioned corps ahead of you, with you alone to pursue them. Now he will be able to reinforce the former Corps of Saint-Cyr with his Guard and attack Count Wittgenstein with superior forces.' For Kutuzov, Napoleon's departure from Russia was a stroke of good fortune compared to which he doubtless considered unimportant whether or not Napoleon would give Wittgenstein a drubbing on his way; but for Alexander, the War of 1812 could be the end of the whole business, and that could be encompassed by taking Napoleon himself prisoner. For that reason, he concludes his letter: 'I call your attention to this danger which is so obvious, and I remind you that you will be personally responsible for all the misfortunes which may result.'

The 'misfortunes' which, according to Alexander, resulted from the fact of Napoleon's escape from Russia were the year 1813, which was bloodier than 1812, and the years 1814 and 1815. But Kutuzov had no intention of 'liberating' Europe; this he regarded as the business of Europe itself, and he had no need to surround and catch Napoleon. Kutuzov did not even desire a close contact with the rear-guard of the retreating French Emperor. His reluctance did not arise from 'cowardice.'

From his point of view, which he had adopted after profound meditations, new engagements were unnecessary. Alexander, sly, distrustful, and hating Kutuzov, suspected, though he was far from the scene, that Kutuzov was deliberately trying to 'spoil' and make impossible the very things the Tsar so much hoped for, that he was deliberately pushing Chichagov and Wittgenstein into a disadvantageous position, and that in their catastrophic battle with Napoleon, he would not come to their assistance . . . But his sharp letters were all in vain. When the decisive hour struck, when the next act of the great drama began to unfold on the banks of the Berezina, Kutuzov acted exactly as Alexander had feared he would, and as he himself considered necessary and useful.

Kutuzov's conduct at Maloyaroslavets illustrates his strategic plans.

. . .

At 11 o'clock on the night of 22 October, a mounted courier sent by Dokhturov arrived at Kutuzov's headquarters with the information that Napoleon was advancing on Maloyaroslavets. Kutuzov's slowness in coming to Dokhturov's assistance was later sharply criticized by some military writers who had taken part in the battle of Maloyaroslavets. 'Why did the army stationed at Tarutino,' asks one witness, 'which received the information of Napoleon's advance on Maloyaroslavets at 11 o'clock on the night of 22 October, only reach the threatened point 38 hours later, though the distance it had to cover was only 28 versts?' The truth is that Kutuzov wanted to avoid engagements; he regarded a new Borodino as unnecessary and harmful in any circumstances. Even at Tarutino he wanted to build

a 'golden bridge' for Napoleon, and tried to avoid unnecessary losses of men. He knew that his flanking 'parallel' march would be a surer method of destroying the
enemy's live forces. Neither Bennigsen at Tarutino,
nor Dokhturov at Maloyaroslavets, nor Wilson at his
own quarters, nor Alexander acting from St. Petersburg
could shake his resolve.

Near Maloyaroslavets Kutuzov adopted the same tactics as he had six days before near Tarutino. Of course
he knew that he must not let Napoleon enter Kaluga—
and not because he feared that he would march through
the southern governments: it is more than probable
that Kutuzov knew as well as Clausewitz and Napoleon
himself that ultimately the French army would have
to take the 'prepared' route. But if Napoleon had
seized Kaluga and everything that had been prepared
there for the Russian army, he would have been able
to reach Smolensk in much better condition.

On 22 September, Kutuzov had ordered Dokhturov
to advance to Fominskoye and attack a French detachment which, according to information brought by
scouts, numbered 10,000 men. But on his way there
Dokhturov received startling new information: first, at
Fominskoye and near Fominskoye, there was not a detachment of 10,000 men, but an immense army, almost
all of the French forces with Napoleon at their head;
second, the French had already occupied Borovsk, far
south of Fominskoye and on the straight line to Kaluga.
It was necessary to abandon the advance on Fominskoye,
to turn sharply southward, and proceed beyond Borovsk
to the town of Maloyaroslavets, situated between
Borovsk and Kaluga. By a straight line, Maloyaroslavets
is one third of the distance from Borovsk to Kaluga. It
was clear that the Russian armies must try to reach

Maloyaroslavets before Napoleon. But Dokhturov feared
Kutuzov, and he sent a special messenger to the Field
Marshal asking for permission to advance on Maloyaroslavets. While the messenger galloped to the Commander-in-Chief and back, much time was lost. The
Russians marched all night almost without rest, but
when they reached the city at 4 o'clock in the morning of 23 October, the whole of Napoleon's army was
approaching. The Russian chasseurs were soon driven
out of the suburbs. That day, Maloyaroslavets changed
hands eight times. The cannonade did not cease for a
moment; now the Russians, now the French recon-
quered the disputed positions by bayonet charges.
Dokhturov was near complete destruction, but at the
last moment, at 2 o'clock in the afternoon, Rayevsky came
to his rescue with his corps, and at 4 o'clock Kutuzov himself approached with the entire Russian army. Kutuzov
went round the town and took up positions on the road
from Maloyaroslavets to Kaluga. At sunset the French
had captured the town after eight assaults, and awaited
a general battle. The cannonade had stopped. The
town was on fire, filled with the blood-curdling wails
of inhabitants and wounded soldiers caught in the burning buildings and littered streets. The French could not
help them: the fire was so fierce that the centre of the
city and some of the outskirts were absolutely inaccessible.

All that terrible night, the Russians beheld the glow
of the burning town, heard the wails of the trapped
inhabitants, the shouts of the French army. Now and
then there was an exchange of rifle fire. They were prepared for another Borodino on the following day. But
early in the morning, the Field Marshal suddenly issued orders for a retreat from Maloyaroslavets.

Kutuzov knew that by giving this order he would incur the silent anger of his general staff, the frank insolence of Robert Wilson and Bennigsen, and more reproaches from the Tsar. Yet he did not hesitate. 'The officers of Your Majesty's army,' wrote Robert Wilson to the Tsar about the battle of Maloyaroslavets, 'fight with dauntless courage, but I consider it my unhappy duty to declare that they deserve and need to be led by a more skilful commander.' Yet Kutuzov in his retreat barred Napoleon's way to Kaluga. Whether he planned to give battle if Napoleon tried to break through to Kaluga, we do not know. Napoleon did not try, but from the point of view of Wilson, Bennigsen, and the Duke of Württemberg, Kutuzov, in refusing to drive Napoleon out of Maloyaroslavets and give him a general battle, had committed another crime.

Kutuzov's ultimate purpose and the radical difference between his ideas and Wilson's were clearly revealed at that point. On 25 October, 3 versts from Maloyaroslavets, Wilson wrote a letter to Alexander, exactly formulating the two irreconcilable points of view: that of exclusively Russian interests represented by the Field Marshal, and that of all Europe, headed by England. 'The Field Marshal's age and physical decrepitude,' wrote Wilson, 'may somehow excuse him, and for that reason one may regret the weakness that makes him say that "he wants only one thing, that the enemy leave Russia," when the salvation of the whole world depends on him. But such physical and moral weakness renders him incapable of filling his present post, because it undermines the respect that is due to superiors, and gives promise of disaster at a moment when every hope and ardent assurance of success should get the upper hand.'

For Wilson, that is, for England, the only thing that really mattered was the death or capture of Napoleon, after which the fall of his Empire could be expected. For Kutuzov, the only thing that mattered was the liberation of Russia with the smallest possible losses for the Russian army. He was of course shrewder, slyer, subtler, and more profound than Robert Wilson. The fatuous English brigadier regarded Russian soldiers as mere material on which to found the new post-Napoleonic greatness of the British Empire. Kutuzov knew this perfectly and clearly understood what Wilson meant by the 'salvation of the whole world.' According to Wilson, Maloyaroslavets should have been the scene of a new attempt to 'save' the London merchants, the Liverpool shipowners, the Manchester textile manufacturers, from the effects of the Continental blockade. But Kutuzov was not concerned with their salvation, and again disappointed Wilson's hopes.

There was an unbridgeable gulf between Kutuzov's conception of the war and that of foreigners, particularly Englishmen. 'The unfortunate withdrawal from our positions above Maloyaroslavets' wrote Wilson to Lord Cathcart, the British Ambassador, on 31 October, 'saved the enemy from inevitable destruction and deprived Russia of the glory and Europe of the advantage of ending the revolutionary war . . . All the blood that has been shed, all the difficulties Russia may suffer will fall on Field Marshal Kutuzov's head.' In contrast, Bennigsen's advice, which the Field Marshal refused to follow, 'could have saved the universe!'

Kutuzov was concerned with the salvation of Russia; at the same time he knew perfectly well (and once even said so to Wilson's face) that the British were interested not in the 'universe' but exclusively in saving England from the Continental blockade. What probably irritated Wilson most was his realization that 'the old Russian fox' saw through him. Cathcart knew why the battle of Maloyaroslavets was part of a 'revolutionary war,' and his correspondent Wilson did not find it necessary to explain the strange words in his letter. Napoleon, the strangler of the revolution, was to them both the incarnation of the French big bourgeoisie, borne on the crest of the Revolution. Even since 1793, this class had been fighting England, first in western Germany, then in Belgium, Holland, Italy, Egypt, Syria, Austria, Germany, Poland, Spain, Portugal, again in Austria, and finally in Russia. For twenty years French industry had fought London, Manchester, Birmingham, and Liverpool, with fire and steel. Sir Robert Wilson unhesitatingly wrote to Cathcart that the decrepit Kutuzov had allowed the 'French Revolution' to escape at Maloyaroslavets.

Such was Wilson's concern over the 'universe.' 'The Field Marshal's conduct infuriates me!' Wilson repeatedly wrote. Why not organize a new Borodino at Maloyaroslavets? Why not sacrifice another 60,000 men?

In 1812, Kutuzov had had many opportunities to observe the generosity of foreigners in shedding the blood of Russian soldiers. He could also remember the curious letters with which Francis, Emperor of Austria, had honoured him in November 1805. At that time, Napoleon had routed one Austrian army and was preparing to rout another. Kutuzov threw out covering forces, which were fated to perish, and hastily retreated toward Olmütz. Capture, disgrace, rout pressed hard on his heels: Napoleon's forces were three times stronger than his own. 'If irresistible pressure forces you to retreat,' Emperor Francis wrote to Kutuzov, 'do so only step by step and in the direction of Krems . . . there *at any cost* you must cover the construction of a new bridge, which will take a few weeks.' At any cost! The cost would have been only the lives of 35,000 Russian soldiers, who would not have perished in 'a few weeks,' as Francis and his Court Military Council thought, but in a few days. But Emperor Francis had courageously agreed in advance to the sacrifice: there were plenty of men in Russia! Even then, Kutuzov did not pay the slightest attention to the letter, though he showed no disrespect to our Austrian ally. Now, in 1812, he had no intention of following the insistent advice of Robert Wilson, also extremely generous in spending Russian blood, and this time he showed no disrespect to our British ally. Kutuzov rarely indulged in arguments; he even more rarely ceded to other people's representations.

At daybreak on 25 October, Kutuzov ordered the Russian army to withdraw from Maloyaroslavets two and a half versts to the south. Miloradovich's vanguard retired only a small distance from the town. Napoleon saw that if he persisted in his intention of breaking through to Kaluga, he would have to accept a general battle on as large a scale as Borodino.

He decided against it.

For the first time in his career, Napoleon withdrew from a general battle. For the first time in this bloody Russian campaign, he turned his back on the Russian army, and decided to flee. The real retreat of the Grand Army did not begin on 19 October, when Napoleon led it out of Moscow, but on the night of 24 October, when he decided to give up Kaluga and move back to Borovsk.

At a war council in a peasant house in sight of burning Maloyaroslavets, Napoleon listened silently to the assembled marshals. Marshal Bessières insisted on the impossibility of attacking Kutuzov in the positions he occupied: 'And what positions! We have just learned its strength. And against what an enemy! Didn't you see yesterday's battlefield, didn't you see the fury with which Russian recruits, scarcely armed, scarcely clothed, marched to their death?' Bessières strongly advised the Emperor to withdraw, to decline battle with Kutuzov's entire army, which barred the road from Maloyaroslavets to Kaluga.

Napoleon followed his advice.

On 25 October, at daybreak, the Emperor rode to Maloyaroslavets. With him a small retinue: Marshal Berthier, General Rapp, and a number of officers. Suddenly a detachment of Cossacks came galloping with their pikes atilt, heading straight for Napoleon and his retinue. With shouts of 'Hurrah!' they charged into the small group of mounted men. Their shouts saved Napoleon from death or capture: his retinue had not recognized the horsemen in the distance and took the Cossacks for a squadron of French cavalry. But on hearing the characteristic 'hurrah,' the retinue of about 25 officers clustered round the Emperor. One Cossack managed to swoop down on General Rapp, piercing his horse with his pike, but two French squadrons arrived in time to throw back the Cossacks, who quickly vanished in the woods taking with them a few French artillery horses and disorganizing a part of the French camp on their way.

Napoleon remained outwardly calm in the face of this terrible danger. He rode into Maloyaroslavets. The town was a heap of ruins. Several thousand charred corpses littered the streets. These were the inhabitants of Maloyaroslavets and Russian and French wounded. The town was still burning in some places. Napoleon returned to the camp. The French army was ordered to back up on the old Kaluga road, whence it had come. In the evening Napoleon summoned Uvant, chief physician of the Old Guard, and ordered him to prepare a phial of poison immediately. Napoleon drew his inferences from the Cossack raid. From that moment on, he never parted from his phial: it spared him the threat of being taken alive.

Napoleon retreated from Maloyaroslavets to Borovsk, Vereya, Mozhaisk. This time he gave orders to requisition from the population absolutely everything that could be of use in the campaign, and ruthlessly to burn cities, towns, and villages lying on his army's route of retreat. It is true that after the first passage of the Russians and the pursuing French armies, little remained to be burned. Yet some places, such as Borovsk, had escaped destruction. But now, after Napoleon left it on his way to Vereya, Borovsk was burned to the ground. The same fate befell Vereya, where Napoleon had stopped only for a short while. In this town he united with Marshal Mortier, who had brought with him (from Moscow) 8,000 cavalrymen, of whom only 2,000 had horses.

In Vereya, Mortier reported to Napoleon that before leaving Moscow his detachment captured General Wintzengerode and Captain Naryshkin, who had ventured into Moscow, claiming to have come for a parley. Wintzengerode was a German who had gone into the Russian service, and Napoleon fell into a rage when he heard of his capture. In his view, the Englishmen and Germans who surrounded the Tsar and Kutuzov exerted an evil influence and stood in the way of a peace.

Napoleon ordered the two prisoners brought before him. 'Then,' writes Naryshkin, 'the most terrible scene began, the like of which even the oldest French officers serving with Napoleon had not seen . . .' 'You are in the service of the Russian Emperor?'—'Yes, Sire,' answered Wintzengerode.'—'And who gave you permission? You are a scoundrel! Must I meet you everywhere! And why did you go to Moscow? To spy, no doubt!'— 'No, Sire, I trusted in the honour of your troops.'— 'And what business have you with my troops? You are a scoundrel! Look at the condition Moscow is in! Fifty scoundrels like you have brought her to that condition! You induced Emperor Alexander to make war on me! Caulaincourt told me about it! You organized the killing of my soldiers on your way! Oh, your fate is sealed! Guards, take him, have him shot by a firing squad, rid me of him! A fight with me is an unequal fight! In six weeks I shall be in Petersburg! As to you personally, you are through. Shoot him on the spot! Or rather, court-martial him! If you are a Saxon or a Bavarian, you are my subject and I am your sovereign. In that event you'll be shot. If not, it's a different matter.'

Then Napoleon turned to Naryshkin. 'Are you Naryshkin, son of the Chamberlain? Oh, your case is different. You are a brave man who does his duty. But why do you serve such scoundrels as this? You should serve your own Russian people!'

Luckily for Wintzengerode, he was able to prove that he was a Prussian subject. This saved him from execution.

From Maloyaroslavets to Smolensk, the retreating French army passed through devastated towns and villages, and fired everything that had escaped destruction. 'On 2 November,' writes Robert Wilson from Vyazma, where he was with Kutuzov's staff, 'we again advanced by forced marches. The enemy's movements could be distinguished by an uninterrupted line of flames and smoke, several versts long.' There was a gigantic glow of fires ahead and on the sides; the ground was littered for miles with dead men and horses.

On both sides the bitterness grew. Peasants hunted lagging Frenchmen and pitilessly exterminated them; the French, too, showed extreme cruelty. After Napoleon with his Old Guard had passed Vyazma and advanced towards Smolensk, Davout, Murat, and Ney beat off attacks by Miloradovich, Platov, and Orlov, and the Russians did not enter Vyazma until the main French forces had left the outskirts of the burning city. It was only by accident that General Choglokov with his detachment, which had somewhat outrun the main Russian forces, reached Vyazma in time to free 300 Russian wounded and prisoners whom the enemy had locked in the church before setting it on fire.

Frost had not yet set in, but the weather was much colder. Miloradovich and Platov closely followed the French rear-guard, harrying it without interruption; Cossack detachments and partisans harassed the flanks of the retreating French, capturing baggage trains, cutting up lagging units in sudden raids. 'Today,' notes Robert Wilson on 5 November in a village situated 40 versts from Vyazma on the road to Smolensk, 'I saw a scene of horror rarely encountered in modern war. Two thousand men, naked, dead or dying, and a few thousand dead horses, mostly fallen from starvation; hundreds of unfortunate wounded crawling out of the woods and imploring the pity of even the angered peasants whose avenging shots resound everywhere; two hundred blown up carts; every habitation set on fire; remnants of all sorts of armament littering the roads; the severe winter climate—'

Even before reaching Smolensk, the retreating army was starving. Here is an account by a French officer (he wrote it in Smolensk, on 7 November): 'Three or four times a day I passed from extreme misery to extreme pleasure. I must admit these pleasures were not refined: for instance, one of the keenest pleasures was to find at night a few potatoes, which we ate unsalted, with our moldy bread. Can you realize the depths of our misery? This went on for 18 days. I left Moscow on 16 October and arrived in Smolensk on 2 November.' He had been ordered to convoy 1,500 wounded evacuated from Moscow before the retreat of the Grand Army. The guard consisted of about 300 men. On the way they were attacked by Russian partisans and regular troops. They were also fired at from a distance, but somehow managed to repel the attackers. 'We resolved to form a small square and rather be killed to the last man than fall into the hands of the peasants, who would have murdered us at once by cutting our throats or by some other pleasant method.'

The hunger in the French army assumed catastrophic proportions.

Somewhere between Vyazma and Smolensk, the Russian General Kreitz marching with his regiment perceived a noise in the woods on the right side of the road. He rode into the woods and to his horror found Frenchmen eating the flesh of a dead comrade. This incident took place before the frosts, before the complete disorganization of the French army, before the unprecedented disasters after Smolensk. Kreitz's testimony is confirmed by a number of others. 'They have nothing to eat except horse meat. Since their departure from Moscow and Smolensk, they have been eating human bodies.'

'. . . Hunger has compelled them to eat horses' carcasses, and many of us have seen them roasting the flesh of their compatriots . . . The Smolensk road is covered, at every step, with dead men and horses,' writes Voieykov to the aged poet Derzhavin, from Elna, on 11 November. This note, too, refers to the beginning of the retreat, before Smolensk. Any number of witnesses attest that the eating of corpses at the end of the disastrous retreat was a common occurrence.

Yet even before the frosts, the hunger among the French was frightful. It was hunger and not frosts that rapidly destroyed Napoleon's retreating army.

General Kreitz, who took part in the whole campaign, wrote: 'French writers unjustly declare that the cold was the cause of the destruction of Napoleon's army. From Maloyaroslavets to Vyazma, the weather was quite warm. Between Vyazma and Smolensk we had light frosts, and near Elna the first snow fell, but it was light. The Dnieper, however, was covered with a thin crust of ice, which no one ventured to walk on before Ney arrived there. Between Smolensk and Borisov, the cold was more intense but still bearable: we camped at night without shelter.' General Kreitz spent his first night under a roof at Borisov. 'Between Borisov and Vilna the frost was extremely severe, and most of the French died on that stretch. They died chiefly from hunger, exhaustion, disorder, and the loss of all discipline; the cavalry perished for the same reasons, and in addition the horses were inadequately and stupidly shod.'

For the time being, the purely French units maintained discipline. We have an account by one Aupias, a captured French general of the Cuirassiers, written for Emperor Alexander a month after the end of the great retreat and describing impartially the horrors suffered by the Grand Army. The passage refers to Napoleon's order—extremely painful to a great number of French soldiers—to *burn* the entire baggage train containing the valuables looted in Moscow, because of the military danger involved in dragging all this wealth: 'Many units, many generals carried out the order the very day it was issued. The soldiers experienced a voluptuous joy in doing their duty towards the Emperor as strictly as possible. The harder and more critical conditions became, the more his soldiers loved him and clung to him as to the only pilot capable of saving the ship.'

In the German and Italian units, however, and partly among the Poles, menacing symptoms of indiscipline began to appear.

The retreating French dragged with them several thousand Russian prisoners captured at the beginning of the war. They had almost entirely ceased feeding them. Orders were issued to shoot those who were too weak to march. Thus, out of one party of prisoners driven by the French from Moscow to Smolensk, 611 men (among them 4 officers) were shot as 'weak.' Prisoners were killed at the slightest sign of their lagging behind, and many thousands perished in this way. Corpses of shot Russian prisoners were found mingled with the French dead along the whole road of the retreat. An eyewitness with the Russian army tells of seeing a long line of dead Russian prisoners disposed in regular intervals, all of them with their heads bashed in. The

Russian prisoners could not help lagging behind their captors: exhausted from hunger, they collapsed on the ground. Then they were finished off by a bullet, bayonet, or a blow with a rifle butt. These and other bestialities aroused the most rabid fury on the part of the Russians.

The national war, hitherto marked by the action of the regular army and the unorganized peasants, assumed a new form: the partisan movement.

.   .   .

The idea of guerrilla warfare was largely suggested by the example of Spain, and the Russian guerrilla leaders recognized this to be so.

Colonel Chuykevich, who wrote his *Reflections on the War of 1812* during the war itself (though the book was published only in March 1813), recalls the Spaniards and cites them as a model: 'The rapid successes of the French arms in Spain are explained by the fact that the inhabitants of that country, burning with the desire to take revenge on the French, relied too much on their personal bravery and the justice of their cause. Hurriedly mobilized recruits were opposed to the French armies and were beaten by an enemy superior in numbers and experience. These disastrous lessons induced the brave Spaniards to change their methods of fighting. They magnanimously chose a protracted struggle that would be to their advantage. Avoiding general battles with the French forces, they divided their men into small units . . . frequently interrupted communications with France, destroyed the enemy's supplies, and exhausted him with ceaseless marches . . . In vain did the French captains cross Spain from one

end to the other, conquering cities and entire regions
. . . The great-hearted nation did not cease fighting,
the Government did not lose courage and remained
firm in its determination to free Spain from the French,
or to be buried under her ruins. No, you will not fall,
brave Spaniards!'

As I have had occasion to note, the Russian national
war was different from the Spanish. It was waged chiefly
by peasants in army or militia uniforms. But this made
it no less national.

One manifestation of the national war was the partisan movement.

Five days before Borodino, Lieutenant-Colonel Denis
Davydov, who had served as Prince Bagration's aide-de-
camp for five years, came to see his superior. He ex-
pounded his plan: to disrupt Napoleon's extended lines
of communication by sudden raids on his stores,
couriers, baggage trains. In Davydov's eyes the small
cavalry detachments, whose function was to make sudden raids and remain in hiding until a new opportunity
for action, could become nuclei for the mobilization
and arming of the peasants. Before Borodino, the 'general opinion at that time,' as Davydov says in his *Journal
of Partisan Actions,* was that after winning a victory
Napoleon would conclude peace and march on India
with the Russian army. 'If we cannot escape destruction,' Davydov told Prince Bagration, 'I should rather
fall right here; in India death awaits me and 100,000
of my countrymen without glory and for a cause alien
to my Fatherland, while here I shall die under the flag
of independence . . .' Bagration reported Davydov's
plan to Kutuzov. The Field Marshal was extremely cautious and little inclined to flights of heroic imagination, but he authorized Davydov to take 50 Hussars and

80 Cossacks. Bagration was dissatisfied with this miserly grant. 'I don't understand His Serene Highness's fears,' he said, communicating the modest results to Davydov. 'Is it really worthwhile to bargain over a few hundred men when, in the event of success, he may deprive the enemy of indispensable supplies, and in the event of failure, he would lose only a handful of men? After all, war is no kissing business . . . I should have given you 3,000 men to begin with, for I don't like to do things in a fumbling way, but that is now out of the question: the Prince himself fixed the strength of your detachment: we must obey.' Bagration said this five days before he was mortally wounded in battle, and after his death Davydov had even less chance of obtaining more men. With his 130 men, he set out round the Grand Army to harry Napoleon's rear.

Such were the modest beginnings of a guerrilla warfare, which was to play so great a part in the second half of the war.

The organizers of the guerrilla detachments were not always officers of the regular army. On 31 August 1812, the Russian rear-guard began a fighting retreat from Tsarevo-Zaimishche, while the French were entering the town. Ermolay Chetvertakov, a private in a regiment of Dragoons, had his horse wounded under him and was taken prisoner. In Gzhatsk, Chetvertakov succeeded in making his escape. He arrived at the village of Basmany, situated far to the south of the Smolensk highway along which the French army was advancing. In Basmany, Chetvertakov conceived a plan similar to Davydov's: he tried to gather a partisan detachment consisting of peasants.

Several years before, in 1804, when Chetvertakov had 'his skull shaven,' that is, when he was drafted, he fled from his regiment, was caught and whipped. But now, in 1812, he decided to fight the enemy with all his strength, and to induce others to do the same. The peasants of the village of Basmany did not trust him, and he found only one follower, with whom he went to another village. On their way, they encountered two Frenchmen, whom they killed, donning their uniforms. Later, in the village of Zadkovo, they encountered two French cavalrymen, killing them, too, and taking their horses. The village of Zadkovo assigned 47 peasants to help Chetvertakov. Under his leadership, this small detachment first wiped out a group of 12 French cuirassiers, then partly destroyed a French half-company of 59 men, putting the survivors to flight and capturing their conveyances. These successes produced an enormous impression, and as a result 253 volunteers from the village of Basmany joined Chetvertakov. Though illiterate, Chetvertakov revealed himself a first-class administrator, a brilliant strategist and tactician. By harrying the enemy with sudden raids, by shrewdly and carefully tracking down small French detachments and exterminating them in lightning thrusts, Chetvertakov saved a large territory round Gzhatsk from French marauders and looters. Chetvertakov was pitiless, and the peasants were so incensed against the invaders that they could scarcely have been restrained in any case. They took no prisoners—but the Frenchmen also shot on the spot, and without trial, any partisan who fell into their hands. In the village of Semionovka, the peasants of Chetvertakov's detachment burned 60 French marauders. As we have seen, the French committed similar deeds.

Chetvertakov became famous. One day a call from him sufficed to raise about 4,000 peasants, who joined his permanent detachment of 300 in an open attack against a whole French battalion equipped with cannon. The battalion was forced to retreat. After this engagement, the peasants scattered to their homes, but Chetvertakov's detachment continued to fight. Only after the danger was over, and the French had left, did Chetvertakov return to his regiment, then stationed in Moghilev (in November 1812). Generals Kologrivov and Emmanuel investigated the matter and were convinced of Chetvertakov's remarkable achievements and the great services he had rendered. Wittgenstein requested Barclay to reward Chetvertakov. His reward was—'a military medal' (not even a St. George cross). This settled the matter. Real distinction was barred to a serf, regardless of his exploits.

The historic significance of the partisans has been a subject of frequent dispute. Immediately after the war, when memories were still fresh, Davydov, Figner, Seslavin, Vadbolsky, Kudashev, and their exploits were spoken of with enthusiasm. The boldness and skill of the brave little detachments captivated everyone's imagination. Later, a certain reaction set in. The generals and officers of the regular army, the heroes of Borodino and Maloyaroslavets, were reluctant to accept as their equals these daring raiders who submitted to no one, who came from nowhere and spent half their time in hiding, who captured baggage trains and shared the spoils, but were incapable of standing up in a pitched battle with regular French units. Moreover, Ataman Platov and the Cossack circles claimed that the Cossacks were the principal force of the guerrilla detachments and that the fame of the guerrillas really belonged to them. The French helped to strengthen this view: they spoke much of the damage inflicted on them by the

Cossacks and scarcely mentioned (or mentioned with contempt) the partisans. In all fairness, it must be recognized, however, that the guerrillas rendered great and indisputable services from the middle of September to the end of November, when the French crossed the Berezina.

The guerrillas were magnificent scouts, often recklessly bold. Figner, the prototype of Tolstoy's Dolohov, actually rode into a French camp wearing a French uniform, and repeated the exploit several times. Seslavin actually crept up to a French sergeant, hoisted him on his saddle, and brought him to Russian headquarters. Davydov, with a group of two to three hundred men, created panic in detachments five times stronger, putting them to flight, capturing their supplies, freeing Russian prisoners, and sometimes capturing guns. The peasants were on much better terms with the partisans and their leaders than with regular army units.

Of course some guerrillas exaggerated in describing their exploits, and the future Decembrist Prince Sergey Volkonsky, who for a short time commanded a guerrilla detachment, judges them rather severely: 'In describing the actions of my guerrilla detachment,' he writes in his *Memoirs,* 'I shall, unlike many partisans, refrain from mystifying my readers with stories of unprecedented exploits and dangers. Thus, by scrupulous avoidance of the exaggerated accounts of other partisans, I shall inspire confidence in my notes.' But all the heroism was not exaggeration. The guerrillas have an indisputable record of resourcefulness, intrepidity, self-sacrifice, and will be remembered for ever for their part in the defence of the country against the foreign invader.

Even brave fighters and leaders of extremely active

detachments sometimes indulged in boastful exaggerations, which harmed them in the eyes of army circles. One of these partisan leaders, Seslavin, was the first to report Napoleon's advance to Maloyaroslavets: 'The enemy has been forestalled,' he wrote, 'the French destroyed, Russia saved, Europe liberated, and universal peace concluded—such are the consequences of that important discovery.' Not Kutuzov, not Bagration, not the whole people, but he, Seslavin, alone saved Russia and Europe.

Denis Davydov, the 'poet-partisan' also boasted occasionally, but he was much more moderate. The truth always won the upper hand in his notes, and to this day, regardless of what his enemies may have said, they are a precious source for the history of 1812. They must, of course, be treated critically, but can by no means be rejected. He describes a number of audacious enterprises by partisan detachments attacking the French rear-guard and the wagon trains of lagging enemy units, but he definitely recognizes that partisan attacks on larger bodies, such as Napoleon's Old Guard, were absolutely beyond their strength. 'I am second to none—and no one will deny it—in my hatred of the enemy who attacked my country's independence and honour . . . My comrades remember, if not my modest successes, at least my attempts to injure the enemy during the National War and the foreign expedition; they also remember the admiration and enthusiasm aroused in me by Napoleon's exploits, the respect for his army, which I retained in my soul even in the heat of battle . . . As a soldier, with arms in hand, I have never ceased to do justice to the greatest soldier of all time; I was held spellbound by bravery, regardless of the garb it assumed or the country in which it appeared. The "bravo" in praise of the enemy, which escaped Bagration's lips in the very heat of the battle of Borodino, found an echo in my heart, and did not surprise me.' Such were Davydov's feelings. He conducted himself chivalrously towards captured enemies. The same cannot be said of many other partisan leaders, among whom Figner (who perished in 1813) was distinguished by particular ruthlessness.

Peasant aid was particularly important for the partisans at the outset of the guerrilla warfare. The peasants of the Bronnitski district of the Government of Moscow, those of the village of Nicola-Pogorely near Vyazma, of Bezhetsk, Dorogobuzh, and Serpukhov rendered substantial services to the partisan detachments. They tracked down enemy groups and detachments, destroyed French foragers and marauders, readily supplied partisans with food and fodder. Without this help, the partisans would not have achieved half the results they did.

Then came the retreat of the Grand Army, beginning with the senseless blasting of the Kremlin. Those who returned to Moscow and found the whole city in ruins were filled with rage. The destruction of the Kremlin was felt as a wanton insult. By Napoleon's orders, the retreating French armies systematically burned all the towns and villages along their road. All this, and the sight of Russian prisoners slain by the retreating French, inspired a pitiless fury in the peasants.

Aside from helping partisan detachments, the peasants often engaged in direct military operations. Guerasim Kurin of Pavlovo (near Bogorodotsk) formed a group of peasants, armed them with weapons taken from dead Frenchmen, and with his assistant Stulov led them in an attack on a French cavalry detachment, which was put to flight.

Peasant women were also active, and distinguished themselves by their cruelty to the enemy. There were several authentic and verified cases of rape committed by Frenchmen on women who fell into their hands, and this contributed to the fury of the peasant women. *Starostikha* (village elder) Vasilisa (of Sychevski district in the Government of Smolensk) took several French prisoners, killed a number of French soldiers with her pitchfork and scythe, and was said to have attacked lagging wagon trains. She was by no means an exception. All sources note the participation of women in the National War. Unfortunately the records concerning their activity are very incomplete. There were whole legends about Vasilisa, but it is hard to distinguish historical truth from fantasy. Official historiography had long neglected to collect and verify material concerning the National War, almost exclusively dwelling on the actions of the regular army and the partisans (though scarcely mentioning women guerrillas); and after the witnesses died out, it became difficult to obtain authentic data. Offensive actions, like those of Kurin, Stulov, or Chetvertakov, were, of course, relatively rare; as a rule, the peasants limited themselves to tracking down small enemy detachments, and defending villages and entire districts from attacks by French marauders. These activities were infinitely more destructive than any raids, even the most successful ones. Not the burning of Moscow and not the frosts—there were no frosts until Smolensk—but the Russian peasants inflicted the most terrible blow on the Grand Army.

Yet the Government looked on this peasant activity with misgivings. Captain Naryshkin was stationed near

Klin with his cavalry detachment. Exploiting the peasants' ardent desire to help fight the enemy, he distributed among them some spare weapons belonging to his detachment. Other peasants had armed themselves with French weapons taken from slain marauders and foragers. Small peasant groups thus armed roamed round Moscow and pitilessly killed Frenchmen trying to find hay and oats for horses stationed there. These peasant guerrillas rendered enormous services. Suddenly Naryshkin received from his superiors 'an order [these are his own words], inspired by mendacious reports and base slander, to disarm peasants and execute by firing squads those convicted of rebellion. Surprised by this order, so unworthy of the magnanimous conduct of the peasants, I replied that I could not disarm hands I had myself armed and who were serving to destroy my country's enemies, nor treat as rebels men who sacrificed their lives to defend their freedom, wives, and homes; and that the name of traitor by right belonged to those who in such a sacred hour for Russia dared slander her most zealous and loyal defenders.'

There were innumerable such cases. We have many documents showing that the Government obstructed the peasant partisans in every possible way, fearing lest they turn their arms against the landlords. Alexander, Arakcheyev, Balashov were frightened; the super-patriot Rostopchin terrified the Tsar with the spectre of Pugachev. Luckily for Russia, the peasants did not obey these orders to disarm, but went on fighting against the enemy until he was finally expelled from Russia.

The guerrilla warfare, the peasant attacks, the Cossack raids, intensified the shortage of food and horses among the French, and compelled the invaders to abandon their guns and a large part of their treasure. It

forced them to abandon sick and wounded comrades to
the cruel death that awaited them if they did not have
the luck to fall into the hands of the regular army.
Near Mozhaisk, the retreating army passed an immense
plain, cut by a ravine and a little river, bordered by
little hills and the charred ruins of two villages. The
whole plain was littered with the rotting, decomposed
corpses of men and horses, wrecked cannon, rusty sabres.
At first the soldiers did not recognize this place of horror. It was Borodino, with all its still-unburied dead.
Marching towards torture and death, Napoleon's men
cast a last glance at their perished comrades.

Not far from Borodino, somewhere between Mozhaisk
and Gzhatsk, Caulaincourt indignantly reported to Napoleon that a French army unit marching ahead had
for no reason bludgeoned out the brains of two thousand Russian prisoners. Russian prisoners were constantly being killed in other units, but this mass slaughter shook even the hardened nerves of Napoleon's staff.
'This is a horrible cruelty,' Caulaincourt told the Emperor. 'Is this the civilization we brought to Russia?
What effect will this barbarism have on the enemy? Are
we not abandoning our wounded and a mass of prisoners to him? Will he not take a terrible revenge?' 'Napoleon kept a gloomy silence, but from the following day
these murders were stopped,' writes Ségur—but this is
a complete lie. No one even thought of stopping the
killing. On the contrary, with each stage of the retreat,
the horrors increased.

But Caulaincourt was right in foreseeing that the
French army would have to pay for its bestialities.

The Emperor with his Guard marched in the van.
Having left Vereya on 28 October, he was in Gzhatsk
on 30 October, in Vyazma on 1 November, in Semlevo

on 2 November, in Slavkov on 3 November, in Dorogo-buzh on the fifth, in Mikhailovo on the seventh, and on 8 November he entered Smolensk. The other units of his army reached the city between 8 and 15 November. During all this calamitous march, Napoleon and his army placed their hopes in Smolensk, where they expected to find food, supplies, and a resting place. Kutuzov marched along a parallel line south of the French route, with a slowness that astonished the French. This 'parallel pursuit,' conceived and carried out by Kutuzov, was the surest way of destroying the Napoleonic army. At the time, of course, the French staff was unaware of this. In Smolensk, they thought, there would be a good rest, the soldiers would pull themselves together and recuperate from the terrible sufferings they had gone through.—But the reality was otherwise. In the dead, half-gutted city, a shattering blow awaited the retreating army; there were virtually no supplies in Smolensk.

From that moment on, the retreat began to turn into a flight. All the sufferings between Maloyaroslavets and Smolensk paled in comparison with the abyss that opened before the Grand Army after Smolensk, and swallowed it almost entirely.

10

BEREZINA AND THE DESTRUCTION OF THE GRAND ARMY

THE last days of the bloody struggle were approaching. The agony of the French army lasted from 11 November, when it set out from Smolensk, to the night of 14 December, when Marshal Ney, at the head of a few hundred soldiers in fighting condition and a few thousand disarmed, wounded, and sick, crossed the Niemen. During that time, every day brought Napoleon new, unmistakable evidence of the terrible dimensions of his defeat. The French officers and soldiers who managed to survive the war confirmed that hard as the first stage of their retreat had been (Maloyaroslavets-Vereya-Vyazma-Smolensk), it could not even compare with the horrors they had experienced during the second and last stage (Smolensk-Krasnoye-Berezina-Vilna-Kovno).

In Smolensk, the army found no adequate food or rest. Some members of Napoleon's retinue tried to make a pleasantry of the bitter disappointment. 'You can see,' wrote Duroc to Montesquiou on 10 November 1812, 'that all our preparations to spend the winter in Moscow have proved unnecessary, and that our hopes for pleasures and spectacles have vanished. Not entirely, however, for we are still dragging our troupe of actors with us, and if they don't drop out on the way, we shall have the pleasure of witnessing comedies at our future winter quarters. For the moment we do not know where this will be possible; it all depends on the events and the enemy's movements. Smolensk is no better preserved than Moscow; it has been burned to the same extent as the capital.'

The abundant stores the retreating forces had expected to find in Smolensk were practically non-existent. Almost all the horses perished, for neither in Smolensk nor round Smolensk was it possible to get fodder. The march battalions that had passed through Smolensk to reinforce the Grand Army, stationed in Moscow between August and October, had eaten up the cattle brought there previously. And yet, if the army entering Smolensk had been even remotely like Napoleon's former armies, the stores would have been sufficient to sustain them for at least 15 to 20 days—on scanty rations, to be sure. But the motley, cosmopolitan mass of starving, frightened, irascible men, with scarcely a bond between them, behaved in such a way that a methodical distribution of rations was out of the question. The Guard received everything it needed. The rest of the army was filled with jealous hatred of the Guard, but as the Guard had preserved its discipline, arms, and solid bonds of comradeship, it was immune to attack. The other troops, having lost all vestige of discipline, threw themselves on the stores like hungry wild beasts, destroyed and carried away everything they found, and no threats and orders on the part of their superiors could stop them.

After three days the stores were gone. Discipline

dropped with terrifying rapidity, the bestiality of the starving German, Polish, and Italian soldiers, and of some purely French units—this was new—assumed unprecedented proportions. French officers wrote in private letters that at dusk or at night a man carrying bread in the streets of Smolensk was in danger of attack and death. Firing squads could no longer restore discipline. The death penalty could scarcely frighten men facing death from hunger and exhaustion. Davout's implacable severity somehow maintained discipline in his corps. The other marshals were completely unable to do so.

Smolensk disappointed the army in still another essential respect. There was virtually no opportunity to rest. The first days were marked by a bitter struggle over the provisions from the looted stores, over the distribution of supplies among the various units; later there were alarms, rumours of approaching Russians (Cossack patrols), and preparations for leaving the city.

As Napoleon entered Smolensk, he was harassed by complex and pressing cares: his starving army had been forced to abandon many guns for lack of horses, and had lost nearly all of its cavalry. Moreover the Russians were close on the heels of the rear-guard. Near the Kolotsk monastery and further on, Davout had been forced to accept battle and had lost nearly 10,000 men, in killed and wounded. On 3 November, the Russian advance guard under Miloradovich had attacked Viceroy Eugène and Marshal Ney, near Vyazma. The battle had continued throughout the night, and the French corps of Eugène, Ney, and Davout had suffered many casualties.

Abundant snowfall began during the last marches before Smolensk, and caused considerable hardship to the soldiers unaccustomed to move over snow. The cold was becoming more and more severe. It was not easy to keep warm in the gutted houses of Smolensk. Soldiers camping in the squares burned carriages, carts, and boxes; they roasted horse flesh on the fire. Even in Smolensk there were deaths and amputations as a result of frost.

From distant Paris alarming news reached the Emperor. A courier reached Dorogobuzh with news of the fantastic 'conspiracy of General Malet.' This Republican general escaped from prison; announced to a regiment stationed in Paris that the Emperor had been killed in Russia; arrested the Minister of Police and wounded the Minister of War . . . True, the disorder had lasted only three hours. Malet was arrested and shot; the whole affair seemed more like a madman's prank than a serious incident; but Napoleon was alarmed and irritated. It seemed to him that he had established a solid order in which such things were impossible. Clearly his presence was needed in Paris . . . Under these conditions he would not have wanted to tarry in Smolensk even if it had depended on his will. But it did not depend on his will. Delay threatened the remnants of the Grand Army with death by starvation.

On 14 November, after five days' stay in Smolensk, Napoleon with his Guard set out in the direction of Krasnoye. He was followed by Eugène, Davout, and Murat, with the remnants of their corps. Next came the rear-guard under Marshal Ney, and after Ney came the Russians.

In the Russian general staff and in St. Petersburg the agitation mounted: was it possible that Napoleon would escape? Would the Field Marshal really deprive Russia of the glory of definitely crushing the enemy? Did he really refuse to liberate Europe from the iron yoke which would remain in full force if the conqueror escaped to create new legions?

The Field Marshal kept silent. Neither Alexander, nor Ermolov, Toll, nor Konovnitsin, learned his true intentions.

* * *

Kutuzov's position had of course greatly improved since Tarutino and Maloyaroslavets. Napoleon's defeat was now evident. The invading army had lost most of its strength and was making every effort to leave Russia as fast as possible, to reach the frontier and escape destruction by hunger and cold. At the same time Kutuzov faced increasing difficulties in putting through his plan of seeing Napoleon out of Russia without unnecessary battles. Kutuzov did not believe that Napoleon could retain his world empire after his defeat in Russia, and he refused to shed Russian blood to obtain a result that was inevitable in any case. It was becoming plainer and plainer that the Field Marshal was following a preconceived plan. The Tsar had long distrusted Kutuzov, and now that everyone was telling him about the Field Marshal's incomprehensible irresolution and 'cowardice,' he knew that something else was behind it.

Alexander's dislike and distrust of Kutuzov, and Kutuzov's antipathy and disrespect for Alexander were so great that both lost all measure of self-control.

The Grand Army was retreating; Tarutino and Maloyaroslavets had brought a critical turn to the war. Yet Kutuzov and the Tsar still found time to exchange pinpricks. Here, for instance, is a 'report' sent by the Commander-in-Chief to the Tsar: 'Cavalry General Baron Bennigsen proposes aide-de-camp Colonel Golit-

sin for promotion to the rank of general in recognition
of his merits in the present campaign and in the engagements of 24 and 26 August. I am submitting this
proposal to Your Majesty *without expressing my own
opinion.* Field Marshal Prince Kutuzov, 26 October
1812.'

Kutuzov knew, of course, that Alexander himself desired the promotion. Alexander knew that Kutuzov
knew it and could not help knowing it. The Tsar replied: 'I reserve to myself the right to choose my ad-
jutant-generals.' But the Tsar feared Kutuzov and
asked him to communicate the message to Bennigsen;
thus the letter looked like a rebuke to Bennigsen.

Though unable to get rid of the Tsar, Kutuzov had
no difficulty in disposing of his less important enemies.
Recalling Bennigsen's slanderous reports on Kutuzov
to the Tsar, we can appreciate the irony of Kutuzov's
brief note to Alexander: 'Consequent upon General
Bennigsen's fits of illness and various other reasons, I
have ordered him to go to Kaluga, there to await further orders from Your Majesty, which fact I am happy
to report herewith.' The routine expression 'I am happy'
acquires a curious significance in this context. Alexander swallowed this insult and did not even inquire
why Kutuzov regarded Kaluga as a suitable spa for the
'sick' Bennigsen.

Barclay had left the army before Bennigsen; on 4
October, Kutuzov gave him 'sick leave.' He went to
Kaluga and from there petitioned Alexander to grant
him his discharge, justifying his request by the 'disorder, exhaustion, and anarchy prevailing in the army.'
Barclay was cut to the quick by his demotion and could
not serve with Kutuzov. He could not forgive him for
having stolen his office, 'his power, and deeply con-

ceived plan,' as many of Pushkin's generation later thought.

'The great task is done. Now it remains only to reap the harvest,' said Barclay taking leave of Loewenstern, his aide-de-camp. 'I have handed over a preserved, well-clothed, armed, and not demoralized army to the Field Marshal . . . He does not want to share with anyone the glory of expelling the enemy from the Empire.' Before leaving the army, Barclay also said: 'The nation, which perhaps would stone me now, will later do me justice.' Both his predictions came true . . . In Kaluga 'a crowd gathered and a hail of stones fell on the carriage. Cries resounded: "Look, there is the traitor!" Only the strictest incognito spared him further insults.' Later, Pushkin recognized Barclay's merits and bowed to his memory in *The Great Captain*. From Kutuzov's point of view, Barclay's departure from the army was almost as necessary as Bennigsen's dismissal.

But his strongest enemy remained. Robert Wilson, observing Kutuzov's conduct, began to suspect him of treason and dreamt of instituting an investigation: 'To my grief I again saw Bonaparte escape,' wrote Wilson to Cathcart. '. . . Much has been done, but it could all have been over. I am of those who think that naval regulations should also apply to the army. Why are they not required to prove that they acted in the best possible way? It seems to me that sooner or later the reason for all these things will be revealed.'

This letter was written after Kutuzov's conversation with Wilson, when Kutuzov told him plainly that his aim was to eject Napoleon from Russia and that he did not see why Russia should waste her forces on the complete destruction of Napoleon, since the harvest of such a victory would be reaped by England, not Russia. Alluding to this conversation, Wilson wrote to Cathcart that, in contrast to Kutuzov, one could have complete trust in Admiral Chichagov. 'I hope that the Admiral will not avoid the enemy but will seriously grapple with him. I have not the slightest fear concerning his political speculations.' The last words are a direct and malicious reference to Kutuzov. If only Kutuzov were replaced! This was the dream of Wilson, the Tsar, and Lord Cathcart.

'Good opportunities to end this war were neglected, though they occurred more than once,' wrote Wilson to Alexander from the village of Lapkovo, on 12 November, five days before the battle near Krasnoye. 'In our present position, having rested, we are losing a day for nothing; if we remain here for another 24 hours, Bonaparte will restore his communications; once he reaches Poland he will be redoubtable, for he will have 100,000 troops. He has suffered much from our detachments and from nature itself, but he has not yet been defeated. On the contrary, he can see that even his weakened power seems terrifying to the general who leads Your Majesty's armies. There is not an officer in the army but is convinced of this, though opinions differ concerning the motives of such useless, irrational, and expensive "caution." '

This, again, is an allusion to Kutuzov's 'political speculations.' But regardless how offensive Wilson was to Kutuzov, the Field Marshal could not send him away, as he had sent Bennigsen. He had to bear with him.

And in his own staff, among persons generally loyal to him, Kutuzov no longer found support.

'The march from Maloyaroslavets to the Dnieper,' writes A. A. Shcherbinin, an officer of the quartermaster department who never left Kutuzov's headquarters, 'was marked by Kutuzov's constant opposition to Konovnitsin and Toll, who wanted to cut off Napoleon's retreat by a swift advance on Vyazma. Kutuzov wanted to build a "golden bridge," so to speak, for the disorganized enemy; he refused to undertake bold actions against the skilfully manoeuvring French; he planned to let Chichagov's fresh troops finish the enemy after he had been further weakened by a long march.' Toll and Konovnitsin were in despair. Kutuzov deliberately refused to overtake Napoleon in Vyazma, and tarried in the village of Polotnianye. 'Pyotr Petrovich, unless we get the Marshal to move, we shall winter here!' exclaimed Toll, disregarding all discipline, and running into an office where Konovnitsin was working with his officers. Kutuzov was far from being 'a tired old man, taking his ease,' as Shcherbinin called him. Kutuzov did not want to catch up with Napoleon, and nothing could change his mind. Toll and Konovnitsin did not intrigue like Bennigsen and Sir Robert Wilson; they loved and respected Kutuzov, but, like his enemies, they refused to understand his tactics.

Near Vyazma, the Russians made a successful attack on the French rear-guard. At that moment, Kutuzov, with the main body of his troops, was only 6 versts from Vyazma. 'He could hear the cannonade as distinctly as if it were taking place in his own antechamber,' writes General Loewenstern who was favourably disposed towards Kutuzov as a rule, 'but despite the insistence of all the higher officers, he remained a mere spectator of that battle which could have brought the destruction of the greater part of Napoleon's army and the capture of the Viceroy . . . At headquarters, everyone was burning with impatience to give battle to the enemy; the generals and officers protested and set fire to their tents to demonstrate that they were no longer needed; everyone awaited the signal to battle. The signal did not come. Nothing could compel Kutuzov to act; he even grew angry with those who pointed out to him the extent of the enemy's demoralization, and he chased me from his study for telling him, upon my return from the battlefield, that half of the French army was rotten . . . Kutuzov kept stubbornly to his plan and advanced parallel to the enemy. He refused to take risks and preferred to expose himself to the censure of the entire army.'

Loewenstern was also unable to understand Kutuzov's basic idea. Wilson, however, clearly understood what Kutuzov was aiming at, and hated him all the more. But as Napoleon approached the border, and as one Russian province after another was liberated, Kutuzov's authority in the army and among the population grew, and the Tsar was in no position to rid himself of the Field Marshal.

Among Kutuzov's staff there were a few who sincerely loved and respected him: Dokhturov, Denis Davydov, Konovnitsin, Rayevsky, and, quite particularly, Toll. On two occasions, their faith in Kutuzov was put to a severe test: at Krasnoye and at Berezina where, according to Kutuzov's closest collaborators, the old Field Marshal allowed Napoleon to escape.

After the battle of Krasnoye, Kutuzov's entire staff became convinced that he had deliberately refused to provoke a decisive denouement by a bloody engagement. 'I do not claim to criticize the actions of our generals during the three days' engagement at Krasnoye,' writes Loewenstern, 'but without doubt, had they displayed greater energy, neither Davout, nor the Viceroy,

nor especially Ney could have escaped. Korf, Ermolov,
Borozdin, and Rosen made not the slightest use of their
favourable position.' And he adds significantly: 'General Korf, a straightforward man, said publicly that
he followed literally the Field Marshal's instructions
to facilitate the enemy's retreat.'

In his *Memoirs,* Wilson definitely abandons his obviously groundless charge of Kutuzov's cowardice and
speaks directly of a 'secret motive' that influenced the
Field Marshal's conduct at Krasnoye: 'To later generations it may seem incredible that Napoleon should have
been allowed to escape under these circumstances. It is
natural to assume that some secret motive influenced
Kutuzov's conduct, and that the mere fear of failure
could not have produced so much pusillanimity.'

'The battle of Krasnoye,' writes Denis Davydov,
'which certain military writers call by the high-sound-
ing name of the three days' battle, should, in all justice,
be known as a three days' search for hungry, half-naked
Frenchmen; insignificant detachments like mine could
boast some trophies, but not the main army. Large
groups of Frenchmen hurriedly threw down their arms
at the mere appearance of our detachments on the highway.' These engagements took place on 15 and 16
November, gathering in intensity on the seventeenth
and eighteenth. At some places, the French retreated
in order, at others they were seized by panic and turned
to flight, throwing away their arms. Napoleon at the
head of his Guard and other units which were more or
less intact, made no attempt at a stand: his only purpose was to get away with as many troops as possible,
and cross the Berezina. He still had thirty to forty thousand soldiers in fighting condition, and only the speedi-
est possible departure from Russia could save an appre-

ciable part of them. Near Krasnoye a kind of selection took place: the troops least fit for battle perished or surrendered—most of them unable to keep up with the retreating units.

Denis Davydov's account of these battles is not entirely just. The engagement actually lasted not three but four days, and brought heavy losses to the Russians as well as to the French.

The Russian army, moving south of Napoleon's line of retreat, did not follow him to Smolensk, but advanced from Elna directly to the town of Krasnoye, southwest of Smolensk, across the line of Napoleon's route from Smolensk to the Berezina. The first skirmish between the Russian General Ozharovsky and the Young Guard was not quite successful for the Russians. On the three days following, Napoleon feigned offensive manœuvres, but actually his sole purpose was to avoid battle. He long awaited Ney, but failing to receive news of him, he ordered his entire army to retreat from Krasnoye.

Tormasov had occupied positions near Dobroye, west of Krasnoye. Kutuzov's staff wanted to move the main forces to Tormasov's assistance, hoping to throw a net round Napoleon's army. Kutuzov, who understood the real condition of the Russian army, did not concur.

Napoleon marched to Orsha. He entered the town, dictating orders, computing his forces, and constantly speaking of Ney, 'the bravest among his bravest,' as he called him. It seemed beyond doubt that Marshal Ney with his rear-guard of 7,000 to 8,000 men had been destroyed. The battles near Krasnoye had been protracted precisely because Napoleon had been awaiting his rear-guard; when it became clear that Ney would not succeed in breaking through the ring of Russian troops,

Napoleon, abandoning all hope of rescuing his rear-guard, had retreated to Orsha.

Ney left Smolensk on 17 November with about 7,000 soldiers (some sources mention 8,500), a small detachment of horse (400 to 500 men), and 12 guns. A disarmed mass of sick and wounded dragged themselves behind him (about 8,000 men).

On 18 November, Ney, not yet knowing that Napoleon had left Krasnoye, tried to force his way through the united Russian forces under Miloradovich, Paskevich, and Prince Dolgoruki. He was thrown back to the woods from which he had emerged.

The Russians were at his rear, Russian infantry occupied positions at both sides, and Russian artillery opened fire from the flanks. Before him was a snow-covered forest, beyond it the Dnieper. The French guns were put out of action. Ney was pressed from all sides. Suddenly a Russian officer appeared before Ney, asking him to surrender: 'Field Marshal Kutuzov would not have dared address so cruel a proposal to so famous a warrior if you had even one chance of escape. But 80,000 Russians are in front of you, and, if you doubt it, Kutuzov asks you to send someone to walk along the Russian lines and estimate their forces.' Ney knew that Napoleon and the other marshals had left and were far away. The words of the Russian officer sounded convincing.

There are several similar versions of Ney's reply: 'The Emperor's Marshals do not surrender! We don't negotiate under fire!' According to another version, he interrupted the officer, saying: 'Monsieur, have you ever heard of a Marshal of the Emperor surrendering to the enemy? No? Well, then please be silent!' To his generals, Ney said: 'Advance across the woods! No roads?

Advance without roads! Advance towards the Dnieper and cross it! What, the river is not entirely frozen? It will freeze! *En avant!*' About 3,000 men followed him through the pathless snow-covered woods towards the river. For a time the Russians lost sight of them and began by capturing the thousands of wounded who had been marching behind the rear-guard. Ney reached the Dnieper, which was covered by a thin crust of ice. 'Forward!' cried the Marshal and stepped first on the unreliable ice.

No one among the local population had yet ventured to walk on the ice. Ney passed first with his corps, but many of his men fell through and drowned. Of his 3,000 soldiers and officers he lost 2,200 during the crossing. The surviving soldiers of his rear-guard later related that many of their comrades had fallen through the thin ice and vanished in the water before their very eyes.

To the dismay of soldiers crossing the Dnieper, several wagons bearing wounded and sick soldiers, and foreigners with their wives and children who had dragged themselves from Moscow after the retreating army, had been left on the other bank of the river. During the entire crossing, the Dnieper resounded with the cries of the drowning, and no one even thought of trying to send the overloaded wagons on the ice. On both banks, there were Cossacks roaming about, suddenly turning up at unexpected places. Induced by cries and entreaties, the officers finally permitted a few wagons filled with the wounded and women and children to attempt the crossing. Almost at once, the ice broke under them and they were all swallowed by the icy water. 'We did not think then that later we would often feel envy for those who had found peace on the bed of the Dnieper,' writes one of Ney's soldiers who witnessed the scene.

The second stage of the retreat was just beginning.

Ney with his remaining 800 men joined Napoleon in Orsha. The Emperor silently pressed the Marshal in his arms. Ney again volunteered to command at the most dangerous spots: at the rear-guard, pressed hard by Platov with his Cossacks, and Miloradovich with his regular cavalry.

At daybreak on 18 November, the French vanguard entered Orsha, and Napoleon with the Old and Young Guards entered Dubrovno. At one o'clock on 18 November, Napoleon and the Guard left Dubrovno and the next day entered Orsha. On 20 November he advanced to Borisov, a town situated on the left bank of the Berezina, intending to cross the river on the bridge that had remained intact.

The number of Napoleon's forces at this most critical moment of his retreat has been subject to some discussion. No exact computations were made in Smolensk or in Orsha. The maximum figure quoted is 90,000 men, of whom 35,000 to 40,000 were capable of fighting (with the almost intact Guard at their head), and 50,000 to 55,000 were disarmed, sick, unfit for battle, and only hindered Napoleon's movement. The minimum figure quoted is 55,000 to 60,000 men, comprising 23,000 to 25,000 capable of fighting and 30,000 to 35,000 disarmed, sick, half-frozen. All sources agree on one point: Napoleon had approximately 30,000 to 35,000 men fit for battle, for the most part French. Behind them trudged tens of thousands of Italians, Germans, Poles, Dutchmen, Illyrian Slavs, men of many nations and languages who did not understand one another, who hated one another and especially their superiors, who constantly fought over food or the miserable substitutes for food with which they tried to satisfy their hunger. They were buried in snow, they froze, stumbled and fell, numb with hunger and cold. They moved like automatons, they fell, froze, died in silence, and their comrades passed by without even trying to help them. All round them the Cossacks roamed, sometimes guerrillas raided them crying 'Hurrah!', slashing, clubbing, or stabbing laggards and the guards of the baggage trains, often cutting off entire units and forcing them to surrender. Napoleon marched on foot in the ranks of his Old Guard, for several kilometres walking silently through the deep snow.

Denis Davydov has left us an account of a scene that he was to remember all his life: '. . . The Old Guard approached with Napoleon himself among them . . . We jumped on our horses and again appeared on the highway. The enemy noticing our noisy crew cocked their guns and went on proudly marching without accelerating their steps. No matter how hard we tried to detach at least one private from these closed columns, they remained unharmed, as though made of granite, disdaining all our efforts; I shall never forget the easy gait and the impressive bearing of these warriors, inured to all manner of deaths. In their tall bearskin caps, blue uniforms with white straps, and red plumes and epaulettes, they looked like poppies amidst the snowy fields . . . Having only Cossacks at our disposal, we buzzed round the passing enemy columns, capturing wagons and guns that lagged behind, sometimes breaking up a scattered or extended platoon, but the columns themselves remained unscathed . . . Colonels, officers, sergeants, many privates rushed at the enemy, but all in vain. The columns moved on, one after another, driving us off with shots from their rifles and jeering at our futile attempts to raid them . . . Napoleon and the Guard passed through our Cossacks like a hundred-gun warship through fishing boats.'

On the third day after Napoleon's departure from Orsha the advance patrols of his vanguard faced a ribbon of muddy water. The river before them was tortuous and rather wide. It was not yet frozen, but the first chunks of ice floated down in its current. Even in ordinary times this river would have been hard to cross; the early frosts made it almost impassable.

It was the Berezina.

. . .

'Berezina! Fateful name, fateful river where the misfortunes of mankind could have ended, but did not end, continuing for three more years! Fateful place where the most terrible blunder was made, a blunder for which Europe paid with hundreds of thousands of lives on the fields of Lutzen, Bautzen, Dresden, Kulm, Leipzig, Troyes, Ligny, Waterloo, with long years of devastation and war!' This quotation from a German memorial typifies the feelings of the generation that lived through the Napoleonic epic. At the Berezina, Napoleon's strategic genius unfolded in all its greatness, saving him from what seemed like inevitable capitulation. Military historians agree with Clausewitz that at the Berezina Napoleon 'not only completely saved his honour but acquired new glory.' And yet perhaps even Napoleon's genius would not have sufficed to save him in these desperate, utterly hopeless circumstances, if a single will had reigned in the Russian camp, or, more accurately, if the will upon which everything in the Russian camp depended had actually been intent upon surrounding and capturing the French Emperor.

At the very beginning of the retreat, when Kutuzov, having taken the old Kaluga road, was still at Krasnaya Pakhra, Alexander Ivanovich Chernishev, aide-de-camp and favourite of the Tsar, appeared at headquarters with a plan worked out by the Tsar's military advisers. The Tsar and his advisers, including Chernishev, drew up this plan in the comfortable study of the Winter Palace, where the Tsar 'fought' the entire campaign of 1812—more accurately, the Tsar drew up no plans at all, but only 'approved' the plans of his bemedaled courtiers. The plan was ambitious, worked out to the last detail, and led 'irrefutably' to Napoleon's encircle-ment and capture. The planners assumed that from Smolensk Napoleon would either march through Vitebsk, Bocheykovo, and Glubokoye—in that case the Russians would have to await him at the river Ula, near Chashnikov, or wherever he would try to cross that river—or, which was much more likely, he would march through Orsha, Borisov, and Minsk, where he had pre-pared large stores of supplies—in that case the Russians would have to await him at the Berezina, which he would try to cross at Borisov or elsewhere. The Ula, which flows northward and falls into the Dvina, and the Berezina, which flows southward and falls into the Dnieper, run so close to one another for a certain stretch that, from purely strategic considerations, it was out of the question to pass between them. Thus, all Russia's military strength on that front (Wittgenstein on the northern flank, and Chichagov on the southern) would have had to meet Napoleon either at the Ula or at the Berezina, to prevent him from crossing; and as

Kutuzov's main Russian army would pursue Napoleon from the east to the west, towards the Berezina or the Ula, Napoleon would be left with no choice but capitulation. Such was the plan in its main outlines. Every detail was provided for, it looked smooth and infallible. In the Winter Palace, at any rate, the plan seemed magnificent.

The drama of the Berezina was just beginning when Chernishev brought this plan to Kutuzov. Kutuzov acted in his customary manner: he made no essential objections and sent the necessary instructions to Wittgenstein and Chichagov. But in reality he did not approve the plan; he did not desire its realization, and thought it impracticable besides. In a letter to the Tsar, he lightly, delicately, hinted at 'difficulties' and pretended to have accepted the plan.

But the Tsar had no illusions about Kutuzov's character and his attitude towards his own Imperial person. The Tsar did not believe a single word of Kutuzov's and embarked on a most dangerous undertaking: behind the Field Marshal's back and without his knowledge, he began to give instructions and advice (which, coming from the Tsar, were equivalent to orders) to Wittgenstein and Chichagov. The result was confusion and disharmony; moreover, if the Tsar had agents who spied on Kutuzov, Kutuzov had his own spies who kept him more or less informed of events in the Winter Palace and at the headquarters of Wittgenstein and Chichagov. The old Field Marshal knew everything and took everything into account. Even at Krasnaya Pakhra, he had been opposed to Alexander's plan: now, when the critical moment arrived, he definitely rejected it.

It would be an injustice to Kutuzov to suppose that

his actions in this connection were inspired by personal feelings alone. Wilson judged him far more correctly than Ermolov, Denis Davydov, and a number of other observers and critics: Kutuzov followed a definite political purpose, which he considered best for Russia. As we have said, this purpose consisted in ejecting Napoleon from Russia and not going a step further. Kutuzov had achieved the destruction of the invading army, and that was all he required.

After all we have said, there is no need to develop the radically opposite view held by the Tsar. The most important thing for the Tsar was to capture Napoleon and thereby remove him from his throne. The Tsar knew that Europe expected this of him.

In his London milieu, old Prince Vorontsov, the Russian ambassador, was certain that Napoleon would perish or at least be taken prisoner, and that in no circumstances would he reappear in Paris. 'At last,' he wrote to his son on 4 December, 'we have begun to beat the tyrant, and we shall continue until his colossal power is destroyed, for I do not see how the monster will escape death or capture.' Mikhail Semenovich did not receive his father's letter until 6 February 1813, when Napoleon had returned to Paris and had begun grandiose preparations for a new war.

Vorontsov, like the Tsar, disapproved of Kutuzov's actions.

But Kutuzov knew better than anyone that to catch Napoleon while sitting in the Winter Palace or in the Russian Embassy at London was far easier than at the Berezina. He knew the terrible losses suffered by the Russian army, through battles, hunger, and cold. True, the spirit of the Russian army was above praise; the soldiers were submitting to discipline of their own free will, and not for fear of lashes. Nevertheless, the size of the Russian army (especially after Krasnoye, when the frosts set in and fodder was hard to find) began to decrease sharply.

No winter clothing was sent to the soldiers and militiamen; they suffered severely from cold during the hard campaign.

Barclay himself gives evidence of the distressing condition prevailing in the Russian army.

Even before Napoleon crossed the Berezina, Barclay did not conceal from Alexander that the Russian army would be unable to continue the war in its present state. 'Your army, Sire, is in bad shape, because an army whose administration is disorganized is a body without a soul. For the time being, it is still functioning for the defence of its country under the influence of patriotism, but after crossing the frontier this army will no longer be equal to its task, if it remains in its present condition.'

In Kutuzov's staff it was said that the Russian army was so weak that its true condition should be concealed 'not only from the enemy but also from officials serving with the army.'

Kutuzov himself furnishes data on the numerical strength of the Russian army at the time of the occupation of Vilna (10 December 1812):

On that day, the Russian 'main army' (which followed Napoleon from Tarutino to Vilna) numbered 27,464 men and 200 guns; on the day of its departure from Tarutino it had consisted of 97,112 men and 622 guns. In two months it had lost 70,000 of its effectives. Of these, only 60,000 were more or less accurately accounted for: 48,000 sick were in hospitals, 12,000 were killed in action or died from wounds or illness. True, there was hope of increasing this insignificant number (27,464 men) by Wittgenstein's and Chichagov's forces (34,483 and 24,488 men respectively). But Kutuzov could not rely on these forces with absolute certainty, and he had no faith in the talents of the two leaders.

In these conditions, Kutuzov could not regard Napoleon's capture as sure, and the Field Marshal's tactics derived from his conviction that his soldiers' blood should not be shed without a definite reason.

The Tsar, of course, counted on the fact that Napoleon's Austrian 'ally' (Schwarzenberg's corps) did not hinder Chichagov's movements and that the whole 'war' on the southern flank was a travesty. Soon after the opening of hostilities, reassuring news arrived from that front. Metternich managed to inform Alexander that the Austrians would not wage a 'real' war against the Russians. As early as 7 July, General Tormasov wrote to General Sacken from Lutsk: 'In conclusion I consider it my duty to inform Your Excellency that, according to the highest sources, we may be reassured about the Austrian frontier. This important secret of our security from the Austrians must not be confided to anyone.' Napoleon himself had soon ceased to expect any real help from the Austrians. This meant that Chichagov was free to take an active part in surrounding and capturing Napoleon.

Wittgenstein on the northern flank was less free. During late summer and early fall, he remained behind the Drissa. Only when the Petersburg militia joined him, did he begin to act. On 19 October, Wittgenstein compelled Saint-Cyr to retreat from Polotsk, whereupon the Russians occupied that town, and the Cossacks began to raid as far as Vitebsk. On 30 October, near Chashniki, Wittgenstein again threw Saint-Cyr

westward, in the process of thrusting back Marshal
Victor's troops, who had come to Saint-Cyr's assistance.
Pursuing the retreating Victor, Wittgenstein occupied
Vitebsk (6 November) and a week later, when Victor
took up positions near Smoliantsi, Wittgenstein once
again forced him back, taking prisoners and capturing
a few guns.

This was the last of Wittgenstein's relatively easy exploits. He knew what the disposition received well in
advance required of him: to pursue Victor *at once*, and
to take part in the imminent pitched battle at the
Berezina. But Wittgenstein was paralyzed by his insurmountable fear of Napoleon. He was an inferior general, and later, in the spring of 1813, Napoleon routed
him at Lutzen and Bautzen (to Russia's misfortune,
Alexander appointed Wittgenstein Commander-in-
Chief after Kutuzov's death). After Bautzen, Miloradovich presented himself to Wittgenstein and said: 'The
good of the Fatherland requires that you be replaced.'
But at the Berezina, no one even thought of replacing
Wittgenstein. He was left to do what he saw fit, and he
'came too late.' The chief part, however, was entrusted
to Chichagov.

Pavel Vasilievich Chichagov was an admiral. He had
been Minister of the Navy and it was by sheer accident
that he had been given the post of an army comander.
In 1811, the Tsar, who liked him, had appointed him
to a rather odd office: 'Commander-in-Chief of Moldavia, Walachia, and the Black Sea Fleet.' He occupied
this post when the War of 1812 broke out. When entrusted with the extremely difficult task of 'capturing'
Napoleon, Chichagov had 24,500 men under his command. Hot-headed, foolhardy, inept at commanding
large masses, Chichagov disgraced himself for ever by

his ill-starred attempt to prevent Napoleon from crossing the Berezina. Generations of Russian children learned from Krylov's fable of *The Pike and the Cat* how the rats had bitten off the pike's tail—or how the admiral suffered a defeat on land. Generations of history students have learned that Chichagov spoiled the end of the National War by letting Napoleon slip out of his hands. Later military historians, both Russian and Western European, have a different view of the matter, according to which the 'guilt' was shared by three persons: Chichagov, Wittgenstein, and Kutuzov. In the light of our previous remarks, it is clear that Kutuzov's 'guilt' did not consist in his failure to capture Napoleon, but perhaps in his failure to assert his ideas openly and directly.

On 16 November, Chichagov's vanguard, commanded by Count Lambert, occupied Minsk, where enormous stores of provisions and military supplies had awaited Napoleon. Napoleon learned of this two days later, before entering Orsha, and was soon startled by the news that Chichagov had also occupied Borisov. Napoleon began sending urgent orders to Dombrowski, Oudinot, and Victor to concentrate as many troops as possible near Borisov, in order to secure his passage by the Borisov bridge. Marshal Oudinot, whom Napoleon had ordered to advance on Borisov, proved the most active and successful of the three. Chichagov detailed Count Pahlen to bar Oudinot's road, but the French marshal completely routed Pahlen's detachment, and the French cavalry forced the Russian infantry to take cover in the woods near Borisov. Chichagov moved his army back on the right bank of the Berezina, and the French entered Borisov. The remnants of Pahlen's defeated force managed with some difficulty to cross a short distance above Borisov and unite with Chichagov on the right bank.

On 25 November, Napoleon, by various manœuvres and feints, succeeded in diverting Chichagov's attention to Borisov and the banks of the river south of Borisov. While Chichagov concentrated his forces there, Murat, Oudinot, and two prominent engineer generals, Eblé and Chasseloup, were hastily building two bridges near Studianka.

On the night of 25 November, the Imperial Guard entered Studianka, followed at daybreak by Napoleon. He gave orders to begin the crossing at once. At that moment he had no more than 19,000 armed men at his disposal. The crossing took place during an exchange of fire with a Russian detachment under General Chaplits, who was the first to notice that Napoleon was leading his troops out of Borisov. Napoleon gave orders for strong forces to guard both banks of the river near the Studianka bridges. Throughout the whole day of 26 November, his troops continued to join him, and during the night, Napoleon ordered Ney to cross with the remnants of his corps and the entire Young Guard. All night and all morning of 27 November the crossing went on, and one after another the French battalions passed to the right bank. At two in the afternoon of 27 November, Napoleon and the Old Guard crossed over, followed by Victor's divisions. Having achieved the crossing, the French army began to draw up on the right bank.

That afternoon and night, enormous hordes of unarmed or half-armed men, laggards, sick, many with fingers or even entire limbs frozen, began to reach the left bank, which had not yet been entirely evacuated by the regular French troops. Following them and with them, the baggage train began to cross, and with the baggage train the survivors among those unfortunate foreigners who had accompanied the French on their retreat from Moscow. They were all impatient to cross, they begged leave to pass as quickly as possible, and spoke of the Cossacks who trailed them, but they were not allowed to pass. Napoleon had given orders for the armed men to pass first, and only later, if enough time remained, the unarmed, the wounded, the women and children. If it should prove too late, he gave orders to burn the bridges.

It proved too late.

In the battles of 28 November, the Russians fought stubbornly but without success. Neither Chichagov nor Wittgenstein did what they might have, considering that on the right bank Chichagov had 35,000 men against Napoleon's 19,000, and that on the left bank 25,000 to 26,000 Russians were opposed only by Marshal Victor's 7,000 to 8,000 armed men. At 9 in the morning of 29 November, amidst the wails and entreaties of thousands of wounded, sick, unarmed, and all those who had been dragging themselves with the baggage trains, General Eblé issued orders to burn the two bridges he and Chasseloup had built.

Chichagov had learned of the extraordinary commotion near Studianka as early as 27 November, but decided that it was only a demonstration intended to mislead him, and spent that day in the village of Zabashevichi. About the same time (after the departure of the French troops from Borisov to Studianka), Wittgenstein 'belatedly' reached Borisov. But he came accompanied only by his staff, without his army . . .

•   •   •

The crossing of the Berezina has given rise to a heated polemic which has clarified a few points.

In an anonymous English book translated into Russian in 1833 and dedicated to Chichagov, a decided attempt was made to justify the admiral. The author, who claims to be a witness and participant in the engagement, maintains that Chichagov reached the right bank of the Berezina with only 15,000 infantry and 9,000 cavalry, and that Wittgenstein did not appear on the left bank until after the French had crossed. As to Kutuzov, at that time his vanguard was in Tolochino, almost 115 kilometres east of the crossing place; the main body of his troops was 150 to 160 kilometres away, in the little town of Kopys.

Near Minsk, the French captured a detachment of 50 Cossacks convoying a courier bringing important documents from Petersburg to Chichagov. From the intercepted documents, Napoleon learned that Alexander wanted Chichagov to unite with Wittgenstein near the Berezina. But neither Wittgenstein nor Chichagov, both of whom knew the content of this order, was in a hurry to carry it out, and the anonymous author of the book (inspired obviously by Chichagov himself) tries in every possible way to prove that Chichagov had reasonable grounds for wasting his time as he did. Thus, he explains his several days' stay in Minsk by a need of 'reshoeing his horses' and of distributing provisions, et cetera. But Wittgenstein and Kutuzov could also have produced this sort of justification without difficulty. The plain truth is that none of the three wanted to encounter Napoleon.

Borisov was occupied by the Russians under Lambert as early as 21 November. But, as we have said above, Marshal Oudinot attacked Borisov, routed Pahlen's di-

vision, threw the Russians out of Borisov, and occupied
the town. According to our anonymous author (i.e.
Chichagov), this is what happened afterward: as late as
24 November, Chichagov had not the slightest idea of
Wittgenstein's whereabouts; in the meantime, Napoleon with his main body was approaching the Berezina,
and on 24 November reached the hills between
Nemants and Borisov. Victor marched towards him,
fighting off Wittgenstein. On 15 November, at Smoliantsi, Wittgenstein had successfully engaged Victor
and taken some prisoners . . . After Smoliantsi, Wittgenstein for some reason lost five days in inactivity. And
then, instead of continuing to follow Victor towards
Radulichi, he suddenly took a completely different
route, towards Baran, and at the decisive moment was
far from the scene of action. For the four following
days, Chichagov did not hear from Wittgenstein or
from Kutuzov, who remained motionless at Kopys.

'Kutuzov,' writes Denis Davydov in his *Memoirs*,
'avoided an encounter with Napoleon and his Guard;
he not only failed to press on after the retreating
enemy, but hardly moved at all, and was all the time
far behind him.' This did not prevent Kutuzov,
Davydov goes on, from writing to Chichagov that he,
Kutuzov, was 'on the tail of the enemy forces,' and
from urging him to act decisively. According to
Davydov, Kutuzov indulged in some intricate ruses in
his communications to Chichagov: he antedated them,
so that the admiral was entirely bewildered, and 'often
severely reprimanded the couriers, who justified themselves saying that they had been sent out of General
Headquarters later than the date marked on their
orders, and had arrived in good time.' In reality,
Kutuzov did not move from Kopys.

Thus, Kutuzov's complete silence, followed by incorrectly dated orders, completely confused Chichagov. On 25 November, Napoleon, as we have said above, ordered his forces stationed in Borisov to make great demonstrative movements, to put their heavy guns in position, with a view to deceiving Chichagov (stationed on the right bank) and making him think that Napoleon intended to force a passage at Borisov. After the fact, Napoleon said—and his words were repeated by many military historians—that he had deceived Chichagov by diverting his attention from the place (Studianka) where he had decided actually to force his passage on the Berezina. 'That stupid admiral!' Napoleon said of Chichagov. The anonymous author of the book mentioned above protests against this assertion in a footnote. 'What did the deceit consist in?' he asks with bitterness. Chichagov took into account all the possible crossing places, but he was helpless against Napoleon's forces, because of having been so terribly misinformed. Chichagov had been deceived not by Napoleon, but by Wittgenstein and Kutuzov: 'He was indeed deceived. First in his expectation of General Ertel's arrival [Chichagov had requested his assistance but was refused it]. Second, General Wittgenstein, who was supposed to join him, did not arrive. Third, General Kutuzov did not pursue Napoleon.' The destruction of some of General Partouneaux's division [that failed to cross the Berezina] and the capture of its survivors were not much of a comfort.

On the day following the crossing of the Berezina, Robert Wilson wrote to Lord Cathcart in St. Petersburg (expecting him of course to pass on the information to Alexander), explaining that not Chichagov but Kutuzov was responsible for the failure, because the latter had wasted four days, stopped the pursuit, and had not harassed Napoleon's rear at the critical moment: 'No one says that Admiral Chichagov is to blame. His position was such that he could not attack the enemy. We [that is, Kutuzov, in whose headquarters Wilson was at that time] are to blame because we spent two days at Krasnoye and two at Kopys, thus leaving the enemy's rear free, an important advantage, while effecting a crossing with the pleasant expectation of finding two enemy armies ahead [Chichagov's and Wittgenstein's].'

But regardless who was guilty, it was no use crying over spilt milk. Napoleon had escaped.

* * *

'Do you see the villages of Brilovo and Stakhovo?' writes Martos, an officer in Chichagov's engineers corps. 'There Napoleon gave us a most bloody battle; strong batteries from those sloping banks covered his crossing, and all day long we fought with changing luck. Here, the greatest of all captains attained his end.' After Napoleon had completed his crossing and departed, Martos rode to the bridge with Chichagov: 'Towards the evening of that day, the plain of Veselovski, rather vast, offered a horrifying, unbelievable spectacle: it was littered with carriages and carts, mostly broken, piled on one another, carpeted with the bodies of dead women and children, who had followed the army from Moscow in an effort to escape the misfortunes that had befallen that city and to accompany their countrymen, whom death later struck in several ways. The fate of these unfortunates hemmed in between two opposing armies was inescapable death; many were trampled by horses, others crushed by heavy vehicles, struck by a hail of bullets and cannon balls, drowned in the river during the crossing, or, stripped by the soldiers, thrown naked into the snow where the cold soon put an end to their agonies . . . According to the most moderate estimates, up to ten thousand people were lost in this way . . .'

Along with these tragic pictures, we have statements by other witnesses describing the magnanimous, humane attitude of the Russian troops towards the defeated enemy. 'In the midst of a terrible blizzard, I lost my way and was all alone,' writes General Loewenstern. He finally came, half-frozen, to the Russian campfires. 'In the woods adjoining our bivouac many Frenchmen had sought shelter for the night. Late at night they came out of the woods without arms and approached our fires to warm themselves. Our surprise was great when next morning we saw forty to fifty Frenchmen squatting round each fire, showing not the slightest fear of death. Our splendid good-hearted Karpenko gave orders to build several more fires. Then a few thousand Frenchmen came out of the woods and placed themselves round the fires. Karpenko, who pitilessly killed the enemy when face to face with him, now saved the lives of many unfortunates.'

The same Loewenstern describes the cruel sufferings of the Russian army in these days of severe cold: 'After the crossing of the Berezina, terrible frosts set in. I was unable to remain on my horse for more than ten minutes, and, as the snow made it very hard to walk, I alternately mounted and dismounted, and allowed my Hussars to do the same. To keep my feet from freezing, I stuck them in the fur caps of the French grenadiers, which littered the road. My Hussars suffered terribly . . . The Sumsky regiment had no more than 120 horses capable of charging . . . Our infantry was obviously disorganized. Nothing makes a man so pusillanimous as cold; when our soldiers managed to get under a roof somewhere, it was absolutely impossible to get them out. They preferred to die. At the risk of being burned, soldiers sometimes crawled into the large Russian stoves. One had to see these horrors with one's own eyes to believe them.' The two armies, the pursued and the pursuing, were approaching Vilna in the most lamentable state.

'Human sufferings never held greater horror,' writes Loewenstern. 'All the villages in the vicinity were burned to the ground, their inhabitants had run away, nowhere were provisions to be found. Only vodka sustained our strength. We suffered no less than the enemy.' Less than one third of the Russian army that had begun the pursuit of Napoleon at Maloyaroslavets reached Vilna. 'The task of pursuing the enemy was entrusted to the Cossacks; the Russian army did not go beyond Vilna. It had to have a rest, for it could scarcely move.'

The condition of the French army was catastrophic.

Martos, quoted above, continues as follows: 'An uncontrollable feeling of horror seized our hearts. Imagine a wide sinuous river, covered as far as our eyes could see with human corpses; some were just beginning to freeze. Here was the empire of death in all its horror . . . The first thing that caught our eye was a woman who had fallen half through the ice and had frozen in; one of her arms was cut off and hung loosely, with her other arm she held a suckling baby. The little thing had wound itself around its mother's neck; the woman was still alive, she was staring at a man who had fallen through the ice but was frozen to death; be-

tween them on the ice, another dead child was lying
. . . The wind and the frost were extremely cruel, all
the roads were covered by snowdrifts, crowds of Frenchmen were staggering about on the near-by field. Some
tried to light fires, others were cutting up horses and
chewing the bones. Some roasted them, some tried to
eat the raw flesh. Soon I noticed piles of frozen or freezing bodies.' The endless road was 'paved with dead
bodies.' The Russian wounded fared no better than the
French: 'That day was painful beyond anything I can
remember. The little village was crowded with our own
and French wounded and prisoners whose number became so great that there was almost no room for them.
It was horrifying to see them: adults and children, all
together, men and women, with feet wrapped in straw,
wearing some indescribable rags, without shoes, with
frozen faces, with hands gone white.'

In those days, the hunger reached its utmost limit.

'Witnesses such as Stein, the Muravievs, Fenschau,
and others assert that the French ate their dead comrades,' we read in Alexis Nikolayevich Olenin's *My
Notebook*. 'They related that they had often met
Frenchmen in some barn, sitting round a fire, on the
bodies of their dead comrades, from which they had
cut the best parts to satisfy their hunger. Later, they
grew weaker and weaker, and fell dead only to be eaten
in turn by other comrades who had managed to drag
themselves to them.' There are innumerable such statements concerning the state of the French army in
November and December 1812.

Before the crossing of the Berezina the cold was not
too severe, and there were even some warm days. On
18 November, when Ney accomplished his desperate
and disastrous passage over the Dnieper, the river was

covered with only a thin crust of ice. Between 25 and
28 November, Napoleon was forced to build bridges
over the Berezina.

But after 28 November, heavy frosts set in. The thermometer sometimes fell to 45° below zero (Fahrenheit),
and temperatures of 30° to 40° were common. This
weather continued to 12 December. This new disaster
completely crushed the remnants of Napoleon's army.
Inadequately clothed, countless men were unable to
move; they fell and froze to death. In Marshal
Berthier's report to Napoleon on the last days of the
French army's stay in Russia, we read: 'The day of 8
December was the most catastrophic. The Duke of
Bellune [Marshal Victor] came *alone,* the entire rear-
guard left him, men died of cold. The artillery was lost
because all the horses perished. Everything was lost.'
Wrede's corps, before the extreme cold, had comprised
8,000 men. Now only 2,000 remained. Marshal Ney
formed them into a rear-guard.

Marshal Berthier reports: 'The greater part of our
artillery has been put out of action because the horses
have died and the majority of the gunners have had
their feet and hands frozen off . . . The road is littered
with men frozen to death . . . Sire, I must tell you the
whole truth. The army is in a complete state of chaos.
The soldiers throw away their guns because they cannot hold them; both officers and soldiers think only of
protecting themselves from the terrible cold, which is
never above 30 degrees. Our staff officers and adjutants
are unable to walk. There is hope that we may gather
our Guard today . . . We shall inevitably lose a considerable part of our artillery and baggage train . . .
The enemy is incessantly pursuing us with a great force
of cavalry, with guns on sleighs and a small infantry

detachment.' This report is dated 'Vilna, 9 December, 5 a.m.'

On 12 December, Berthier reported from Kovno: 'The measures taken for organizing our stay in Vilna have come to nothing, through lack of discipline and enemy pursuit. General Wrede has been compelled to retreat. The King [Murat] has given orders to evacuate the city during the night. The Duke of Elchingen [Ney] was forced to burn all his artillery and baggage train half a kilometre from Vilna. The temperature is 35 below zero.'

The cold quickly annihilated the remnants of the Grand Army. Exhausted by hunger and their marches through deep snow, the men perished by the thousands. Their tattered uniforms, their torn shoes no longer protected them from the cold. 'The frosts have worn out everyone; the majority of our men have frozen hands and feet . . . Your Majesty knows that a league and a half from Vilna there is a gorge and a very steep hill; at five in the morning, when they arrived there, all our artillery, carriages, and the army train offered a terrible spectacle. Not a cart could pass, the gorge was blocked with guns, the carriages were overthrown . . . The enemy . . . fired at the road . . . At that place all our artillery, carriages, and train were definitely destroyed, the Duke of Elchingen gave orders to burn all that . . . The extraordinary cold and the immense mass of snow completed the disorganization of the army, the highway was entirely buried in snow; our men strayed from it and fell into the ditches at its sides.' Berthier describes the complete destruction of Napoleon's main army. 'I am compelled to tell Your Majesty that the army is in complete disorder, including the Guard, which comprises no more than 400 to 500 men;

the generals and officers have lost everything they had, the majority have had one or another part of their body frozen, the roads are littered with corpses, the houses are filled with them.' Every vestige of discipline and order had vanished. 'The entire army is one column stretched out along several leagues; every morning it sets out and every night it stops without orders; the Marshals march with the rest, the King [Murat] does not think it possible to stop at Kovno, for there is no army . . . At the present moment, Sire, not the enemy but the most terrible season of the year is waging war against us, we hold out only because of our energy, but everything round us is freezing and hostile. Amidst all these disasters, you may be assured, Your Majesty, that everything in human power will be done to save the honour of your arms. A frost of 35 degrees and the abundant snow that covers the ground brought about the disaster of the army which is no more.' Of Marshal Bessières' (Duke of Istria) corps, '11 officers and about 1,000 soldiers froze to death'—before the cold set in, he had only 1,200 men under his command.

These reports essentially agree with Berthier's report intercepted by the Cossacks and published in Russia shortly after the end of the war.

Ségur, who lived through these days with the French army, maintains that the total number of troops who crossed the Berezina with Napoleon, including the unarmed, the laggards, the wounded, and the sick, was 60,000 men; that on the right bank between the Berezina and Molodechno they were joined by another 20,000 (from the units that had remained on the flanks); that of these 80,000 men, 40,000 perished between Molodechno and Vilna, and that many others were fated to die between Vilna and the Niemen. The frost was savage between the Berezina and Molodechno. The thermometer was never higher than 26° below zero, and between Molodechno and Vilna the cold was even more intense. When the army entered Vilna, the temperature was nearly 40° below zero.

None of the participants ever succeeded in describing the days of the retreat from the Berezina to Vilna and from Vilna to Kovno. They would break off their accounts explaining that it was impossible to render in words what they had seen. For dozens of miles the roads were littered with corpses. Soldiers built shelters with the corpses of their comrades, piling them like logs.

On 9 December, the first crowds of starved, half-frozen men entered Vilna. As though drunk, they began at once to break into the stores and loot, in an effort to warm and feed themselves before those who followed them could deprive them of their share. The very next day the first Russian detachments began to approach Vilna. General Loison, part of whose corps was still capable of fighting, tried to defend the city, but 12,000 of his 15,000 men had perished from cold in the three days preceding his entry into Vilna. The detachment of the Bavarian General Wrede was as weak. Ney took over the command of the retreat from Vilna to Kovno. Platov and his Cossacks were already in the suburbs of Vilna. Ney set out, exchanging fire with the Cossacks who were hot on his trail, and the road was soon littered with the corpses of his men. On the night of 13 December, he entered Kovno where he was able to feed his exhausted troops.

Denis Davydov had orders to report to Kutuzov in Vilna. On 12 and 13 December, he rode thither from Novye Troki. 'From Novye Troki to the village of Pokari we travelled without incident. Beginning with

Pokari, at the point where the road forks into two branches, one going to Novye Troki the other to Kovno, piles of dead men and horses, a large number of carts, gun-carriages, and caissons nearly barred our way; a large number of enemy wounded, lying in the snow, or sheltered in carts, awaited death from hunger and cold. My path was lighted by the glow of two burning inns in which many unfortunates found their death. My sleds bumped into the heads, arms, or legs of frozen or freezing men. This went on along the entire road from Pokari to Vilna. My heart was rent by the groans and wails of sufferers of many nations. This was the hymn of the liberation of my fatherland from the invader.'

The news of Napoleon's defeat did not reach Vilna and Kovno until the very last days.

On 2 December, Kovno solemnly celebrated the anniversary of Napoleon's coronation, and on 6 December the city received a report of the Emperor's alleged victory at the Berezina. According to this report, the combined Russian forces of Wittgenstein and Chichagov lost 9,000 prisoners and 12 guns. 'The news was announced in the city to the sound of drums,' says the diary of a Kovno burgher. 'Placards with the announcement were posted at street corners, and at night the city was illuminated.'

Even at the sight of the starved, freezing, wretched French soldiers, not everyone realized the definite and irretrievable rout of Napoleon's army. The inhabitants of Vilna and Kovno continued to submit to Marshal Ney. There were stores in Kovno, and the soldiers refreshed themselves during the few hours of their stay in the city.

At daybreak on 14 December there was an exchange

of fire with a small detachment of Russians who approached Kovno and tried to prevent Ney from crossing the Niemen. A part of the Russians passed over the frozen river to meet Ney with shots from the western bank. Ney succeeded in beating them off. He spent the day in preparation for the crossing. He had several thousand men with him, but no more than 1,000 to 1,500 armed soldiers at the most. Some sources maintain that he had less than 800 men in fighting condition. At eight in the evening of 14 December 1812, after having sent his detachment across to the Prussian side, Marshal Ney with a retinue of a few officers crossed the bridge.

Napoleon learned of all these tragic events in Paris: on 6 December, he took leave of his army in the little town of Smorgonia, handing over the command of its remnants to Murat.

When Napoleon gathered his marshals at Smorgonia and announced his intention of leaving, some of them feebly objected, arguing that the Emperor's departure would definitely disorganize the army. But the army had actually ceased to exist, and the argument was dropped. Neither Napoleon nor the marshals regarded his departure as a flight to save himself; the army was on its way to Vilna and Kovno, and Napoleon had preceded it only by eight days (he left on the sixth, and the last detachment crossed the Niemen on the fourteenth). During these eight days Napoleon would have been in no personal danger, and his presence could not have improved the situation. But from the military and political points of view, Napoleon's departure was indispensable for the rapid creation of a new army to replace the army destroyed in Russia; it was obvious that the defeat suffered by the Emperor in Russia would rouse against him all Europe, or at least a part of it, and above all Prussia, which Russian troops were bound to enter soon.

Napoleon travelled in a sled with Caulaincourt, a Polish officer named Wonsowicz, and a Mameluke servant. In his *Memoirs,* Caulaincourt related that the Emperor was completely calm during the entire journey. Napoleon was apparently little upset by what had happened, and he was entirely absorbed by plans for the great new war, the war of the coming year of 1813. He passed through Vilna, Kovno, Warsaw. In Warsaw, he sometimes seemed gay and calm, he even joked and said among other things: 'I left Paris intending not to carry the war beyond the Polish frontiers. I was carried away by events. Perhaps I made a mistake in going to Moscow, perhaps I should not have stayed there long; but there is only a step from the sublime to the ridiculous, and it is up to posterity to judge.'

What he found ridiculous in the horrors that marked the end of his invasion of Russia remained his secret. But that phrase, which would have been monstrous coming from any other man, was so much in Napoleon's spirit and style, that it seemed natural and failed to arouse indignation or even surprise. That phrase even became proverbial.

For Napoleon, the Russian campaign was but a lost gamble. He was now absorbed by his next venture, not suspecting that the wound inflicted by the Russian people would prove the undoing of his empire.

．　．　．

The Russian campaign was over. During the second half of December, surviving units of Macdonald's forces and groups of lagging soldiers who had been lost in Lithuanian forests continued to cross the Prussian frontier. All told, nearly 30,000 men remained at the disposal of Murat, whom Napoleon had entrusted with the supreme command before his departure, and later, after Murat's departure, of Eugène Beauharnais, Viceroy of Italy.

That was all that remained of the Grand Army, of the 420,000 men who had crossed the Niemen on 24 June 1812, plus the 150,000 men who had gradually joined them later.

On 10 December, Platov and his Cossacks entered Vilna, followed by Prince Kutuzov himself with his entire staff and a numerous suite. Almost immediately it became known that the Tsar, too, was leaving Petersburg to join the army in Vilna.

In Polotsk, on his way to Vilna, Alexander wrote to Kutuzov that he would be in Vilna the following day, 22 December, and that he desired no reception. 'I am impatiently looking forward to seeing you, to tell you personally how greatly the new services you have rendered to your country, and, we may add, to all Europe, have strengthened the respect I have always had for you. Wishing you well as ever. Alexander.' In reality, the Tsar had never before been so irritated with Kutuzov and so firmly resolved to get rid of him as at that very moment.

On 23 December, the Tsar arrived in Vilna, accompanied by Arakcheyev. The Tsar was forced to act a part before the public, to praise and reward the hated Kutuzov in every possible way, to fête him as the embodiment of the Russian people's triumph, of Russia's salvation from a terrible danger. The Tsar acquitted himself of this task with his customary self-control and gift for saving appearances. Only recently the Tsar had expressed his true feelings towards Kutuzov by marking one of the Field Marshal's reports (the report on Yashvil and the Kaluga militia) with the words: 'What a piece of knavery!' Now he found the most gracious words and the tenderest modulations of voice to greet the 'saviour of Russia'—as it had become customary to call Kutuzov—but the Tsar and the Field Marshal disagreed more than ever in their political views, and their judgments of what was to be done next.

For Kutuzov, the war with Napoleon ended at the moment when Ney with his few companies crossed the bridge over the Niemen. For Alexander the war was only beginning. He was for saving Europe and helping England.

On the morning of 24 December, Alexander invited Wilson to his residence and thanked him for his letters. The scene is described in Wilson's book, *Narrative of Events during the Invasion of Russia:* 'You have always told me the truth, truth I could not obtain through any other channel. I know that the Field Marshal has not done anything he ought to have done . . . All his successes have been *forced* upon him. He has been playing some of his old Turkish tricks, but the Moscow nobility support him and insist on his presiding over the national glory of this war. In half an hour I must, therefore [and he paused for a minute], decorate that man with the great order of St. George . . . But I will not ask you to be present. I should feel too much humiliated if you were; but I have no choice—I must submit to a controlling necessity. I will, however, not again leave my army, and there shall be no opportunity given for additional misdirection by the Marshal.'

The only way Wilson could interpret these last words

was that Kutuzov would remain Commander-in-Chief in name only, and that the real commander would be the Tsar.

Such was the Tsar's hatred of the Field Marshal that he failed to see how ironic it was for him, Alexander Pavlovich, Tsar of All the Russias, to apologize to the British agent for decorating Kutuzov.

.   .   .

The departure of the French did not immediately arouse the feeling of joy and relief that is mentioned by later writers. Moscow celebrated a sad Christmas: 'Yesterday's holiday was singularly quiet,' says a report to the Minister of the Interior. 'The events have extremely depressed the inhabitants. They are not erased by their sequel . . . The removal of dead bodies continues . . . Rumours that piles of corpses have been buried in shallow graves in Moscow and the environs fill everyone with apprehension for the spring.' Corpses were rotting in the outskirts of Moscow and on the Kaluga road. The epidemics did not await spring: in November, December, and January death from infectious diseases decimated the army and the civilian population.

According to Kutuzov, it was hard and dangerous to undertake a new war against Napoleon, and it was entirely unnecessary. The Russian people had asserted their rights, vanquished the invincible enemy, and won immortal glory. Why liberate and strengthen the Germans, who as Russia's neighbours were potential enemies? Why shed Russian blood for the Germans, who would one day perhaps shed the blood of the grandsons and great-grandsons of the very Russian soldiers who were now to be driven to fight Napoleon for the liberation of Germany? Not only Kutuzov, but many, many others thought along these lines. But a terrible anger against Napoleon prevailed in Russia, and this strengthened the Tsar and Wilson. 'Let us take revenge on the brutal invader, come what may!' was a common sentiment.

Even in the summer of 1813, when the Allies began to negotiate with Napoleon, there were men in the depths of the Russian provinces who absolutely opposed peace and laid their hopes in the intransigent Spaniards.

The news of Spanish successes against the French 'produced general joy here,' writes a certain Babaev from Tula on 4 August 1813, when the June armistice between Napoleon and the Allies was still in force. No one in Tula, in the heart of Russia, wanted peace with Napoleon: 'As a rule, everyone, assuming that a truce with this monster, and even a peace, would be insecure and entail pernicious consequences, impatiently awaits the resumption of military operations, placing all hopes in the power of their beloved Fatherland!'

'Russians! You have torn half a world out of the jaws of the monster who devoured mankind by the millions. Half a world celebrates your heroic valour!' This was the theme of church sermons all over Russia in 1814, after the collapse of Napoleon's empire. But as early as December 1812, many people in Moscow, Petersburg, on estates, and in provincial cities held the same view, anticipating the remote consequences of the War of 1812. They regarded the liberation of Europe as imminent.

Kutuzov did not oppose this current with great energy, though he knew that it was carrying Russia in

an undesirable direction. A. S. Shishkov, the Secretary
of State who had contrived to rid the army of Alexander's presence at the beginning of the war, was now
in Vilna with the court. He, too, feared a continuation
of the war and believed that it was not in Russia's interest. Having conversed with Kutuzov and learned that
the Field Marshal shared his views, Shishkov asked him
why he did not defend them before the Tsar with
greater determination. Kutuzov's reply to this question
is quoted literally in Shishkov's *Memoirs:* 'I [Kutuzov]
expressed this view to him [the Tsar], but, in the first
place, he sees the matter from another angle, and his
approach cannot be entirely refuted; in the second
place, I must tell you frankly and openly that when he
cannot dispute my arguments, he embraces me and
kisses me; and then I just cry and agree with him.'—
'You saved not only Russia, you saved all Europe,' Alexander said to the Field Marshal on 24 December, when,
surrounded by an enormous suite, Kutuzov came to
congratulate the Tsar on the occasion of his birthday.
In accepting this greeting, which clearly outlined the
program of transferring the war beyond the frontiers,
Prince Kutuzov tacitly accepted the mission of 'saving
Europe.'

On 12 January 1813, Kutuzov published a proclamation to the Russian army: 'Brave and victorious soldiers! At last you have reached the frontiers of the Russian Empire! Every one among you is a saviour of our
country. Russia hails you by this name! Your impetuous
pursuit of the enemy, and the extraordinary labours
you have accomplished in this campaign have astounded
all nations and covered you with immortal fame . . .

'. . . Let us cross the frontiers and endeavour to
complete the enemy's defeat on his own ground. But

let us not follow the example of our enemy in committing acts of violence and savagery unworthy of a soldier
. . . Let us be generous, let us carefully distinguish
between the enemy and the peaceful population. Our
just and kind treatment of the population will clearly
demonstrate that we do not strive to enslave them and
win a futile glory, but that we are trying to liberate
from misery and oppression even those nations that had
taken up arms against Russia.'

The foreign campaign began. The Prussians went
over to the Russian side. Two years of European slaughter were ahead, during which the Russians incurred
greater losses than any other nation. Only on his death-
bed did the old Field Marshal resolve to say frankly
what he thought of this new bloodshed.

In April 1813, Kutuzov was gravely ill in Bunzlau,
Prussian Silesia. Napoleon, at the head of large forces,
was marching on the Russians and Prussians, but Kutuzov was not fated to take part in the operations against
him.

On 27 April, he was near death. Alexander I came to
Bunzlau to make his farewells. Krupennikov, an official
attached to Kutuzov, was behind the screen placed near
the dying man's bed. This is the dialogue he overheard
and later reported to the Tsar's steward, Tolstoy: 'Forgive me, Mikhail Illarionovich!'—'I forgive you, Sire,
but Russia never will!' The Tsar did not reply.

The next day, 28 April 1813, Prince Kutuzov died.

The news of the Field Marshal's death reached Alexander in Dresden. 'This is a great and painful loss not
only for you but for the whole Fatherland,' wrote Alexander to Kutuzov's widow (who, incidentally, had no
illusions about the Tsar's tears). 'You are not alone in

shedding tears for him; I weep with you and all Russia is weeping. May God, who has summoned him, comfort you with the thought that his name and his achievements will remain immortal. His grateful Fatherland
will never forget his merits.'

The country was slow to regain faith in the Tsar and
the Supreme Command, which had suffered such terrible blows at Smolensk and Moscow. In the spring and
summer of 1813, Napoleon, at the head of his newly
created army, defeated the exhausted Russian and Prussian forces in the bloody battles of Lutzen, Bautzen, and
Dresden. Many recalled the deceased Field Marshal's
objections to carrying the war against Napoleon beyond
Russia's frontiers; and there was general alarm and dissatisfaction. When Moscow learned that Napoleon had
routed an allied army near Dresden and thrown it back
beyond the Elbe, the alarm in the capital, which was
still a charred ruin, became general: 'The news of our
retreat behind the Elbe,' wrote Rostopchin in a letter
dated 7 June 1813, 'produced fear and dismay . . . If
our uncertainty regarding our military operations continues, and is not interrupted either by victories or the
reoccupation of Dresden, there will be much unrest
here. The people most unfavourably disposed towards
the Tsar and the government are the Dissenters and the
merchants; the former demonstrate this by their deeds,
the latter by their words.'

At that time the mood of the Russian army was divided. When the allies concluded a temporary truce
with Napoleon after his victories at Lutzen, Bautzen,
and Dresden in June 1813, Caulaincourt visited the
Russian outposts: 'The Russians organized a celebration in honour of Caulaincourt,' writes a witness. 'The

duke proposed a toast: "To the Russian Army!" The Russian officers replied with a toast: "To the courageous French Army!" and thrice emptied their glasses. A Prussian general was present, but the Prussian army was not mentioned.'

CONCLUSION

THE War of 1812 had colossal consequences and left a deep mark on history.

For Europe, it was a signal for an uprising against Napoleon's domination.

Napoleon's invasion of Russia was the most openly 'predatory imperialistic' war ever undertaken by the dictator who had solidly based his rule on the interests of the French upper middle class. As early as 1803, and particularly after 1805, Napoleon's rule was economically oppressive to Austria and all the German states. It was maintained by a policy of open violence, conquests, arbitrary annexations, and military and police terror. The dictator deliberately strove to hamper the economic and technical development of all the countries he had conquered in Central and Northern Europe. In Italy, the oppressive character of his rule was felt as early as 1796, and with particular force after the 'second conquest' in 1800. Beginning with 1807, this oppression increased to an incredible extent. It began to stifle the economic development of countries that had hitherto managed to defend their trade and industry. Napoleon's annexation of Holland and the Hanseatic cities; his seizure of all the North German principalities; his attempt to seize Portugal and Spain; the arrest of the Pope and the occupation of Rome; finally, the drastic new methods, applied after 1810, to impose the

Continental blockade—all this, in the eyes of the middle classes of the conquered countries, clearly proved that the European continent was helplessly succumbing to monopolistic exploitation by the French bourgeoisie.

In the first years of the Continental blockade, though the commercial bourgeoisie complained, the industrial bourgeoisie exulted. Freed from English competition, they did a flourishing business. But soon the industrialists, too, began to complain. It was difficult to do without English colonial products, without cotton, indigo, sugar cane (despite the successful experiments with beet sugar). And then, in 1810-11, the subordinate position of the bourgeoisie in the conquered countries was fully revealed: to his own merchants and industrialists, Napoleon granted licences to buy the required raw materials from the English on certain conditions; but he forbade the merchants and industrialists of the conquered countries to do the same. The prevailing sentiments among this bourgeoisie were now rage, humiliation, and a sense of impending ruin.

The peasants of Central and Southern Europe had been entirely or partly liberated from serfdom by Napoleon's conquests and the overthrow of feudalism. But now (between 1807 and 1812) the Grand Empire became an insatiable monster exacting a 'blood tribute' in the form of conscripted recruits. Napoleon boasted of having lost 'no more than' 50,000 'real' Frenchmen in the Russian campaign—the remaining hundreds of thousands were Germans, Italians, Dutchmen, Poles, Spaniards, Dalmatians, and other nationalities. According to the Emperor, there was consequently no reason to be aggrieved. After all, the 'blood tribute' was paid by the peasants and workers, the privileged classes bought themselves off, supplying substitutes.

All these hardships resulting from Napoleon's rule in Europe were felt with particular acuteness because of the implacable measures by which this rule was maintained. The European press was completely stifled; no German, Italian, Dutchman, could exist in peace if he had the misfortune to arouse the suspicion of the omnipotent, ubiquitous, omniscient imperial police.

When the first detachments of Russian troops crossed the border to Prussia in January 1813, they were greeted, first in a half-whisper, and then aloud with the joyous words: 'The Russians, the liberators are coming!' All through 1813, this cry, in various languages, resounded.

It is true, of course, that the Prussian uprising had been prepared by the patient work of Stein, Hardenberg, Scharnhorst, Gneisenau, and other patriots. But it is also certain that without the Russian victory of 1812, Prussia and the rest of Europe would scarcely have liberated themselves so soon from Napoleon. Let us quote Field Marshal Gneisenau, one of the most important organizers of the Prussian movement against Napoleon, a straightforward man not addicted to flattery. In the summer of 1814, after Napoleon's first abdication, he wrote to Alexander: 'Without the excellent spirit of the Russian nation, without its hatred of foreign oppression, without the noble stubbornness of its exalted sovereign, the civilized world would have perished beneath the despotism of the brutal tyrant.'

Yet today Hitlerite textbooks relate the liberation of Prussia in 1813 with practically no mention of the War of 1812. When they do mention 1812, it is chiefly to say that without the accidental coming of cold weather, Russia would have been sunk without a trace.

The position of England was different. She never

depended politically on Napoleon, as did the European
continent. But the Russian victory put an end to the
Continental blockade, and a stream of English goods
flowed into all the countries of Europe so long closed
to them. What happened was exactly what Kutuzov,
who was not only a remarkable strategist but also a
profound political thinker, had foretold in his conversation with Wilson between Krasnoye and Berezina:
England profited most from Napoleon's destruction.
England's economic primacy, which Napoleon's most
desperate efforts could not wrest from her, now remained uncontested for decades. Russian exports, imports, and exchange became strongly dependent on London. In St. Petersburg, Tsar Nicholas's Chancellor,
Count Nesselrode, from time to time graciously received
English merchants, members of the English colony in
the Russian capital, and 'deigned' to explain to them
the Russian policies; in Odessa, up to the Crimean War,
the Tsar's satrap, the Governor-General, feared nothing more than the protestations and complaints from
English ship owners, skippers, and wholesalers. The
same could be observed in Riga, Kronstadt, Reval. After
the collapse of the Continental blockade, the English
merchants treated the Russian Government with the
same self-assurance and independence as did their representative Sir Robert Wilson in his time.

· · ·

For Russia, too, the consequences of the National
War were immense. Not the cold and not Russia's vast
expanses conquered Napoleon, but the resistance of the
Russian people.

The Russian people asserted their right to an inde-

pendent national existence; they asserted it with an indomitable will to victory, with the true heroism that despises all phrases, with a surge of spirit unequalled by any other nation save the Spanish.

The Russians revealed greater physical strength and material potentialities than Spain. Within six months Napoleon's hordes were dispersed and destroyed in Russia, while the Spaniards, despite their equally indisputable heroism, took five years, even with the immense help given them by England, to get rid of Napoleon—and ultimately succeeded in 1813 in direct consequence of Napoleon's defeat in Russia.

The popular character of the Russian war was manifested in the heroic conduct of the Russian soldiers on the battlefield, in the armed peasant attacks on the conqueror, in their successful efforts to starve him out; in Spain, the popular character of the war was manifested in independent fighting enterprises on the part of irregular peasant masses. This required a great deal of heroism, but the results could not be as quick and considerable as they would have been if Spain had preserved a regular fighting organization. Such an organization was created in Spain only at a later stage of the struggle; in Russia it existed from the beginning to the end, and could usefully exploit the surge of the national spirit.

The victory of 1812 inspired the nation. Certain contemporaries maintained that after it Russia became 'new,' like Moscow, which divides its history into the 'pre-French' and 'post-French' periods.

The War of 1812 is also associated with the first revolutionary upsurge of Russian modern history—the uprising of 14 December 1825—not only because in 1812

certain Decembrists rose in arms against Napoleon for
Russia just as in 1825 they rose in arms for Russia
against Nicholas I; the reasons for the association are
deeper.

The War of 1812 was interpreted by the younger
generations between 1812 and 1825 and later, as a struggle for freedom, as a liberation from the additional,
the foreign oppression, which Napoleon was bringing
to Russia.

The powerful impulse which the victory gave to the
Russian people was echoed in the first awakening of
the revolutionary consciousness. Lenin's formula: 'The
Decembrists awakened Herzen' can be expanded: 'The
immediate consequences of the War of 1812 awakened
the Decembrists.' This complementary formula is less
precise than Lenin's because we should speak not only
of 1812 but also of 1813, 1814, and 1815, when the war
against Napoleon was waged in Europe. Even the years
after Waterloo must be taken into account, for the
Russian armies remained in France for a long time.

But all these consequences were conditioned by the
victory of 1812. Not only the Decembrists are associated
with the War of 1812; long ago the thought was expressed that 'without 1812 there would have been no
Pushkin.' In this form, the thought seems paradoxi-
cal. We know that great poetic geniuses are often born
and often develop in periods of national humiliation,
as Dante, Goethe, and Schiller bear witness. But Pushkin's poetry does indisputably reflect the proud joyous
awareness of the moral force of his people, which overthrew 'the idol oppressing the kingdoms.' It is more
than likely that without the War of 1812 Pushkin would
not have been what he was, would not have spoken of

Russia as he spoke when, like Peter, 'he knew her destiny.'

Pushkin is only one of many possible examples. The whole Russian intellectual movement, the Russian national self-awareness received a powerful impulse in the terrible year of invasion.

'Not the noisy talk of French journals destroyed Napoleon,' wrote Chernyshevsky. 'He did not allow any talk. He was destroyed by the campaign of 1812. Not the Russian newspapers awakened the Russian nation to a new life, it was awakened by the glorious perils of 1812.'

Russian serfdom continued to be in force after 1812; the necessary social and economic conditions for its collapse were not yet ripe. But, as we have said, Napoleon did not come to Russia to break the old chains; on the contrary, he came to add new chains to the old.

The Poles at the beginning of the seventeenth century, the Swedes at the beginning of the eighteenth, and Napoleon at the beginning of the nineteenth—all these attempted to destroy Russian independence. Napoleon's threat was the most formidable, for since the days of Alexander of Macedonia and Julius Caesar, the world had not seen such monstrous power concentrated in one hand. He dominated an immense empire, inhabited by the most diverse, wealthy, civilized nations. His power over them was unbounded, his military genius was and still is regarded as unsurpassed in the history of mankind. The Russian people smashed this giant.

'Read the history of Russia, it is a very useful occupation!' the late German publicist Maximilian Harden urgently advised his compatriots in 1918, when the Germans so successfully (so it seemed to them) spread over

the Ukraine, the Crimea, the Caucasus. He greatly
feared the results of this invasion, but the Berlin military censorship did not permit him to express himself
more clearly. This advice would be very useful to our
neighbours even now.

A NOTE

ON THE AUTHOR'S SOURCES

IN addition to the published works on the subject of Napoleon's invasion of Russia, Mr. Tarlé has had access to, and has here utilized for the first time, a vast amount of contemporaneous documents which exist only in manuscript form, and are preserved in various libraries throughout the U.S.S.R. The majority of these documents are in the Russian language. They include letters to and from the Tsar, the Russian Commander-in-Chief, Kutuzov, generals, ministers, and other important personages, including Rostopchin, Governor-General of Moscow. The documents in French consist chiefly of private letters and official dispatches intercepted by the Cossacks in frequent raids during the retreat of the Grand Army. The author's sources also include innumerable diaries and eyewitness accounts recorded by the guerrilla fighters who played so important a part in the campaign. The greater part of these original manuscript accounts are contained in the famous Schilder, Voyensky, Vorontsov, Dubrovin, and Semenovsky archives.

Scholars who are interested in learning the source of quotations appearing throughout the text may locate them by referring to the original Russian edition, which is available in the more important libraries in the United States under the title: *Nashestvie Napoleona na Rossiyu—1812 god.*

INDEX

415